WIRED TOGETHER: THE ONLINE CLASSROOM IN K-12

VOLUME 4: WRITING, READING, AND LANGUAGE ACQUISITION

edited by

Zane L. Berge
University of Maryland-Baltimore County

Mauri P. Collins
Northern Arizona University

HAMPTON PRESS, INC.
CRESSKILL, NEW JERSEY

Printed in the United States of America

Library of Congress Cataloging-in-Publication Data

Wired together : the online classroom in K-12 / edited by Zane L. Berge, Mauri P. Collins
p. cm.
Includes bibliographical references and indexes.
Contents: v. 1. Perspectives and instructional design -- v. 2. Case studies -- v. 3. Teacher education and professional development -- v. 4. Writing reading and language acquisition.
ISBN 1-57273-092-7 (v. 4 : cloth). -- ISBN 1-57273-093 5 (v. 4 : pbk.).
1. Educational technology--United States--Case studies. 2. Computer-assisted instruction--United States--Case studies. 3. Teachers--Training of--United States--Cast studies. 4. Teachers--In-service training--United States--Case studies. 5. Language arts--United States--Case studies. I. Berge , Zane L. II. Collins, Mauri P.
LB1028.3.W56 1997
371.33--dc21 97-22976
CIP

Hampton Press, Inc.
23 Broadway
Cresskill, NJ 07626

CONTENTS

PREFACE

In July 1992, when we sent out the call for chapters for the three previous volumes in this series, *Computer-mediated Communication and the Online Classroom* (Hampton Press, 1995; which we refer to by their project title: CMCBOOK), we received only a handful of submissions that related to computer-mediated communication (CMC) in primary and secondary schools. These mainly described bulletin board systems and other relatively unsophisticated CMC applications. In those days of text-only Web browsers there was little out there to be browsed and, in the CMCBOOK series, only a single, short paragraph was included about the Web. It is hard to imagine that it was such a short time ago. The popularization of easy-to-use graphical interface browsers for the Web such as Netscape and Mosaic have been the catalyst for explosive, exponential growth in the use of the Internet.

INTENDED AUDIENCE

We offer these books to a broad audience of classroom teachers and teacher educators, administrators, and policymakers. The chapters in these books were written with the K-12 practitioner in mind. There are a number of books currently available that examine computer-mediated communication theory and its application in higher education. This is not intended as a theoretical work, but as a series of practical case studies that could be used as models for classroom use. The common thread that unites these books is the classroom use of computer-mediated communications in all its iterations.

As with our previous books we asked the authors to focus on the pedagogical problems they had discovered and to relate how they had used CMC to solve those problems. This seemed to be the most right-headed course. Although technology changes rapidly, the pedagogical issues remain fairly constant. Additionally, teachers and principals continue to emphasize how difficult it often is to provide justification for large funding requirements in the area of CMC to school boards and other central administrators. They have often found that these decision makers are convinced by the weight of the case studies in printed books, as several users of the CMCBOOK series have since informed us. It can be overwhelming to start online, and a seemingly impossible experience if a teacher waits for the complete infrastructure to be installed before beginning. We suggest a good idea is for you to start somewhere—*anywhere* that makes sense! Choose a project that excites you and that will help create the learning environment of which you have a vision. Figure out a way to do it!

THE PROCESS USE FOR THE K12BOOK

When we attended the Association for Curriculum and Development (ACSD) conference in San Francisco in March 1995, we noticed a tremendous interest among these primary and secondary school teachers and administrators in computer-mediated communication in all its forms and the Web in particular. The volumes in the CMCBOOK series were received well in higher education, and there now appeared to be a definite call for a similar set of books to meet the needs of K12 educators and teacher educators. This became *Wired Together: The Online Classroom in K-12* (the project title is simply "K12BOOK").

On May 1, 1995, Zane distributed a call for chapters to selected online discussion groups with a Kindergarten through Grade 12 (K-12) focus. We also distributed, via e-mail, a number of personal invitations for submissions. The closing date for proposals was June 30, 1995, and we received nearly 100 proposals. These were reviewed by an editorial panel of elementary, secondary and higher education faculty, and in July 1995, we issued acceptances to the authors of 73 chapters. At the time, it appeared the content would sort into 3 books. Rather than each of the editors reading all the chapters in all the books (which we found to be a very time-consuming process with the CMCBOOK), we assumed primary responsibility for one book each and invited Patricia Dieter Reidell, a middle school English teacher, to work with us on the third. Of course, as with all such efforts, for a variety of reasons throughout the months following acceptance, several chapters were subsequently withdrawn from the editorial process.

The entire editorial process of the CMCBOOK project up to page proofs had been conducted online, and we found that to be both a time-efficient and effective process, well accepted by our CMCBOOK authors. We decided to use the same process for the K12BOOK, with the addition of a series of Web pages. The first step was to set up a closed discussion group (we used Listserv) so that we could quickly communicate with all the authors, and they with us and each other. The author guidelines from CMCBOOK were revised in light of our prior experience and distributed over the list. We also distributed drafts of two chapters: Santoro's defining of CMC and Collins's explaining of the common terms and terminology of the Internet. We limited authors to approximately 3,000 words and directed the authors to refer to the Santoro or Collins chapters rather than redefine terms and concepts.

Mauri had learned to annotate documents with HTML and felt that a series of Web pages would considerably ease electronic document management. A K12BOOK home page was created, and the Author Guidelines and Santoro and Collins chapters were linked to it. We sent the URL to the authors, via the mailing list, with text versions of everything on the Web pages for those who did not have Web access. An index page with authors and chapter titles was created for each of three books, and as first drafts came in, they were linking to the appropriate entry. Each book was initially divided into two sections, and the authors were invited to read the chapters in their section and to adjust their own content in light of what others had written. First drafts were received electronically during the fall of 1995. Editorial comments were e-mailed back to the authors, and final drafts were received via e-mail through January 1996. The glossary from the CMCBOOK was sent to the authors, and suggestions for additions and annotations were received back. When all the final drafts were received we consulted with the publisher, and the chapters were rearranged into the present four volumes.

The online working process was new to most of the authors, some of whom had not published book chapters before. Even for those authors who had previous publications, they were used to working only with an editor and were often not aware of the other authors nor the contents of other chapters. We had found with the CMCBOOK that authors appreciated a more collaborative mode of working that also kept them updated on the status of their chapters and the general progress of the books.

Using electronic mail, the Listserv group, and the Web pages, we were able to go from the call for chapters to their final delivery to the publisher in 10 months, an impossible feat were we required to do it using conventional mail. Although most of our authors were from the United States, we also have authors from Canada, Australia, the United Kingdom, Israel, Germany, Russia, Singapore, and India. It became obvious to us as we read their chapters that using CMC in the classroom raises the same kinds of issues and is applied to similar pedagogical problems, regardless of the physical location of teachers and students.

WHAT THE AUTHORS THOUGHT OF THE PROCESS

We asked the authors to comment on the editorial process used in the K12BOOK, especially how it compared to other authoring processes in which they had been involved. Several remarked about this being "somehow new." They could not articulate well what that "new" was. The words used to give a sense of how this editorial process was significantly new were "access," "freedom," and "connectivity." Several authors, although seasoned computer-mediated communicators, noted that at first even they felt a little "clumsy." Hardly any of the authors felt they had taken the time or made the effort to interact with other authors to the extent this process would have allowed. There were expressions of regret at this in most cases.

K12BOOK authors expressed concern with the same kinds of limitations as had the CMCBOOK authors. They cited things such as wishing they had more time to take advantage of the flexibility and possibilities of this process, technical problems with sites going down, and lack of convenient access to e-mail or Web sites. Overwhelmingly, though, authors found this process useful because of the ease and convenience in communication between themselves and the editors especially, as well as among other authors. Authors commented that the regular updates from us were important in giving them a sense of "ownership" or "community" in this effort compared with other edited works to which they had contributed.

The Web site, for those having convenient and low-cost access, allowed authors to judge such things as what terminology they need not duplicate, the style being used, and the scope of this work. Several commented that, if nothing else, the review of others' work was reassuring—they were using the appropriate style for the intended audience, and they were not using too much jargon—and that this access served to provide models of writing useful in producing their own contribution to K12BOOK.

The process has proven itself now with seven volumes, and we will continue to refine and elaborate it as we strive to implement the model of collaborative and interactive work, unbound by time and space, that computer-mediated communication fosters so well. We feel this writing and publishing process can be applied within classrooms, schools, or businesses using internal, private Web servers, or openly, across the world, as we have used it.

ACKNOWLEDGMENTS

We raise our keyboards in salute to the late Gerald M. Phillips in recognition of his encouragement and his inspiration that put the words "Berge," "Collins," "book," and "edit" all together in one sentence for the first time on the scholarly discussion group, IPCT-L. (Incidentally, it was on IPCT-L that we met!) Academically and professionally, we hope that all we do carries with it a small spark of his genius. We thank our authors for making their deadlines, regardless of full lives and personal trauma. We acknowledge, with sincere thanks, the help given in the selection and editing processes of the K12BOOK by Nancy Biggs Berge (Fairfax County Virginia Schools) and Patricia Dieter Reidell (The Pennsylvania State University).

DEDICATION

These books are dedicated to the most important people in our lives: our families. It is with special note we dedicate the K12BOOK to Zane's father, Mark R. Berge, who passed away soon after the CMCBOOK was first published.

We also note Nancy Biggs Berge, who again bore the brunt of dealing with two harried editors underfoot for days at a time with patience, tolerance, and hospitality; our parents, who read our books and voice pride in our accomplishments; and to all our children: Jenna Berge; Mark Berge; Doug Collins; Kim and Mike Snyder and their boys, Derek and Sean; Sarah Waghorn; Paul Simon Waghorn; Krys and Scotty Hosmer; Jay Strebel; Benjammin Strebel; Nori Strebel; and Josh Strebel.

Z.L.B.
M.P.C.

Baltimore, MD
1997

ABOUT THE EDITORS AND CONTRIBUTORS

Zane Berge is Director of Training Systems, ISD Graduate Programs, University of Maryland Baltimore County. His scholarship and consulting work is in computer-mediated communication, especially in computer-conferencing. berge@umbc2.umbc.edu

Mauri Collins is a Doctoral Candidate in Adult Education with majors in both Distance Education and Instructional Design at the Pennsylvania State University. She is an experienced online discussion list moderator and facilitator. mauri@cac.psu.edu

* * * * *

Junko K. Ady teaches Japanese at the high school level and is one of the technology resource teachers at the Punahou School (K-12), Honolulu, HI. jkady@punahou.edu

Charoula Angeli is a doctoral student in Instructional Systems Technology at Indiana University in Bloomington. Her research interests are Computer-Based Instruction in K-12 and Problem-Based Learning in secondary education. Angeli@indiana.edu

Tom Brush is currently an assistant professor in educational technology at Auburn University in Auburn, AL. He received his PhD in Curriculum and Instruction from Indiana University. Prior to his appointment at Auburn, he was Director of Instructional Technology at Mt. Clemens Community School District in Mt. Clemens, MI. brushta@mail.auburn.edu

Bob Bulik is a Coordinator of Curriculum & Faculty Development for Ohio University. He has taught secondary special education and conducted research in the areas of school-to-work transition, education of marginalized learners, and attitudes of juvenile offenders toward learning. bobbulik@macc.wisc.edu

Annette Christy is a media specialist at Wren Middle School in Piedmont, SC. She designs programs that use telecommunications in middle and high school curriculums. Christya@fcae .acast.nova.edu

Donald Cunningham is Professor of Education, Cognitive Science and Semiotic Studies at Indiana University, Bloomington. His interests include semiotic models of cognition and multimedia. cunningh@ucs.indiana.edu

Mary Louise Cunningham teaches second grade at Highland Park Elementary School in Bloomington, IN. She is very interested in integrating computers into her classroom. cunningh@ucs. indiana.edu

Jeri H. Dies is an Assistant Professor of Applied Linguistics and Foreign Languages at the Florida Institute of Technology. Her research focuses on the application of technology and the Internet for language learning and teaching, and the assessment of language learning and study strategies. jdies@fit.edu

Werner Dobner is the German/American Student Exchange Coordinator, Host Nation Coordinator, and press officer for the German Foreign Office which organizes seminars on Germany for American teachers. For the past three years he has been teaching AP GERMAN via the computer. Werner_Dobner@odedodea.edu

Patrick Fullick is lecturer in Science and Technology Education in the School of Education at the University of Southampton. His work focuses on young people's understanding of the nature of science, and the use of new technologies in mediating this learning. plf@soton.ac.uk

Robert Hawk Geeslin, EdD (Florida State University, 1969), is Research Associate at Oklahoma State University College of Osteopathic Medicine where his major research interest is the part played by attention, especially anticipatory attention, in the process of learning to read. rhawk@galaxy.galstar.com

Patricia R. Grimes is an Advanced Placement English Teacher at Woodbridge Senior High. She is also an AP Reader and Adjunct Professor at George Mason University. Involved in the Northern Virginia Writing Project, she researches writing with technology across the disciplines. pgrimes@PEN.K12.VA.US

Bob Hall is district technology coordinator for the Napoleon Area Schools, Napoleon, OH. NAP_ACA_BH@NWOCA.OHIO.GOV

Justus Lewis is a Senior Lecturer in the School of Accountancy and Business, Nanyang Technological University, Republic of Singapore. Her research interest is in the use of computer-mediated communication to facilitate teaching and learning. jhlewis@SINGNET.COM.SG

Robert Longpré teaches French in Saskatchewan, Canada. His work focuses on using CMC to meet the needs of linguistically isolated rural learners. longpre@sasknet.sk.ca

Uta Morse is a Teaching Fellow in the School of Civil and Structural Engineering, Nanyang Technological University, Republic of Singapore. Her focus is on integrating cultural and linguistic understanding of foreign languages. cumorse@NTUVAX.NTU.AC.SG

Mary Lou Morton is presently teaching at Joy Elementary School in Fairbanks, AK. She works with students with learning disabilities and continues with her work of computer-mediated instruction which she began at Indiana University. mlmorton@ northstar.k12.ak.us

Mary O'Haver teaches fifth grade social studies, reading/language arts, and science at Fairland Elementary School in Montgomery County, MD, where she has been active in integrating technology into her classroom since the late 1970s. mohaver@umd5.umd.edu

Tom O'Haver is professor of analytical chemistry at the University of Maryland at College Park where his professional interests include spectrocopy, instrumentation development, science education, and teacher training. to2@umail.umd.edu

Jun Ohashi is a lecturer at the department of Japanese and Chinese, University of Melbourne. He is also a part-time doctoral student focussing on SLA in the Japanese language. jun_ohashi@muwayf.unimelb.edu.au

Patricia Reidell is completing graduate work in Adult Education/Distance Education at the Pennsylvania State University. She is a secondary level English teacher interested in Creative Writing and interdisiplinary computer use. par8psu.edu

Elizabeth Stacey is a lecturer in the Education Faculty at Deakin University, Victoria, Australia. She has wide experience teaching and researching the use of computer-mediated communication, including audiographic technology, in education. estacey@deakin.edu.au

MaryAnn Tille is a senior English and speech teacher at Ayersville High School, Defiance, OH. She uses a variety of technologies to help students feel comfortable in an electronic environment. AYR_ACA_MT_@NWOCA.OHIO.GOV

Sherry Wulff is an Associate Professor in the Professional Communication Department of Alverno College where she teaches courses in Media Studies, Communication Theory and Research, and Speech Communication Methods for secondary education teachers. swulff@stu.wisc.edu

Stephen Zsiray is Assistant Superintendent for secondary education in the Cache County School District. His interest is in the integration of technology into curriculum delivery to improve instruction, thus enhancing student opportunities to learn. Steve.Zsiray@m.k12.ut.us

1

CMC AND THE READING WRITING CLASSROOM

Patty Reidell

This volume is intended to be read by a wide audience of teachers, including teachers of literacy, language, and second languages in the kindergarten through 12th-grade levels. In U.S. public and private school systems, kindergarten to high school students' ages may range from 4 to 18 years of age. This volume is intended to be a concept map and does not specifically focus on teaching methods. Rather, it deals with the different goals and outcomes of learning that are specific for each learner age group. This volume is a compilation of reports of successful distributed learning programs and projects in varied settings delivered by teachers who all use computer-mediated communication (CMC) in their classrooms. The hope is that ideas from these contributions may impart both broad concepts and practical models for application in a variety of classroom settings.

The authors of this volume are teachers who are publishing the results and conclusions of their own projects and studies that have already taken place. In so sharing, the teachers as authors have expanded their roles from the one strictly defined as "classroom expert". They have become collaborators with their peers after reflecting on their own teaching, evaluating their own work, and publishing successful course projects through this text.

In this introduction, topics and themes relevant to teachers of language, second language, and literature are discussed. All issues that impact schooling today are accentuated by adding distributed learning using computers in schools. Some issues are magnified just by adding computers to the schools and classrooms.

GENERAL ISSUES

At local levels, school boards are representatives of parents and the community and also reflect the standards and expectations of the community. Whether in urban, suburban, or rural remote settings, school districts and administrators have concerns related to the efficient operation of the school as an institution. One major concern directly related to managing CMC is the cost of acquiring and maintaining the personnel and technology hardware including software, phone lines, fax, and multimedia equipment. In the usual school organization, the political power rests with the decision makers and the administrator who allocates resources. Resources may be defined as either time or money: as the salary for district distance education facilitators, inservice time for teacher training, remuneration for formal education in credit or noncredit computer courses, shared time in computer labs, availability of phone lines for Internet connections, computers in classrooms, computer labs, option for a teacher to arrange her daily schedule to use a computer lab, or time for additional organizational planning or course design.

Access to the technology is the primary factor in a successful program. Chesbro and Bonsall (1989) document the investment in computers in U.S. public school systems. She reports that in the 1981-82 school year, 38% of all school districts had some microcomputers. In 1988, 94.9% of all schools had microcomputers for use by students. They quoted a Quality Education Data (1988) report that stated: "There are now 1,250,000 computers in public schools that serve over 39 million students, for an average density of 32 students per micro" (pp. 155-156). According to the 1994 Office of Technology Assessment report, this estimated ratio is now one computer for every nine students (O'Neil, 1995). The low density can be interpreted as an indication of the lack of hands-on time for student learners and an increased need for more software and hardware. Type and frequency of use, either for games, word processing, or drill-and-practice programs seem to be the main focus of computer use at the date of the report publication.

THE LANGUAGE AND LITERACY CLASSROOM

Several intersecting factors recently have influenced changes in the traditional teacher role in language teaching. During the last decade, a paradigm change in the traditional teacher philosophy occurred that promoted different classroom behaviors by language teachers. The "teacher" role has been redefined. It has evolved from the "expert," the traditional "lecturer" or "master" in a teacher-centered environment. In contrast, in a learner-centered setting, the teacher is more of an advanced, actively engaged learner who also models reading, writing, researching, and acquiring new skills and ideas.

The authors who first had an impact on teaching styles and approaches wrote about learner responses to literature and the social aspects of learning. They were: Nancie Atwell (1987); Stephen Tchudi (1986); Charlotte Huck, Susan Hepler, and Janet Hickman (1987); and Frank Probst (1987). Their concepts and collections of innovative ideas have been accepted as credible methods to energize and sustain the classroom teacher in multiple approaches to English language teaching.

Robert Probst (1984) wrote about the learner responses to text. He expanded on Louise Rosenblatt's (1983) term *transaction,* which was assigned to the private interpretation of reading done outside of class. Probst also stated that by viewing reading as an act of creation rather than a search for "one true meaning", the traditional authority of the pedagogue is relinquished. Probst suggested guiding techniques that the teacher of literature might use in looking for patterns in learner responses. Frank Smith (1987) addressed issues of emerging learners "reading to write" and about learning as a collaborative activity. In his book *Joining the Literacy Club*, he provoked thought and discussion among teachers of reading and writing.

English and second-language classrooms have not been the same since these teacher educators published their research about reading and writing. The whole language movement coincided chronologically with many of the advances in computer technology, availability or cost, and user ease. Young adult literature for middle school students became more available in the past decade. This increase in literature specifically written for the adolescent has given the reading and writing teacher more material for learners, based on contexts and themes related to adolescents' interests.

ADULT LIFELONG LEARNING

Ronald Gross (1982) edited a collection of essays written about adult learners. A recurring thread in all chapters is the simple, unheralded natural occurrence of informal learning that ultimately has the greatest impact on the individual. The themes of study, learner autonomy, and the social nature of learning are presented for adults to adopt into their lifelong education plan. In the collection of essays, Gross includes a chapter by Paulo Freire on the social and political implications of learning and the importance of setting the context for making a lesson in literacy relevant. Cyril Houle's study of adults and their common characteristics gives insight into his approach to adult education. Malcolm Knowles's (1980) contribution relates pedagogy to andragogy. This interesting essay relates theory to practice and then elaborates on the evolving loop in which current andragogical theories make a circular return to pedagogy. Gross quotes Knowles as stating that adult education practices have to be used successfully younger learners.

Collaboration, interdisciplinary learning, and contextual learning are not reserved for adults, but in reforming pedagogical theory, these concepts have been a force in engaging learners in primary and secondary schools. The individual learner connecting to a community of learners is a social context that reflects some of the themes in this book.

Lindeman (1961) has written about the individual as a creative and motivated questioner and on the social implications of learning. The impact on one's life of continually acquiring new information, solving problems, and transmitting social and political attitudes is restated by the contributors in this volume. The teacher who incorporates CMC into a classroom must become a self-directed learner to gain new knowledge about the technology and the best applications of instructional system design and distance education theories.

Learning about CMC, as written about in Volume 4 of this series, may take place in a formal structured environment at teacher education colleges and universities or in higher education graduate courses for credit. Informal learning environments for CMC include continuing education, community education classes, conferences, journals, or inservice teacher training. This type of intense learning takes time. Some experts state that two to four years are required for a teacher working full time to gain expertise and reach a comfort level with computer use and gain the skills necessary to make the technology transparent. The teachers who successfully learn about the technology and then adapt their teaching style and lesson plans to incorporate the latest technology into their classroom lessons should be recognized as creative and innovative.

In actual practice, the number of responsibilities of the classroom teacher increases and expands with the introduction of technology. Organization and preparation time increases greatly. The time is necessary to gain comfort with the technology, to first set up and then to maintain the computer and other technological connections, adapt lessons, and, finally, to teach learners.

Adult education research models based on setting, process, and context for continuing education of adults take multiple roles and interactions into consideration. Tight (1985) compares four accepted models and elaborates on the interrelated factors. He concludes that the interactions between each element is more multifaceted than previously thought. Adult education research will have an impact on the changes in roles and responsibilities of teachers as teacher education, either formal or informal, becomes more structured in the future. Inservice and district education programs to continually update teachers in applications of CMC to the highest standards possible will become more prevalent.

Reform, Relearn, Restructure

Reforms in education in the last decade have made lasting changes. The whole language movement and teacher-relearn approaches to teaching have brought teachers, slowly, out of the isolation of single classrooms into the collaborative process with peers. Whether this collaboration is highly structured with formalized interdisciplinary teams at certain grade levels or as informal as a casual meeting in the hall, the process of sharing new knowledge, new approaches, and successful methods that have a solid theoretical grounding can only benefit the learners. The authors of chapters in this volume explain their successful projects using interdisciplinary teaching, team teaching, and problem-based teaching approaches combined with distance education.

The organizational methods and techniques used in the classroom of an English teacher change with the adoption of a computer. Organizational methods and evaluation processes are different. Instead of stacks of papers, students' computer discs are inexpensive, easily used, easily stored, and accessible for retrieval and evaluation. Using computers for the six-step writing process makes tracking and evaluation of individual learners progress simpler during each stage of the writing process. Individual student progress with assignments can be monitored and evaluated utilizing the computer as an organizational tool. In addition, the Internet and Web connections and online discussion lists have enabled the teacher to reach beyond the confines of an isolated classroom. At his or her own convenience, the teacher can collaborate with other like-minded teachers and to access and integrate material into long-term projects and plans.

Lessons from Distance Education

To understand better some of the values inherent in teaching with computers, I will turn to the literature and theory of distance education, much of which has been conducted using computer mediated communication.

Moore (1983; Moore, Thompson, & Dirr, 1991) developed a theory of independent learning composed of two dimensions: transactional distance and learner autonomy. Dialogue and structure, the two variables that describe "transactional distance," are classic definitions in distance education. *Dialogue* is described as "the extent to which, in any educational program, the learner, the program, and the educator are able to respond to one another" (Moore, 1983, p. 157). *Structure*, the second variable, is "the measure of an educational program's responsiveness to learner individual needs" (p. 157). Learner autonomy, according to Moore's theory, is a positive quality or attribute in the separation of teacher and learner (p. 158).

The perspective of the self-directed learner is central to the program emphasis. Moore (1989) examined interactions in instructional settings. He distinguished three types of interaction: learner-instructor, learner-content, and learner-learner. The definition and analysis of these distinct exchanges has maximized the meaning and focus toward the learner and learning in distance education as new technologies are developed. In *Contemporary issues in American Distance Education* (Moore, Cookson, Donaldson, & Quigley, 1990), Moore, as one of the editors, assembled chapters that provide a valuable resource on distance education as the field of study evolves into issues beyond the initial theories.

Cheryl Amundsen (1994) suggests the evolution of thinking in distance education is "the teaching and learning, with learning, not the learner or the notion of distance, occupying the central position" (p. 73), in a triangular figure with the traditional teacher, learner, and content set at the corners. Amundsen elaborates on the definitions of teacher, content, and learner as the discipline of distance education moves the focus of inquiry to microanalysis. Gunawardena and Zittle (1995) wrote about research that shows "social presence" to be a positive factor in improving the effectiveness of the instructor in both traditional and CMC courses. An elaboration of Moore's theory, according to Gunawardena and Zittle, shifts emphasis today to learner-centered instruction. Meaning is derived also from learner-learner interactions. The setting, the connection, and learner comfort are factors that contribute to positive instructor-learner interchanges.

Implications from Distance Education for Elementary and Secondary Schools

The interrelatedness of the topics and recurring themes in this introduction brings theories, concepts, and practice together into a circular three-dimensional figure. Distance education, as an evolving field, pulls together andragogy and pedagogy and indicates they are anchor points on a continuum of self-directed learning. Theories from adult education carry over to teacher education; lifelong learning theorists find informal learning, a social context, has the most meaning. Any K-12 learner would agree. Learner responses have been emphasized in the teaching of literature and science and now are being recognized in distance education as an indication of the acquisition of course content. Research seems to support findings that the instructors must abandon traditional roles and focus on interactions with the learner in order to promote interchanges and to encourage learner self-directedness. The developments in recent years in distance education, as a distinct field of study, have challenged and fascinated educators. The contributors to this volume will have various successful programs and courses of study that will further expand and elaborate on the topics I have briefly introduced.

SUMMARY OF THE CHAPTERS IN VOLUME 4

The first section in the book generally addresses reading and writing online and is followed by two chapters that look at student publishing and four examples of online correspondence projects. Foreign language learning is the topic of the fourth section, and the book concludes with two chapters on the use of audiographics in foreign language learning. Audiographics is the use of computers linked by software and phone lines, with audioconferencing occurring simultaneously on a second phone line.

Writing and Reading

According to Bulik and Wulff, computer-based technology in curriculum and the classroom has the potential to open the world to marginalized learners. This technology also holds the potential to overcome and/or remove environmental and personal learning barriers associated with marginalized adult learners. Moreover, the competent use of well-designed technology in curriculum and the (virtual) classroom can create forums for historically unheard whispers to become heard voices. Indeed, technology can provide a channel for traditionally marginalized and excluded voices to be heard and can be a medium and/or tool for effective communication interaction. They use the term *marginalized learners* as an umbrella for categories of students in the public school system that are labeled at-risk, learning disabled (LD) and emotionally disturbed (ED) in special education programs for juvenile offenders in correctional settings.

Technology can offer marginalized K-12 learners opportunities to see how others think and feel; it can provide places and spaces for an exchange and interaction of ideas, thoughtful analyses, and creative problem solving. However, there is no guarantee that technology, by itself, will accomplish any of these goals. Technology interactions require skill development and a command of specific knowledge and practice—a literacy—that all learners (especially marginalized learners) need in order to communicate and act effectively in technological societies. Bulik and Wulff's chapter critically explores the potential for technology to engage and/or alienate marginalized learners as well as to serve as a component in developing lifelong learning habits. Furthermore, they consider technology to be a unique and specific literacy, within a bundled concept of general communication literacy, that all adult learners need for effective communication interaction in the Third Millennium.

Bubble Dialogue, a HyperCard application, was tested as a potential tool for literacy development by Cunningham, Angeli, Morton, and Cunningham. Over a period of three months, 28 students from Highland Park Elementary School in Bloomington, IN, used Bubble Dialogue for reading and writing stories. Scripts were collected and evaluated with the help of two teachers. Findings show that Bubble Dialogue has great potential as a literacy development tool as it promotes articulation and development of the thought processes, development of word meaning, provision of natural language teaching, and acquisition of sentence structure awareness.

The dual histories of drama and educational technology converge to produce an instructional tool for language arts that is available, free of charge, on the Internet. This tool resembles the "frametale" in structure and the video game in enjoyment. In this chapter, Geeslin draws on his experience in cognitive rehabilitation with the traumatically brain damaged to offer this practical method for motivating "reluctant readers." A touch of the two histories is given to ground the exercise in historical perspective without being pedantic or boring. A list of URLs is given to lead you to "live" examples of "just fiction," "almost active fiction," "lonely fiction," and the real stuff: "Inter(net) Active Fiction."

Student Publishing

O'Haver and O'Haver have developed and tested a number of projects for fourth- and fifth-grade students in which they use technological tools to produce curriculum-related educational products, including print, multimedia presentations, and electronic publications, that are targeted to and have value for people outside the classroom. Many of the projects are designed for lower grades in the school. With the introduction of computer-mediated communications via the Internet, the target audience for student products expands to include students and classes in other schools all over the world.

The World-Wide Web provides a means of publishing student writing and artwork, and electronic mail provides an avenue for readers outside the classroom to provide feedback to the students regarding their work. They have found that these projects increase students' motivation for writing and encourage them to think of themselves as producers and not just consumers. The motivational benefits apply to the teachers as well as the students. Development of the Internet as a curriculum resource has been slow in the United Kingdom. In part, this has mirrored the lack of availability of Internet connections to those outside the higher education community. During 1995 this situation began to change, with a rapid increase in the numbers of individuals subscribing to Internet providing services.

Fullick indicates that schools were slow to respond to these changes. In part this was due to technical problems related to the machine-compatibility issues in U.K. schools. But the main reason that schools failed to respond is actually structural—a lack of investment, combined with a neutral or even hostile attitude to information technology in all its forms, especially global networking. This chapter describes a project in which teachers and a university education department produce a journal in which elementary and secondary school science students publish the outcomes of their experimental and investigative work on the Internet. Fullick's chapter describes the possible outcomes of this project in terms of student learning, gives an account of the development of the project to date, and suggests a number of lessons that can be drawn from the introduction of the Internet into the classroom.

Online Correspondence Projects

Christy provides advice and direction for educators beginning to use online services to teach communication skills to primary-, middle-, and secondary-level students. The writer discusses what factors to consider when choosing an online service, basic equipment needs, and training methods for teachers and students. The kinds of strategies to use when organizing this type of learning project from student records, online behavior standards, recordkeeping, key pal sources, and closure activities are discussed in detail. Her step-by-step instructions and advice help make these projects doable, for even a novice Internet user.

In his chapter Brush describes the implementation and evaluation of a CMC project that linked elementary students and senior citizens in the community. Fifth-grade students in one elementary school established relationships with electronic "pen-pals—senior citizens who would correspond with students electronically and share their vast wealth of knowledge. Using electronic mail, students were able to share written information, academic problems, pictures, drawings, and school projects with the senior citizens. Through their electronic discussions with senior citizens, students were able to: (a) receive firsthand knowledge of the applicability of the concepts they were learning in school to the problems being faced by citizens in their community, and (b) acquire a wider array of perspectives and viewpoints regarding the historical, social, and political issues they were discussing in the classroom.

Connecting to a Meaningful Life was a senior English project completed by students of Ayersville High School (in Ohio). Tille and Hall report the purpose of the project was to introduce students to the use of CMC as a tool for research and interpersonal communication. They further outline the project as involving several phases: (a) student training on e-mail procedures and protocols, (b) development of an acceptable use policy, (c) use of listservs to gather addresses of potential contacts, (d) online interviews and correspondence between students and subjects, and (e) completion of a final essay describing the essential qualities of a meaningful life. Tille and Hall suggest the project results indicate that CMC is a viable tool in the high school classroom that enhances the writing process, augments collaboration, develops new and valuable communication skills, and provides exposure to unique resources and global viewpoints.

Patricia R. Grimes, Woodbridge Senior High School, and Miriam Owens, Pattie One Elementary School, have had their students exchange letters via the Internet. The elementary students initiated the two-part letter exchange. Having conducted research, the fourth graders wrote letters to historical figures, roles assumed by the twelfth-grade students. In preparation for answering the elementary students' letters, the high school students examined primary sources. Once the letters came in, they then replied to the fourth graders' questions. In addition, the twelfth-grade students provided the fourth graders with new information. The fourth graders then incorporated this new information into their research papers.

In the second part of the letter exchange, the elementary students, having completed the reading of historical fiction novels, again initiated the letter exchange. This time, the fourth graders addressed their letters to fictional characters. The twelfth graders, having read the same books, assumed the roles of the literary characters and responded. In their letters, they included questions that require the elementary students to reexamine their texts.

Foreign Language Learning

CMC has the potential to revolutionize the teaching of foreign languages. According to Dies, CMC allows an increased number of interactions with speakers of foreign language, culture, and texts to engage learners. Once access is established, professional discussion with peers permits teacher to leave the isolation of a classroom This collaboration and social contact via CMC also increases the number of authentic resources for teaching and learning about the cultural aspects of foreign languages. Many projects are being developed and shepherded by groups with similar goals on Web pages. Possible uses of a well-constructed Web page as a teaching and learning resource are given as examples. Real-time synchronous communications with video via the Web will become the ultimate communication venue for language instruction. Dies stresses the social and cultural elements of interactions between teachers—between teachers as well as teachers and learners.

The teaching of French as a second language is undergoing a process of change in Saskatchewan and across Canada. Curriculum offerings within smaller rural schools are affected by budget reductions, lack of trained subject specialists, rural isolation, and declining student enrollment. French language programs either adapt or are abandoned. The distance education format was considered as a resolution to provide second language programs for learners. This three stage study by Longpré reports findings of a communicative/experiential model for instruction that documents the positive influences of CMC interactivity.

During the study, Longpré and others noted that CMC provided an audience and a voice for learners. The study recognized that the two prerequisites for genuine interaction resulted in increased collaboration and a sense of community for both instructors and learners. Longpré stresses the interactivity and collaborative elements of CMC as motivating factors for learners in the second language program. As a means of learner evaluation, student responses to questionnaires had an impact on plans to incorporate CMC into official curriculum of the French programs.

Based on the joint project between Tsukuba (Japan) and Stirling (U.K.) Universities on teaching and learning Japanese using e-mail correspondence, Ohashi reconsiders the use of e-mail in learning second languages in a wider pedagogical context. The main proposal of this chapter is to recognize the movement from computer-aided instruction to computer-mediated communication in second language acquisition (SLA) models, particularly looking at the difference between the notion of comprehensible input and comprehended input, and to discuss the practical application of e-mail correspondence to facilitate the learner's acquisition of Japanese.

Ady discusses a case study using computer-mediated communication in a high school Japanese novice-level classroom. CMC was utilized in part of an activity called "the survey project." In this activity, students conducted their surveys on their own interests electronically and orally to many Japanese people. Students compiled the results, presented the results orally, and turned in written reports.

This activity was created to promote four skills (reading, writing, speaking, and listening), communicative competence, and cultural awareness. According to students' reflections, this task-based, student-centered activity was highly motivating, and the use of CMC helped to overcome some shortcomings of traditional classrooms through bringing elements of the target culture into the classroom. This activity can be used for any language and at any level. Internet access for CMC use can be minimal; only one account is necessary.

Lewis and Morse describes how a computer group-conferencing facility was used by beginning German language students in Singapore to create their own "gossip" column. The students used the column to discuss matters of general interest as well as language issues arising from their studies. Lewis and Morse found that participation in the gossip column improved the group dynamics of the classroom, fostering a sense of pride, an interest in things German, and an environment for cooperative learning. Although the column involved a substantial commitment of nonclass time, students felt the benefits outweighed the costs.

Lewis and Morse highlight the need for training to make best use of such opportunities for computer-mediated communication, its potential as a forum for students to express academic problems and receive peer counseling, and its capacity to provide true-life language practice that adds relevance to what is learned in class.

AP German/telecom is a course Dobner designed for Juniors or Seniors in high school who plan to take the AP German Language Exam administered by the College Board usually sometime in May of each year. Students taking this course must be fluent enough in advanced German to be able to largely dispense with speaking and listening exercises, and they should have a German teacher in a high school who can monitor their progress and correct the text assignments. The emphasis is on improving writing skills. The work is done on a computer at home or in a high school and consists of exercises that are similar to those found on the AP German Language Exam. The exercises for this course comprise writing assignments on given topics and in a prescribed format, grammar work, and sample tests. Some of the work is monitored by a teacher, some of it is self-programmed (correcting is done by means of an answer sheet), and at times the work may be done in conjunction with other students around the world who are concurrently subscribed to the same course.

Audiographics in Second Language Learning

Students who learn in small-sized groups, in rural isolation or unevenly distributed populations, are often denied the opportunity of learning in curriculum areas that require a content specialist as interactive teacher. The cost of providing specialist teachers in curriculum areas such as foreign languages led school authorities in Australia to seek answers to this inequality. Stacey is a pioneer in the use of audiographic technology, a form of synchronous computer-mediated communication that enables an instructor to teach a larger number of students without the necessity of a face-to-face presence.

Audiographic technologies are explained as a medium particularly well suited to the teaching and learning of foreign languages. Stacey describes a university working in partnership with three clusters of schools teaching three different languages. The aim of the partnerships was to establish a pedagogical model for language learning using this form of synchronous CMC. Stacey concludes that these models of effective strategies for introducing audiographic technology and incorporating the technology into language learning programs were successful. Issues of professional development and staff support were also discussed.

Zsiray is in a position to know that teaching over a audiographic distance learning system poses many administrative and pedagogical challenges. These include setting up and testing hardware and software, developing administrative policies, training users, designing meaningful interactive instruction, engaging students in dialogue with fellow students who are located in remote locations, and evaluating the effectiveness of the instruction.

The elements of the current distance learning system are introduced and future implications of teaching the Russian language over this imposing technology are discussed. Students from five rural and suburban high schools in various parts of Utah have participated in the Russian language program. Future operational scenarios are described on the effective use of this emerging technology for use in high school instruction.

Collins completes this book with a "tools" chapter that introduces the tools that teachers and students need to be aware of to make the best of surfing the Internet. this chapter is followed by a Glossary.

REFERENCES

Amundsen, C. (1991). The evolution of theory in distance education. In D. Keegan (Ed.), *Theoretical principles of distance education* (pp. 61-79). New York: Routledge.

Atwell, N. (1987). *In the middle, writing, reading, and learning with adolescents.* Upper Montclair, NJ: Boynton/Cook.

Chesboro, J.W., & Bonsall D.G. (1989). *Computer-mediated communication, human relationships in a computerized world.* Tuscaloosa: University of Alabama Press.

Gross, R. (Ed.). (1982). *Invitation to lifelong learning.* Chicago: Follett.

Gunawardena, C.N., & Zittle, R. (1995, May). *An examination of teaching and learning processes in distance education and implications for designing instruction.* Paper presented at The Invitational Research Conference in Distance Education, Penn State University, University Park, PA.

Houle, C.O. (1984). *Patterns of learning.* San Francisco: Jossey-Bass.

Houle, C.O. (1992). *The literature of adult education, a bibliographic essay.* San Francisco: Jossey-Bass.

Huck, C.S., Hepler, S., & Hickman, J. (1987). *Children's literature in elementary school* (4th ed.). Chicago: Holt, Rinehart and Winston.

Knowles, M. (1980). *The modern practice of adult education from pedagogy to andragogy* (2nd ed.). New York: Cambridge University Press.

Lindeman, E. (1961). *The meaning of adult education.* Montreal: Harvest House, Ltd.

Moore, M.G. (1983). The individual adult learner. In M. Tight (Ed.), *Adult learning and education* (Vol. 1, pp. 153-168). London: Croom Helm.

Moore, M.G. (Ed.). (1989). Editorial comments: Three types of interaction. *American Journal of Distance Education, 3*(2), 1-6.

Moore, M.G., Cookson, P., Donaldson, J., & Quigley, B.A. (Eds.). (1990). *Contemporary issues in American distance education.* New York: Pergamon Press.

Moore, M.G., Thompson, M.M., & Dirr, P. (1991). *Report on the Second American Symposium on Research in Distance Education.* University Park: Pennsylvania State University, American Center for the Study of Distance Education Annenberg/CBP Project.

O'Neil, J. (1995). Teachers and technology: Potential and pitfalls. *Educational Leadership, 53*(2), 10-11.

Probst, R. (1984). *Adolescent literature: Response and analysis.* Columbus, OH: Merrill.

Quality Education Data, Inc. (1988). *Micro-computer and VCR usage in schools, 1982-88* (2nd ed.). Denver, CO: Author.

Rosenblatt, L. (1983). *Literature as exploration* (4th ed.). New York: The Modern Language Association of America. (Original work published in 1938).

Smith, F. (1987). *Joining the literacy club.* Portsmouth, NH: Heineman.

Tchudi, S. (Ed.). (1986). *English teachers at work: Ideas and strategies from five countries.* Upper Montclair, NJ: Boynton/Cook.

Tight, M. (1985). Modeling the education of adults. *Studies in the education of adults, 17*(1).

I

WRITING/READING

2

EVOLUTION OF A WHISPER

Robert J. Bulik and Sherry Wulff

Students with exceptional educational needs (EEN) have been provided with both the structure and the support of an Individual Education Plan (IEP), specially certified teachers, limited class sizes, and transition support. Students classified as "at-risk" of dropping out of school and other marginalized groups of learners have also received very specific support. Yet, follow-up studies show that a large number of these same students, upon graduation from high school, are unable to find employment or to enter postsecondary education with any significant degree of success (Wagner, Newman, Blackorby, & Cameto, 1994; Whitsett, DiOrio, Williams, & Edmiaston, 1994). What these studies do not determine, however, is exactly why such grim transition statistics exist. Hence, this chapter takes a critical look at the potential for technology to engage or to further alienate marginalized learners by raising the question: If teachers only incorporate technology into the classroom but do not address the underlying literacy, should outcomes improve for these learners?

We use the term *marginalized learners* as an umbrella for categories of students in the public school systems that are labeled at-risk, learning disabled (LD), and emotionally disturbed (ED) in special education programs and for juvenile offenders in correctional settings.

We believe that it is the uncritical acceptance of technology that has the potential to silence voices that have barely risen above a whisper in our society; technology also has the potential to engage marginalized groups of learners by raising their voices from a whisper to where they can be heard by all.

We will raise questions throughout this chapter about the appropriate use of technology in the classroom. We ask questions that cross learning theories, challenge reified assumptions, and range from elementary skill development to transition issues for postsecondary placement of high school graduates. Central to the concerns of this chapter are 3 factors:

1. The historical view of marginalized learners;
2. The literacy imbedded within classroom technology—specifically, computer literacy; and
3. The assumption that technology, as an artifact, engages marginalized learners.

BACKGROUND

Willinsky (1990) wrote from a historical perspective:

> Widespread reading and writing skills were not always welcomed by those in position of power or comfort. This new literacy repeatedly gave voice to an independence of spirit and thought, within a class which many of their betters thought had no apparent need for these disrupting elements. (p. 185)

National surveys show that by 12th grade regular education graduates have earned 15 of their 22 credits for graduation in academic classes, whereas special education graduates have earned an average of 12 of their 22 credits in academic classes (U.S. Dept. of Education, 1994). Lipsky and Gartner (1989) argue that when marginalized students are tracked into "special" programs, they are generally excluded from the "frills" of art, computer literacy, music, and even physical education. Interestingly, only 27.1% of all 12th-grade LD students and 14.3% of all 12th grade ED students have their primary placement in regular education classes. The remaining ED and LD students have their primary placements in resource and self-contained classrooms, segregated from the mainstream (U.S. Dept. of Education, 1994). Wagner et al. (1994) found that special education graduates earned fewer academic credits than their nonhandicapped peers, with ED students earning the fewest academic credits toward graduation.

MORE THAN A STYLE OF LEARNING

The picture is quite different for most "regular" high school seniors. For regular high school seniors, instruction has gradually become more varied and less dependent on structured content, encouraging critical thinking, service learning, and multiple literacies (Terenzini, Springer, Pascarella, & Nora, 1994).

Current research, however, indicates that there is an emphasis on behavior management and control in dealing with marginalized learners, often to the exclusion of teaching content subject matter or providing prevocational or vocational training (Bulik, 1996; Lipsky & Gartner, 1989; Ross, 1991). Using linear approaches to teaching low-level content, instead of diverse learning strategies, inhibits the development of problem solving, critical thinking, self-directed learning skills, and fosters a dependency on teachers. Teacher-generated learning objectives set up an environment in which students are spoon fed and hand held during most learning experiences. It is the conditioning effect of these types of classroom environments, based on a stimulus-response (S-R) model, with rewards for successive approximations for appropriate learning and behavior, that insidiously promotes not only compliance but dependency.

If the educational system produces these dependent learners, unable to think critically or to problem solve, will they survive in the self-directed environment established by adult educators?

The disillusioning postsecondary employment outlook for mildly handicapped youth (Fairweather & Shaver, 1991), the limited success of marginalized youth in postsecondary education (Shor, 1987; Wagner et al., 1994), and our personal classroom teaching experience with K-12 and postsecondary learners have raised doubts about the effectiveness of "special" education in general. Steele (1992) argues for a "de-conditioning" process that would make education meaningful for marginalized students.

The question becomes: If marginalized groups of learners are "simply" presented with computer technology, will they learn more effectively and will follow-up surveys show that school-to-work transition results have improved?

The use of well-designed technology in the (virtual) classroom with marginalized learners can create pathways for unheard whispers to become heard voices. Technology can also offer marginalized learners an opportunity to see how others think and feel; it can provide a forum for new ideas, for thoughtful analysis, and for better information—but, there is no guarantee that students will accomplish any of these goals. Before teachers place students in front of computers, they should be aware of the effect of technology in the following three areas: literacy, transference, and technology.

LITERACY: KNOWING AND DOING

Learning a particular subject with computer-based technology involves grasping a basic understanding of both knowledge and skill—becoming literate in a specific subject-skill area. However, literacy, as a learning outcome, is not an easy term to examine. Perhaps John Dewey (1916/1964) defined it best in 1916 when he wrote: "To be informed . . . is to have at command the subject matter needed for an effective dealing with a problem, and for giving added significance to the search for solution and to the solution itself" (p. 367).

The concept of owning a body of information, along with the ability to use it in a meaningful way, would seem to be the most appropriate understanding of literacy. If we assume that Dewey's "to have at hand the subject matter" constitutes an equivalent to learned subject-matter content, then literacy itself is only partially explained. The concept of literacy also revolves around experience and actually having the capacity for "effective dealing with a problem."

Lazerson, McLaughlin, McPherson, and Bailey (1990) provides an analogy, from Mark Twain's *Life on the Mississippi*, to provide a rather straightforward look at literacy that incorporates learned skills and knowledge and the capacity and commitment to go beyond the basics of a subject field:

> Twain's getting to know the river, Joseph Featherstone tells us, is a classic American expression of a metaphor for learning. Twain learns how to navigate the river at a young age. He learns every shoal, snag, and sandbar. These are the basic skills. But no sooner has he memorized their locations and peculiarities than he has to modify or forget them, and learn other spots, for the river never stops changing its course. Twain must simultaneously remember the reality of what existed in the river and imagine how different forces and conditions are likely to change it. . . . In the process of learning, we, like Twain, continually remake our education, ourselves, and our ways of coping with and understanding the world. (p. 67)

The knowledge or content of a particular subject area is insufficient to qualify an individual as literate. An ability to use that knowledge in a generation and interaction of ideas in critical analyses or in creative problem solving is also necessary. Yet, without the content knowledge to support skill training, learning a set of employability tasks does not make one literate either. What we mean by literacy ought to involve an emphasis on the possession of both knowledge and task skills. The questions continue: Can computers (or technology in general) provide both aspects of literacy in specific subject matter areas such as math or writing?

TRANSFERENCE: BRIDGING THE ABYSS

The second broad area we consider is the overall outcomes expected of public school education. Perhaps what most confounds teachers of marginalized students is the transferability of classroom learning to postsecondary environments. Students will often question the value or relevance of a particular subject or skill. We not only recommend a critical look at what constitutes appropriate subject matter, but also how that material is presented. For example, are educators' teaching strategies and learners' learning strategies designed to serve marginalized students a lifetime? Studies with both special education students and adjudicated youth indicate significantly lower abilities to be self-directed in their learning than their peers (Bulik, 1996). Yet, educational programs for both special education students and incarcerated youth emphasize very structured learning environments. We argue that if 12 years of public school education does not meet an individual's needs, then it should at least pave the way for continued learning as an adult.

It has been our experience that there is not a continuum of learning that bridges all levels of education. Historically, secondary and postsecondary educational institutions have developed with distinct philosophies and a sharp divide that have precluded collaborative efforts in curriculum building. Greenberg (1991) describes this sharp divide as a legacy of distrust that includes colorful descriptors such as *gulf, abyss,* and the *San Andreas Fault,* with each on opposite sides.

Most adult education principles and practices are based on adults becoming more self-directed (Knowles, 1980) and autonomous (Merriam & Caffarella, 1991) as they mature or age (Chene, 1983). Merriam and Caffarella also note that self-directed learning is the way most adults acquire new ideas, skills, and attitudes; all necessary attributes for upward mobility and enhanced quality of life.

It needs to be emphasized that the assumptions, embedded in adult education and practiced by adult educators, instructors, and trainers, cross both formal postsecondary educational institutional settings and informal workplace training programs. For example, employers are now seeking individuals who have taken the initiative to continue their education by obtaining formal degrees and advanced credentials. Long and Morris (1995) noted that "self-directed learning in the workplace is a reality and a growing phenomenon with more business opting for its inclusion yearly" (p. 375). The accelerating pace of technological and social change now makes ongoing workplace education a requirement of most businesses (Knox, 1993). Both formal institutional education and informal credentials that, in turn, have social and economic implications for the individual and competitive advantages for the employer.

In contrast to adult education practitioners, elementary and secondary teachers are required not only to tell students when to learn ("Don't be late for your First Period class!"), but what to learn, and even how to learn it. Teacher-generated learning objectives, intensive tutoring, and immediate feedback all have the unintended side effect of leaving students more dependent on external reinforcement as a reward for learning. The price for failure to conform to these external controls is much higher than "just" failing grades. Students are acculturated into a specific kind of learning process, but then are told "You're on your own!" upon graduation (Piskurich, 1992).

More than any specific level of content literacy, becoming a self-directed learner (SDL) or a self-regulated learner (SRL) may be the key to improving follow-up study statistics. If marginalized learners are to compete successfully in the postsecondary environment, transition planning must be concerned with more than just "placement" on a job or into another classroom. Graduates of special education programs must be prepared to continue learning—to be as self-directed as their peers. Furthermore, if continuing education (in its broadest terms) is in fact no longer a choice, but a condition necessary for both continued employment and advancement, then self-directed learning needs to be a skill that all elementary and secondary school students need to develop. If this is indeed the need, does the structure of the computer learning program enhance or hinder the development of self-directed learning strategies?

TECHNOLOGY: MULTIPLE PURPOSES

The third broad area we consider is technology itself. Although considered separately here, technology should not be considered in isolation in the classroom but as part of a set of literacy skills. A technological society requires a "bundled" concept of communication literacy versus a traditional approach to teaching discrete reading and language skills. Traditional teaching approaches for marginalized learners involve linear models of teacher-directed instruction involving lecture, drill and practice, and testing for recall; these pedagogical approaches are too narrow and do not take into account the added dimension of computer hardware and software.

Learning a particular subject with computer-based technology involves not only grasping a basic understanding of both subject knowledge and practical applications (i.e., becoming literate in a specific subject-skill area), but also developing a basic understanding of the underlying technology. A computer may be a tool to construct, examine, and evaluate communication (e.g., a word processing program to compose a letter or essay); it may be a medium for communication itself (e.g., a mode through which we receive and send communication); and/or it might be part of the content of communication (e.g., learning the hardware and software operations and applications or use of the Internet). Teachers and students must see technology as a way to learn, to communicate, and to think critically.

We have found, in working with a variety of computer programs and with a range of learners from elementary to postsecondary education, that the design of packaged computer programs often assumes that users are passive receivers of expert opinions. Instead of developing the critical thinking and self-directed learning skills needed for success in transition to post-school settings, computer technology actually "requires" some students to become more dependent learners.

Dependency is developed in two ways: First, computers can create impoverished, artificial environments, with limited truths (e.g., rationalized reconstruction of the real world). For example, many predetermined and closed ended assumptions or "answers" are presumed by programs (e.g., Oregon Trail). A second problem inherent in these kinds of programs is that students are treated as generic individuals. Assumptions are made within the structure of the program that uniformity of student responses are possible from diverse individual experiences. Embedded within these assumptions is the idea that concrete training and structured feedback are more important to student learning than reflective, divergent, and self-directed thinking. Is this a goal we should pursue? Can computer technology model diversity and multicultural interaction? Should it be nongeneric—and, if yes, how? These and similar questions need to be addressed before technology is simply inserted into the classroom for marginalized learners.

On the other side of the proverbial coin are programs that provide different phases of writing (such as the *Writing Partner*). Questions such as "Do you want your composition to persuade or to describe?" or "What is the topic of your composition?" and "Wouldn't it be better to move this information to the front?" engage learners in ways that encourage formative thought. The interactive nature of this program not only teaches students about writing, but also aids in the development of internal feedback conditions that help students learn the content and the process. We feel that this form of formative feedback encourages both writing proficiency and self-directed learning.

DISCUSSION

We have argued that the computer has the potential to either create an enriched or an impoverished environment for marginalized learners in the public school setting. The problem appears to reside in the structure of computers and computer programs. Bolter (1991) captures the essence of the problem when he declares that the computer user must "learn to read (and write) in a new way, by cooperating with a text that is directed by its own economy of interpretation" (p. 196).

If teachers simply have marginalized students sit at a computer, they, like Kellogg (1994), will find that "there is no published evidence that reports a reliable correlation between the use of word processors and productivity" (p. 158). Like a pen or pencil, or any other writing instrument, computers are simply a tool: "word processors encourage continuous editing of surface features and formatting of text" (p. 156). Students become involved in the busy work of writing (thinking that they are making progress) and may not fully develop ideas or critical analysis of their presentations or arguments. Quality comparisons "show no difference between composing on a computer or with pen and paper" (p. 160). Students will not necessarily become better writers because they use computers.

The use of a computer to write a paper, for example, addresses only one aspect of Dewey's concept of what it means to be literate; too often, marginalized learners only learn how to use specific skills in isolation. As discussed earlier in this chapter, Dewey's definition of literacy centers on a command and use of knowledge. Likewise, a "bundled" concept of literacy refers to a command and use of the different strands affiliated with language and communication, for example, reading, writing, speaking, listening, media, and computer technology. "Bundled" literacy involves teaching students, across the breadth of the curriculum, how technology (multiple symbol systems and codes) interfaces with both the subject matter and the learning process.

CONCLUSIONS

When marginalized learners "cooperate" with the constraints of very structured computer programs, there is the danger that they will be further de-skilled in terms of becoming self-directed, self-regulated, lifelong learners. Compliance with one teaching strategy (linear models of teacher-directed instruction involving lecture, drill and practice, and testing for recall) is simply traded for another—computer-generated structured responses. We believe that teachers, at all levels, should be critically aware of the assumptions and constraints used to engage marginalized learners. Literacy should be a lifelong pursuit, aided in the next millennium by technology.

REFERENCES

Bolter, J.D. (1991). *Writing space: The computer, hypertext, and the history of writing.* Hillsdale, NJ: Lawrence Erlbaum Associates.

Bulik, R.J. (1996). Are self-directed learning skills the missing competency in the special education curriculum? In H.B. Long & Associates (Eds.), *New dimensions in self-directed learning* (pp. 177-192). Norman: College of Education, University of Oklahoma.

Chene, A. (1983). The concept of autonomy: A philosophical discussion. *Adult Education Quarterly, 34*, 38-47.

Dewey, J. (1964). The nature of subject matter. In R. Archamgbault (Ed.), *John Dewey on education: Selected writings* (pp. 359-372). Chicago: The University of Chicago Press. (Original work published 1916).

Fairweather, J.S., & Shaver, D.M. (1991). Making the transition to postsecondary education and training. *Exceptional Children, 1*, 264-270.

Greenberg, A.R. (1991). *High school-college partnerships: Conceptual models, programs, and issues* (ASHE-ERIC Higher Education Rep. No. 5). Washington, DC: George Washington University, School of Education and Human Development.

Kellogg, R.T. (1994). *The psychology of writing.* New York: Oxford Press.

Knowles, M.S. (1980). *The modern practice of adult education: From pedagogy to andragogy* (2nd ed.). New York: Association Press.

Knox, A.B. (1993). *Strengthening adult and continuing education: A global perspective on synergistic leadership.* San Francisco, CA: Jossey-Bass Publishers.

Lazerson, M., McLaughlin, J., McPherson, B., & Bailey, S. (1990). *An education of value: The purposes and practices of schools.* New York: Cambridge University Press.

Lipsky, D.K., & Gartner, A. (1989). *Beyond separate education: Quality education for all.* Baltimore: Paul H. Brookes.

Long, H.B., & Morris, S.S. (1995). Self-Directed learning in business & industry: A review of the literature, 1983-1993. In H.B. Long & Associates (Eds.), *New dimensions in self-directed learning* (pp. 367-380). Norman: Oklahoma Research Center for Continuing Professional and Higher Education.

Merriam, S.B., & Caffarella, R.S. (1991). *Learning in adulthood: A comprehensive guide.* San Francisco: Jossey-Bass.

Piskurich, G.M. (1992). Preparing the learner for self-directed learning. In H.B. Long & Associates (Eds.), *Self-directed learning: Application and research* (pp. 309-321). Norman: Oklahoma Research Center for Continuing Professional and Higher Education.

Ross, D. (1991). *The origins of American social science.* New York: Cambridge University Press.

Shor, I. (1987). *Critical teaching & everyday life.* Chicago: The University of Chicago Press.

Steele, S.M. (1992). Evaluation and self-directed learning. In H.B. Long & Associates (Eds.), *Self-directed learning: Application and research* (pp. 287-307). Norman: Oklahoma Research Center for Continuing Professional and Higher Education.

Terenzini, P.T., Springer, L., Pascarella, E.T., & Nora, A. (1994, May). *Influences affecting the development of students' critical thinking skills* (Grant No. R117G10037). Paper presented at the meeting of the Association for Institutional Research, New Orleans, LA.

U.S. Department of Education. (1994). *Sixteenth annual report to Congress on the implementation of the Individuals with Disabilities Education Act.* Washington, DC: Government Printing Office.

Wagner, M., Newman, L., Blackorby, J., & Cameto, R. (1994). *The transition experiences of youth with disabilities: A summary of findings from the National Longitudinal Transition Study of special education students.* Menlo Park, CA: SRI International.

Whitsett, M.D., DiOrio, R., Williams, H.C., & Edmiaston, R.K. (1994). *Transition outcomes and issues for students receiving special education services.* Dallas: Texas Education Agency.

Willinsky, J. (1990). *The new literacy: Redefining reading and writing in the schools.* New York: Routledge.

3

LANGUAGE AWARENESS SUPPORT STRUCTURES: TOOLS FOR LITERACY*

Donald J. Cunningham, Charoula Angeli, Mary Lou Morton and Mary Louise Cunningham

When we first began meeting with the students at Highland Park Elementary School, we were not sure how they would react to two strangers, holding a laptop computer and a printer, entering their classroom for the first time. The first classroom we visited was a classroom of 22 second graders. There we saw students engaged in many different in-class activities; some of them were writing in their journals, some others were drawing, and some others were reading a book with their teacher. Although we entered the classroom very quietly, and sat in a corner waiting for the teacher to finish what she was doing so she could come and talk to us, the children soon started asking us who we were and why we were there. The laptop computer seemed to draw their attention very quickly, and they wanted to touch the screen and use the keyboard to type something.

---

*We would all like to thank Mrs. Karen Clark and all the other teachers at Highland Park, who have let us work with their students and helped us with data analysis.

We were glad to see that the students were comfortable with our presence in their classroom and rather familiar with computers. Before long, the teacher came to greet us, and she formally introduced us to the children. We explained to them that for the next three months we would be in their classroom twice a week, and that they would all have a chance to write stories on the computer with us. That seemed to have triggered their interest, and they wanted to know if they would get to use the computer that same day. We asked them to tell us what kinds of stories they wanted to write on the computer, and they gave us a list of topics ranging from family, friends, to things they talked in class, to pets and animals, and many others. After we answered questions they had for us, we told them that it was time to start, and the teacher asked a student to come and work with us.

So this is how it all started.

One of the first second graders we worked with was Timothy, who wanted to tell us how he was using his imagination to pretend he was someone else, somewhere else, to use his own words. The following is the script of the story we typed on the computer:

> Facilitator: Tell me Timothy, what character do you like to pretend you are the most?
> *Note: I wonder how many different characters he has pretended to be so far.*
> Timothy: I like to pretend I am a general in the army.
> Facilitator: What do you do when you pretend you are a general?
> Timothy: I find other children to play with, and command them.
> Facilitator [thinking]: This is interesting. I wonder what are some of the things he commands them to do.
> Facilitator: What do you usually command them to do?
> Timothy: Tell them to stay down and stay quiet, and tell them to hide.
> Facilitator: Do they obey you?
> Timothy: It depends on who is playing.
> Facilitator [thinking]: I guess not all his friends like taking orders.
> Facilitator: So not all of your friends like taking orders?
> Timothy: Usually friends will do it, but not my sister.
> Facilitator: What do you do when your soldiers don't do what you tell them to do?
> Timothy: We get in a fight.
> Facilitator [thinking]: That's not good.
> Facilitator: Do you think it would be better to have a talk with them teaching them the importance of obedience, instead of fighting with them?

Timothy: I try to tell my sister who I am, but she talks back, and I can't talk because she starts fighting with me, so I fight back.
Note: In the future I will try to talk with her instead of fighting with her.
Facilitator [thinking]: I wonder how serious these fights can get.
Facilitator: Who usually wins the fight?
Timothy [thinking]: Really when we fight, no one wins.
Timothy: Usually no one wins.
Facilitator: You also told me in the beginning that you pretend you are somewhere else. Where is that?
Timothy: Anywhere I want to be. Sometimes I pretend to be a dinosaur.
Facilitator: So you don't have any specific place in mind?
Timothy: No, I don't, and that's all I can say. But each time my mind takes me to different places.
Facilitator: You said before that sometimes you pretend to be a dinosaur. What do you do at that time?
Timothy [thinking]: I don't understand what she means.
Timothy: I don't understand what you mean.
Facilitator: When you pretend you are a dinosaur, what do you do?
Timothy: I walk a lot.
Facilitator: Do you feel powerful when you pretend to be a dinosaur?
Timothy: Yes, I do.
Facilitator: Why do you feel powerful?
Timothy: Dinosaurs are powerful.
Facilitator [thinking]: Good answer.
Facilitator: Do you also have imaginative friends?
Timothy: I have a dog, a turtle, and a teddy bear.
Facilitator: Are they with you all the time?
Timothy: No, they are not.
Facilitator: How often do you imagine you are someone else?
Timothy: It depends on if I start to like it or not.
Facilitator: So if you imagine you are a general, and you get tired of it, you change to a dinosaur?
Timothy: Yeah, right.
Facilitator: Do you want to review what we have been talking about?
Timothy: Sure.

When we showed this script to the teacher she said that the discrepancy between the script and the quality of Timothy's written work in the classroom was overwhelming. She was amazed and quite surprised at the quality and the volume of what Timothy had typed on the computer. She said that his oral language was very well developed just like the script he created with us, but his written work was poor. He had poor muscle coordination; therefore, he had a hard time holding the pencil and writing. It was also difficult to motivate him and to get him to develop his ideas further.

It is exactly this discrepancy between the development of oral language and the development of literacy (e.g., reading and writing) that initiated our research study. We know that children are very successful natural language learners. Before entering school, they develop significant oral language proficiency through natural spoken conversation and real-life experiences (Bintz & Dillard, 1990). By contrast, the acquisition of literacy seems to require considerable effort, resources, and management; unfortunately a considerable proportion of children fail to achieve acceptable levels of literacy. Because a general language facility seems to underlie both speech and literacy, why should there be such a pronounced difference in ease of acquisition?

THEORETICAL BACKGROUND

The theoretical background of this research is based on social constructivist and semiotic theories of learning and cognition. The social constructivist view holds that through constant interaction with parents and others, confronting and solving the host of everyday human problems, children become part of a social network (Cunningham, 1992); they learn to solve problems that make "human sense," and they do so in interaction with others.

According to Downing (1979), learning to read and write are strangely removed forms of communication that are not driven by human interaction; they involve a mark-making process that requires explicit awareness of metalinguistic aspects of language. Awareness of those aspects of language required for literacy does not develop spontaneously from spoken language. Therefore, what is required for literacy is a language awareness support structure, incorporating support for the more conscious, deliberate, meta-linguistic process that makes meaning in reading and writing. The support structure has to be such that it is grounded in the social and physical worlds in which children find themselves, so that the ensuing discussion and knowledge construction is meaningful and driven by their concerns.

Vygotsky's (1981) sociocultural theory affirms that "culture is the product of social life and of human social activity" (p. 168). The sociocultural theory is characterized by the following three themes (Wertsch, 1991). First, an individual's mental processes are shaped by cultural, historical, and institutional factors. Second, higher mental function in the individual has its origins in social activity. And third, language is an important mediator between learning and development. The implications of Vygotsky's theory for today's classroom are significant. According to the theory, we cannot understand a child's development by considering only his or her individual behavior. Teachers need to also study the social world in which that individual life has developed. Learning occurs first on an interpsychological (social) level and later on an intrapsychological (personal) level. Children first learn to do things with the help of an adult before they are able to act on their own. For this reason, language develops because of the child's need to communicate with people in the environment. In fact, Vygotsky believed that language in the form of private speech (talking to yourself) may guide cognitive development. For Vygotsky, culture and language are critical for cognitive development. Thus, like the culture itself, the individual's knowledge is constructed in the course of solving problems that arise in goal-oriented activities and is learned through interpersonal interaction (Wells & Change-Wells, 1992). A similar process takes place in learning how to read and write. Hall (1987) showed that learners develop the appropriate literacy skills when they are involved in joint literacy activities in which the literacy process takes place in the context of meaningful actions.

BUBBLE DIALOGUE: A HYPERCARD APPLICATION[1]

To give a better sense of the research, we describe here the language awareness support structure that is built in Bubble Dialogue in some detail. Bubble Dialogue combines elements of role play, comic strip creation, and reflexive dialogue analysis. A master stack, called BubbleMaker, has been written to create customized Bubble Dialogue stacks for later use. The scene in which the discussion is to take place is established by the participants. A graphic is then chosen, and the setting is described by writing a prologue (see Figure 3.1).

In each customized stack created by BubbleMaker, four icons, representing a speech bubble (public speech) and a thought bubble (inner speech) per character, are presented alongside two characters (sometimes more than two characters) on the screen (see Figure 3.2). The comic genre is so well established in many cultures that even very young children, when presented with empty bubbles, feel compelled to speak for the characters, playing out their roles. One of the features

[1]The software was developed by the Language Development and Hypermedia Research Group at the University of Ulster, Coleraine, Northern Ireland.

Figure 3.1. BubbleMaker

Figure 3.2. Bubble Dialogue

incorporated into the application is a notes field. This feature is powerful in a variety of ways. For example, when users review their dialogues they can use the notes field to add comments about "what's happening" or comments on the motives and feelings of the characters (see script). Teachers and researchers may also use this feature to annotate the dialogues in any manner they see fit such as commentary, reminders, and questions for the users to consider as they review their work.

RESEARCH PROCEDURES

During the period of the three months that we spent at Highland Park Elementary School, 28 students from age 7 to 12 worked with Bubble Dialogue. Bubble Dialogue sessions lasted for about 45 minutes to 60 minutes each. First, second, third, and fourth graders needed more time to get used to the software and to type their responses. Children with special needs were also slower as they needed more time to form and type their sentences. Their scripts were also shorter than those of their classmates but very interesting nonetheless. On the contrary, fifth and sixth graders were able to produce long scripts in approximately 30 minutes.

Over a period of three months we conducted 30 such sessions, 20 of which were dialogues between a student and a research assistant. The remainder were dialogues or role playing between two or more students. In general, older children chose to role play most of the time, whereas younger children chose to engage in a dialogue with the research assistant.

Dialogues Between a Student and a Research Assistant

The research assistant asked the student what he or she wanted to talk about, and the conversation was usually on a topic that the student selected. Then both the research assistant and the student chose the names of the characters, a suitable graphic, and the prologue for the story. Before the beginning of the dialogue, the research assistant briefly pointed out the different features of Bubble Dialogue, and almost 85% of all students were able to guess the functions of those features. The research assistant then initiated the dialogue by asking the student a question on the specific subject he or she wanted to discuss. The dialogue continued until the student had nothing else to say, and at that point a review of the dialogue was conducted. During the session the research assistant encouraged students to use the computer by themselves and type their responses. The research assistant typed on behalf of the student, only when she was asked to do so, but that rarely happened as most students liked the laptop computer and wanted to use it by themselves.

Dialogues or Role Playing Between Two or More Students

These sessions were conducted between students who had used Bubble Dialogue at least once before. Students were invited to construct a dialogue by assuming roles of characters other than themselves. The researcher observed and facilitated the process without participating in the conversation. If the students specifically asked for help in typing, the researcher would type on behalf of the students.

Our first concern when we first started working with children was to develop a process of how they could best be introduced to the language awareness features of Bubble Dialogue and how to use those features appropriately. This process is discussed next.

THE LITERACY PROCESS

The literacy process embedded in this software consisted of four phases. The systematic transition from one phase to the next largely depended on the developmental level of the children we worked with and their familiarity with computers. The four phases were: Initiation and Story Selection, Creation of a Customized Stack, Engagement in Dialogue, and Debriefing.

Initiation and Story Selection

During initiation, we spent some time getting to know the student and making sure that he or she felt comfortable. We then asked the student if he or she knew what the word dialogue meant, and because none of the students knew, we used synonyms such as *conversation* and *discussion* to help them understand the meaning of the word. We then helped the student decide what he or she wanted to talk about.

Creation of a Customized Stack

After initiation, we introduced the software, and with the student's help we established an appropriate scene by selecting a suitable picture and writing a *prologue* for the story. Because none of the students was familiar with the word prologue, we had to spend some time explaining to them its meaning. To help them understand what a prologue for their story could look like, we related it to the prologues of the books they read in class.

Engagement in Dialogue

After creating a stack we were ready to start the dialogue. We first reminded the student what the word *dialogue* meant. We then asked him or her to tell us what people did when they carried out a dialogue (most students told us that people usually take turns). We then explained to the student that Bubble Dialogue supports features that would allow us to take turns in the dialogue, such as the features of speech and thought bubbles. We related these features to comic strips, and most students were able to tell us what the difference between the two types of bubbles were and under what circumstances they were used.

We initiated the conversation by asking the student a question. After two or three speech bubbles we used a thought bubble in order to model the language awareness support structure that was built into Bubble Dialogue. We then stopped to ask the student whose turn was next. Most students answered that it was their turn because we just had our turn. At that point we stopped the online conversation to have a discussion about the differences between talking and thinking.

We continued the dialogue until the student had nothing else to talk about, and at that point we reviewed and reflected on the dialogue that the student and ourselves created.

Debriefing

During the last phase of the process, we asked the student if he or she liked Bubble Dialogue, and why. Students said that Bubble Dialogue was fun, and that they would like to have a computer in their classroom so they could use it to write stories. At that point we thanked the student for working with us and gave him or her a printout copy of the dialogue.

We tried this process with 28 students, and we found that it worked well with all grade levels. The only difference was that the process took more time when the student was in the first, second, third grade, or fourth grade (approximately one hour). Transitions from one phase of the process to the next occurred quite efficiently with fifth and sixth graders (approximately 30 to 45 minutes).

During the three-month period at Highland Park, we approached teachers with whom we had established a working relationship, and we invited them to work with us in evaluating the dialogue scripts. We asked the teachers to read each script and evaluate the student's ability to form sentences, express him- or herself appropriately, and follow and respond to an argument correctly. The result of this collaboration is presented next.

BUBBLE DIALOGUE AND THE DEVELOPMENT OF LITERACY SKILLS

Use of Dialectic Discourse to Articulate and Further Develop Learners' Thoughts

All the teachers we worked with were impressed by the amount of information some of their students typed on the computer and the extent to which they were able to further develop their thoughts. Specifically, one of the teachers said that she would be very happy if [student's name] wrote a sentence more every day.

As Tharp and Gallimore (1988) stated well, "meaningful discourse is the medium in which society creates minds, and by which minds create society. For literacy, meaningful discourse is both destination and vehicle" (p. 93). The dialectic process of Bubble Dialogue allows the learner to be drawn into language by using language.

Natural Teaching of Language

What's needed for literacy are natural communicative learning environments in which a child gradually develops as a reader/writer in social settings. Literacy events are experienced by learners as collaborative social activities with goals embedded in natural activity settings (Tharp & Gallimore, 1988). Teaching reading and writing should not occur as an isolated, decontextualized activity.

One of the first things that we noticed once we started working with children was the fact that they wanted to work with us all the time. They never said they wanted to quit, and we had to somehow end the dialogue to move on to other things. We believe that the reason for their motivation and eagerness was the fact that our literacy lessons were holistic and focused on the discussion of a topic that was interesting to them. Like Krashen (1981), we also reject approaches to literacy that rely on a nonconversational and sequential style for teaching language.

Word Meaning

One of the major tasks of schools is to promote the development of word meaning, as both vocabulary and discourse competencies. Word meaning is socially constructed. The intersubjectivities of social networks are created through discourse, and the social meanings of words are internalized through inner speech. Bubble Dialogue provides features such as speech and thought bubbles that allow learners to develop intermental, social behavior (speech bubbles) and intramental, individual behavior (thought bubbles, notes field).

Oftentimes we had to stop and explain the meaning of a word to our students. For example, Timothy (see earlier script) did not know what the word *pretend* meant when we first asked him the question. Moreover, if there was anything else he could not understand he would use a thought bubble to express his concern. In addition, one of the teachers that we worked with was very surprised to see that her students have used thought bubbles. Out of the 28 students, 5 of them used zero thought bubbles, 6 used one thought bubble, 14 used two thought bubbles, 2 used three thought bubbles, and 1 used four thought bubbles.

Acquisition of Sentence Structure Awareness

In the often seemingly effortless manner in which adults interact with children, a supportive framework evolves between the more mature and the less mature language user. It is this framework that allows the children to operate linguistically in their zone of proximal development (Vygotsky, 1962). Moreover, Rogoff (1990) has explored the concept of cultural learning in terms of the metaphor of apprenticeship. Following Vygotsky, she sees learning as occurring through the participation of a novice in a jointly undertaken cultural activity in which the expert assists the novice's performance.

Therefore, our main goal was to facilitate the literacy process, creating opportunities for the children to learn language without making them conscious that they are learning language (Speidel, 1984). Through questioning we assisted the children to express themselves to the best of their abilities. Through feedback we helped them write grammatically correct sentences and correct spelling errors. Through modeling we used all language awareness support features of Bubble Dialogue, and we explained to the students how to use them appropriately.

CONCLUSION

As Bruner (1983) stated, literacy development is part of a continuum. All aspects of language (i.e., reading, writing, speaking, and listening) develop concurrently rather than sequentially (Teale & Sulzby, 1986). Bubble Dialogue is a tool that promotes that kind of literacy. Bubble dialogue sessions engage the learners into meaningful, goal-oriented activities. During debriefing, students told us that Bubble Dialogue enabled them to speak and write as if they were at home with their parents or with friends. This motivated them to produce scripts that surprised and impressed their teachers. But this should not be a surprise, because higher level thinking develops best in social contexts (Vygotsky, 1962). It is this kind of environment that Bubble Dialogue makes accessible to the student. In addition, students said that the software allowed them to collaborate to solve a problem. They said that by exchanging ideas back and forth with the speech and through bubbles, they were able to solve the problem and actually remember all the steps involved.

We believe that the students' comments about Bubble Dialogue gave rise to the emergence of a new paradigm for literacy, and we hope that the results of this study will be used as the building blocks for the design of future computerized learning environments for the development of literacy skills.

REFERENCES

Bintz, W., & Dillard, J. (1990). Becoming book buddies: Writing dialogue journals in a first grade classroom. *Journal of Teaching Writing, 9*(2), 133-148.

Bruner, J. (1983). *Child's talk: Learning to use language.* New York: Norton.

Cunningham, D. J. (1992). Beyond educational psychology: Steps toward an educational semiotic. *Educational Psychology Review, 4*, 165-194.

Downing, M. (1979). *Reading and reasoning.* London: Chambers.

Hall, N. (1987). *The emergence of literacy*. London: Hodder and Stoughton.

Krashen, S.D. (1981). *Second language acquisition and second language learning.* Norwood, NJ: Ablex.

Rogoff, B. (1990). *Apprenticeship in thinking.* New York: Oxford University Press.

Speidel, G. E. (1984). *Conversation and language learning in the classroom.* Paper presented at the Third International Congress for the Study of Child Language, Austin, TX.

Teale, W. H., & Sulzby, E. (Eds.). (1986). *Emergent literacy: Writing and reading.* Norwood, NJ: Ablex.

Tharp, R. G., & Gallimore, R. (1988). *Rousing minds to life: Teaching, learning, and schooling in social context*. New York: Cambridge University Press.

Vygotsky, L. (1962). *Thought and language.* Cambridge, MA: MIT Press.

Vygotsky, L. (1981). The genesis of higher mental functions. In J. Wertsch (Ed.), *The concept of activity in Soviet psychology* (pp. 144-188). Armonk, NY: Sharpe.

Wells, G., & Change-Wells, G. L. (1992). *Constructing knowledge together: Classrooms as inquiry and literacy.* Portsmouth, NH: Heinemann.

Wertsch, J. V. (1991). The problem of meaning in a sociocultural approach to mind. In E. McKeough (Ed.), *Toward the practice of theory-based instruction* (pp. 31-49). Hillsdale, NJ: Lawrence Erlbaum Associates.

4

ALL THE WORLD'S A STAGE IN THE MUD

Robert H. Geeslin

Does the Internet *really* offer reading experience so rich in adventure that adolescent boys will come back for more, time after time, in spite of struggles with the keyboard, screens that scroll, vocabulary and readability not carefully controlled? Will they persist in staring at the screen until they can make sense of it? Can the Internet *really* provide authentic reading experience? In a word, yes! For over a hundred years, the Knights of the Round Table, the tales of Beowulf and King Arthur, and the Quest for the Holy Grail have kept adolescent boys struggling with the printed page far beyond the limits imagined by their instructors. Now, knights in shining armor rescuing damsels in distress have come alive! Fortunes in gold and jewels are won and lost, and the mysteries of Merlin and his uncommon knowledge may be teased from the fabric of a story line. Where? On the Internet. It has proven to be so much fun that it is sometimes hard to get students, even the "reluctant readers," to take a break.

This is a "how-to" chapter on motivating the reluctant reader with computer- mediated communication (CMC). The discussion includes literature, or "language arts" if you prefer, as well as technology. The technique for motivation is authenticity. I observed students in extracurricular communications (e.g., persuading Mom to give him money, obtaining the family car, or just in the gym or on the playground). Communication in these settings is authentic, derived from a need and a desire within the person. There is no lack of motivation in these communications. It is my assertion that the authenticity of the desire is the key element in motivation, especially of sustained motivation under adverse conditions. Given that a student authentically desires to read some piece of written material, the "reluctance" disappears to be replaced by eagerness (or determination, depending on the relative difficulty of the material).

BACKGROUND

Fiction, Action, Active Fiction, and IAF

To teachers, especially teachers of reading, the word *fiction* calls up mental pictures of one section in the library, its shelves filled with books of historical fiction, romantic fiction, science fiction, adventure, Westerns, mysteries, and others. In this age of multimedia when even popular music has a video to accompany it, the student is more likely to expect film, animation, or a clever mixture of the two, especially if a computer is mentioned in the same breath. Computers have become graphical, and an attitude that "the stodgy old text-based stuff has been left behind" exists among the folks on the cutting edge. However, it is not true that "text is dead." There is still a phenomenal amount of text-based material being written. Much of the fiction available on the computer screen seems to bear more resemblance to the video arcade than to the classroom and has been called *interactive fiction*, so I suggest the term *active fiction* (AF) to distinguish the text-based, computer-mediated material and *Internet Active Fiction* (IAF) for the text-based, computer-mediated material made available by Internet connectivity.

The Bard—Father of Active Fiction?

A bit of background is in order. AF is not a fad but has its roots in literary history.

The frametale of the Elizabethan era may be the literary and structural beginning of AF, although no evidence has come to light to suggest that Shakespeare, "The Bard," actually wrote in this genre. In the frametale, the writer suggests a plot, action, characters, setting. Key lines (jokes) were also included, but the actors were expected to create the actual presentation. Some troops met, decided how they wanted to flesh out the skeleton or "frame," practiced, and adhered to the lines and cues as rehearsed, presenting their unique and consistent version of the tale each time. Others more daring freely improvised the entire production in original and different forms each time they staged the play, purely via ad lib. This literary device produced the first active fiction, but because the audience was not part of the action, the actors had all the fun! (That is a joke, as those of you with a sense of Elizabethan theater will appreciate.)

On the Modern Stage

The unfinished novel of Charles Dickens (ca. 1870), *The Mystery of Edwin Drood*, has been treated as a play (Holmes, n.d.) in which the audience has a chance to vote on various elements: which character was the murderer, which the detective, and which (two) become lovers. In Ayn Rand's (1935/1968) *Night of January 16th*, a jury selected from the audience is given the opportunity to hear a case and may be encouraged to render a verdict. In a similar action, *You The Jury* allows the entire audience to vote (Griffith, 1995). Another murder trial is presented in an adaptation of the play *Scherenschnitt: Kriminalstueck Zum Mitspielen* by Paul Portner (ca. 1964) presented in English as the "wildly successful" *Shear Madness*. The play has the gimmick of having the audience vote during the intermission on which character committed the murder in the first act. The decision influences the following action. The play is a comedy and the jokes remain, they are just told from one perspective rather than another. This is, however, minimum participation akin to a stage comedian asking someone in the audience "Where are you from?" Yet, even this nominal amount of participation seems to improve the audience reaction to the staged event.

On the Screen

The creators of vicarious experience have innovated to enhance the response of audiences. They have found audience participation to work well. (Do you recognize "Come on down!" from *The Price is Right* [Bob Barker] or "Monty! Monty! I wanna make a deal!" from *Let's Make a Deal* [Monty Hall]? (Krause, 1995).

PAPER-BASED TEXT

Reader Response to Print

The value of audience response is seen in the attempt of educators to get overt reader response to printed material as seen in the "programmed reading instruction" materials introduced in the 1960s. These materials followed the operant conditioning model, presenting small bits of information, then requiring a response. They were definitely "interactive."

In reaction to the steps of this method, especially for content area instruction, a presentation protocol was fully developed using a full page of textual material (with illustration where appropriate) followed by a question with possible answers from which to choose. The reader's choice of answers referred to another page that confirmed a correct answer and presented additional information or that corrected a misunderstanding with reteaching. Both of these types of materials represent "self-pacing." In the first, the student works at a comfortable pace in a linear sequence of "frames," whereas the second type used "branching" to present a different series of pages for every different sequence of responses to the questions. In the world of fiction, they represent the "lowest form" of AF, a fixed content disclosed linearly or along different "paths" determined by reader response.

A similar type of reader activity was part of the *Reading Development Kits,* written for adult populations (Smith & Geeslin, 1969). *The Kits* contained material divided into various interest or "subject" areas. We anticipated adult students would demand material of adult content, so lesson content was geared to adult interests. The lessons were printed on individual cards. The student was to choose each lesson according to interest, providing for authentic reading experiences and student involvement, a form of "Active Nonfiction."

Adding Computer Mediation

The lowest level of computer mediation is "store and forward" (S&F). The World-Wide Web branch of the Internet is an excellent example of S&F. Each home page is an S&F publication, an electronic version of the *Kits,* from which the reader makes a selection according to interest. Many, like the "*Adventures of Wells Fargo*" site, are interesting to adolescent males (see Table 4.1).

Hypertext—Minimal Reader Response

The next higher level of computer mediation, as discussed earlier for print material, is the production of some minimum response from the reader. Web pages that use the "branching" method to present a fixed content are available. Their popularity shows that even this minimum amount of user involvement arouses reader interest. As Jeff Breidenbach (1994), a student at MIT, says, "There is an enormous worldwide demand for this type of stuff. (The numbers are amazing) [sic] Go out and write something better." He has available, at the time of this writing, "*Drool* . . . a short game, usually taking a couple of hours to solve."

Table 4.1. Current *Wells Fargo* Titles in Mid-1995.

The Web address for these stories (and additions since this was written) is http://Web.WellsFargo.com/ftr/ftrsty/index.html.

Hold onto your keyboard and ride into the Old West on a Wells Fargo stagecoach. Now you can find out what it was like in the days of the Gold Rush. Authentic stories taken from the historical archives of Wells Fargo that let you discover life as it was on the Western Frontier. Back then, people loved to sit around a fire, front porch, or even a saloon table, swapping tales of the West. Here's your chance to join them.

What a Way to Go
"A Cradle on Wheels"
The Robber
Whiskey-Barrel Banker
Go West, Mr. Wells
Give Fargo Half the Credit
Wells College
Throw Down The Box
The Singing Wires
Oysters & Handcuffs
Original Information Superhighway
All That Glitters . . . Part 1
All That Glitters . . . Part 2
The Army Drafts the Bank
LA Ice Age
$12 Eggs

Beyond Hypertext

World-Wide Web sites fail to tap the full power of computer mediation. Consider a house. Its rooms may be visited in many orders. (One is tempted to say "any order," but that would be an overstatement.) If prompts that identify a place within the house are displayed, the reader may be allowed to discover the details of the setting in as much detail as he or she desires. Was it Mr. Mustard in the kitchen with the wrench? The reader can take a quick look into the cabinets under the sink and find the wrench without a telltale mark, and a further search of the drawers may reveal the knife is in its normal place, but attempting to look in the desk for the pistol is delayed because the key is not yet in the reader's possession (perhaps it is still hidden behind a picture, awaiting discovery). A Web presentation must "give it away" by displaying the possible avenues of exploration as hypertext links, whereas a programmatic handling requires the reader to actively discover the possible links through generative thinking.

This is the level of computer mediation, if not an actual plot, available in the mid-1980s when the first microcomputer programs by Scott Adams (Reilly, 1994) became available. They presented more information as one examined the surroundings, true Active Fiction. To move in the stream of the plot was to solve the riddle. To solve the riddle, the reader must be active as both a thinker and as a writer, as well as a reader. Almost everything in the environment could be examined, with increasing detail leading to increased opportunity for inspection, that is, looking at the dresser might show it had four drawers. The examination could include attempting different commands for opening the drawers and various ways of expressing each, an option allowing examination of the verbs of the story as well as of the nouns. Once opened, the drawers might be searched to reveal a key. Taking the key and examining it might reveal it to be the key to the desk (it was not behind a picture, after all.) Active Fiction, at this level, is beyond the realm of what is possible with paper. Yet, these are the mechanics, not the excitement of discovery!

Stir In Multiple Users

Remember playing hide-and-seek in the early evening? Remember the thrill of near discovery so intense that you nearly wet your pants? That thrill cannot be communicated better than by direct experience. After all, who would believe it? This level of excitement is best achieved when the user (reader) is pitted not against the elements of plot (the writer), but against another character (another user). This level of adventure developed over time but started with the "lonely fiction" of the single user engaged in a solitary struggle.

I remember running the Scott Adams adventure stories on my Radio Shack Model III microcomputer. As characterized earlier, they utilized the medium well enough to rate a place in history, but these stories were not the "first" in computer-mediated Active Fiction. They were just first in a form available to the mass markets. They were preceded by "the original Adventure game," which ran on a big system and was available at first only to MIS staff and later only to corporate staff. In addition, that availability was secret. Playing the original Adventure was a forbidden fruit in most installations, compounding the intensity of the thrill. After all, what if your supervisor caught you at play instead of at work?

This original adventure game began, according to Graham Nelson (1995), himself author of "Curses," when a slender young woman named Patricia Crowther slipped through an almost impossibly tight passageway a hundred feet below the surface of Flint Ridge in Kentucky, to connect the famous Mammoth Cave to the rest of the Flint Ridge cave network (Mullin, 1995). Her husband, Willie, wrote a Fortran program that simulated one of his wife's favorite places in that cave network. (From this beginning comes the use of the now generic "room" to mean a "place" in the story because the caves are narrow passages that open into rooms.) The Willie Crowther simulation intrigued a colleague at work, who added "some adventure" to it (Regents of the University of California, 1991). With this addition of a dash of Tolkienesque, *Adventure* was born.

Adventure was a single person's exploration; although several users could enjoy it at the same time, each had a personal copy. Multiple users did not encounter each other. The adventurer moved about through the cave by typing a direction. If a passageway opened in that direction, the computer would forward a description of the new room to the user. Scattered throughout Crowther's cave were goblins, ogres, gemstones, armor, swords, axes, and other Tolkienesque[1] trappings. The "adventurer" collected the treasure as he or she fought off the evil monster. A genre was born.

Adventure was followed by a host of imitators. In the spring of 1979, Roy Trubshaw, a student at Essex University, wrote a multiuser version of an "adventure game." It was written in MACRO-10, the assembler language for the DECsystem-10 (Bartle, 1990b). The primary purpose of the effort was to write a database definition language (interpreter) that would respond to multiple users. Roy just wanted to be doing something more fun than accounting, so he used the context of an adventure game. This MultiUser Database was the first MUD. Roy had a friend who was as interested in the craft of the story as Roy was in the crafting of the database, or so he says. Richard Bartle (1990a) tells in "Early MUD history" of his help with the design of the game and how he took over when Tubshaw left Essex: "the original game was licensed to CompuServe, where it still runs to this day, laboring under the name of 'British Legends.'"

Add the Internet

The Trubshaw/Bartle MUD was open to the computing public (those with modems) in the wee hours of the morning (2 a.m. until 6 a.m. local time); yet Bartle reports that it "was always full to capacity."

---

[1]J.R.R. Tolkien is the author of the epic trilogy The Lord of the Rings and introduced us to Hobbits and Middle Earth.

Copies were sent to others who were interested in modifying and running a MUD, in Scandinavia, the United States, and as far away as Australia. Why is a shared experience more fun than a solitary one? Is it being able to ask for help from a more experienced person and to offer help to the less experienced (called "newbies")? The fact that most multiuser systems allow "shouts" to be heard by everyone in the vicinity means that victory and defeat, laughter and tears, can be shared along with warnings, instruction, and encouragement. As one student puts it:

> I prefer, in order of preference:
> Exploring interesting new places;
> Solving puzzle adventures by processing clues;
> Competing against other players;
> Defeating tough monsters along the way.
>
> (Note that monster chopping is last on the list, and IRC-style chatting is not on the list at all.)" (Huang, 1992)

Add Cutting-Edge Ideas

"An automated playwright would allow interactive fiction plots to be developed on the fly in the player's computer . . . it seems the stuff of science fiction. The holodeck on Star Trek, for example, is a computer-controlled interactive fantasy that boasts of automated plot generation" (Graves, 1991, p. 10). But that fictional "holodeck" is a graphical, pictorial interface, not a text-based one that encourages reading and writing. Similar use of the power of computer mediation is being applied to textual fiction.

Practical Uses of MUDs

Remy Evard (1993) of Northwestern University in Boston tells of the cutting edge of MUDs, which is a return to the notion of a "MultiUser Database" that provides:

> a metaphor of real life (or virtual life) . . . people and things exist in a place. One interacts with an object as one would in real life. This creates an interesting context for solving problems and indicating real-life situations. . . .
>
> We have considered constructing a version of a new building that the college may be expanding into, and then simulating the physical network connectivity within the MUD. We will do this before the building is built in reality, in order to foresee problems that may crop up. (p. 3)

Today's adolescents will be tomorrow's construction teams. We can prepare them to read, write, and interact effectively with others using the tools of the MultiUser Database, even if it is fun (see Table 4.2).

Table 4.2. Mechanics: The Nuts & Bolts.

Internet Active Fiction (IAF) is available on the Internet, so the first thing you need is an Internet connection, as explained in Santoro (Vol. I) and Collins (this volume). A fiber-optic connection is best, and ethernet is second (<wink><grin>), but a 2400 baud modem is adequate if you have access to the most common tool of character-based Internet access, Telnet.

However you manage your connection, you need a client (see Collins, this volume). A client is a program that takes your keystrokes from your keyboard and sends them "down the wire" to the place (address) you have selected. There are clients that serve general purpose functions (see Collins, this volume). However, there are also some clients that have been built specifically for IAF. If you reach the Internet through an account on a Unix server, you may want to use the TF (Tiny Fugue) client or one of the versions of TinTin. These programs will run on your provider (the local host) and allow the use of scripts (small programs that carry out repetitive actions), or triggers (scripts that "watch the screen" for certain conditions and respond to them in ways you have described).

Desktop machines that are hardwired to a network may have a client such as these that run locally, or they may run TELNET locally. At the least, you can log on using Telnet. I started with a VAX account (no TinTin nor TF) and could only reach out with Telnet. So I know it can be done with minimum configurations, but I found it much more entertaining to tinker with script programming in a client. You may want to start your students with "plain vanilla" and let those who are more power hungry discover the existence of scripts and clients on their own.

The desktop system I used was PC-DOS based. Because there was no client I could run on the VAX-VMS system that was my local access host, I enhanced my local interface, which is simply PCPLUS (DataStorm Technologies). I began running DesqView and ran PCPlus in a window. This allowed me to add local keystroke macros to the MUD's alias system. It is quite workable, by which I mean I can give long, tedious, repetitious commands with a single (or few) keystrokes. I can also open a second window and write a book chapter while my IAF character is in Randall's gym, having a nice swim, guided by one of my Aspect (PCPLUS) Scripts. It is the best of both worlds!

HELPING THE STUDENT GET STARTED: THE NEW CHARACTER

When a student first logs onto an IAF host, a series of questions will be asked. These are one-time questions with lasting consequences. The first is "Name" This is not asking for the student's name but the name of the character the student will play in the IAF saga. The name may or may not be chosen with care. Names are very special, producing automatic responses from other players.

DartMUD allows a new character to wander around, examining things firsthand. New players are encouraged to read the "helps," as most common questions are covered. It is also advisable to use a "disposable" character the first time. Many experienced adventurers will tell you that you *will* make mistakes and that making them "under an assumed name" lets you start over with a clean reputation. DartMUD also allows you to take a different name any time you must re-register. However, my reason for suggesting an introductory period is to suggest that experience with other adventurers will suggest names that are not apparent to those who have never encountered Orcs, Halflings, or Dwarves and their names.

The second question asked of the new adventurer is, of course, a chosen password. If this is the first session, any password used (within limits) will be honored. The IAF system will ask that it be repeated so both the user and the system are sure the entry was as intended. At this point, the password should be written down. After enough use, it will be remembered automatically, but it can easily be forgotten, and *no* amount of pleading will get it back. In secure systems, like DartMUD, a registration password is also required. This password is the one most likely to be lost. Take care to preserve it! Most, if not all IAF hosts, allow additional choices, although they differ in their treatment of these areas. Many ask for a selection of "race." The races available will have different innate abilities, leading to different occupations, in the usual case. Some are strong, resilient creatures built like a linebacker for the duties of a gladiator. Some are frail but quick-fingered, the perfect pickpocket. Others are highly intellectual and make fine clerics and healers. Before choosing a race, it is wise to look over the attributes of the different selections rather than choosing by the sound of the name. Mohnkee, Braman, Rowan, or Dwarf—Orc, Ogre, Catfolk, Gnome—each has its strong points and its weaknesses. Everybody must choose one. None is better than any other overall, but they are all different and suited to different roles.

Some MUDs still ask for a "guild" selection or a "class" choice during the establishment of a character. Most, however, allow some experience before the choice is made. In some IAF, it is a privilege and an honor to be admitted to a guild/class, and considerable effort is required. On the DartMUD, guilds are handled by the characters rather than by the plot. Most other MUDs use a similar system, but you may encounter the question at the time a character is registered.

In a refinement of the attempt to allow individual differences among the abilities of characters, DartMUD allows the new character to allot a percentage of "raw" skills and ability to specific categories. The concept of "buying" and "selling" are used with "points" being the medium of exchange. A student is allotted 500 points of raw skill that can be used to buy strength, night vision, or something from the various skill categories. Conversely, some ability may be "sold" to provide more points for those abilities the student prefers in the character. Systems other than DartMUD may use a similar method, but most either start a new character with a predetermined mix or "roll the dice" and the character gets the result. (Note: on most "roll" systems, you can review your luck and opt to roll again if you did not like it. Be forewarned, though, that three rolls is a common limit. If average or better on any roll, it is best to accept rather than tempt fate with another roll.)

The last thing a new character is asked at the time of registration is to read the help files. "Reluctant" readers may be reluctant to put out the effort. It is dull. There may be a lot of it. It does not often make sense until you have had some experience. You may eliminate some of this difficulty by printing the various topics and compiling a booklet ahead of the registration session. A "walking tour" is another big help. (I remember my first exposure to the Texas A&M site "Lusty MUD." I was allowed to accompany a party of adventurers who were doing a quest. I caught on to a lot!)

The COMMAND LIST

Every IAF has a different list of commands, but almost every IAF has similar common commands. Look, get, drop, and the directions abbreviated as n, s, e, w, ne, se, nw, sw, u, and d are commonly used. Some commands can be long and hard to remember, even harder to get right. For example, DartMUD uses a "Set Combat Allocation" command that is difficult to master. The healers have similarly difficult commands. Such commands can be printed in a booklet or posted on the word-wall. The method for creating an abbreviated command (an "alias" or a "macro") and some useful examples can make life a lot easier. On DartMUD, the alias "alias sca set combat allocation:%1,%2,%3" eases typos, and the example "sca right hand,parry,150" is immediately useful and shows exactly how to use the alias. Another favorite is "alias hrhs hold shield in right hand," which gives the adventurer very fast access to the protection afforded by the shield they wear.

The WORD WALL

A word wall has two uses. The commands encountered can be listed, with an alias suggested. It also allows "teasers" to be entered, that is, words that come from special places that the student may want to find. From DartMUD, the examples that spring to mind are "amulet, Farmtown, quest tokens, and pearl."

GOOD PUBLIC RELATIONS

Communicating With the Parents and Administration

The educator's bane seems always to be communicating to the school administration and to the parents. They both want to know that the students are receiving the kind of attention that produces literate, caring, knowledgeable persons. Every teachers' goals are the same. The usual device for communicating this confluence of intent and desire is the lesson plan. The question really is "How do you know the experiences you are providing are reaching our common goals?" Evaluation is the answer. Try some of these methods of evaluating your IAF users:

1. Before the IAF session, tell the users: "Today (or, this session) you'll need to give me some idea how much progress you make, so let's figure out a way to tell." Here are some ways that might work:

- money in the bank
- number of skill improvements
- new skills learned
- interesting geography or new places visited
- interesting conversations
- a new category we did not think of previously that can be entered here.

2. Talk about images, how the camera sees, how the artist sees, how a writer sees. Ask for images from those who are willing to provide them.
3. Talk about locations and maps. Talk about globes, street maps, and even as simple a map as a room map showing locations. Ask for maps. A sheet of butcher paper for Eristan, another for Tobermore, another for a World Map may be hung. Students pencil in entries. When they agree, the entries may be made permanent.
4. The most straightforward way to evaluate is, of course, to examine the log. A log is a continuous record of an entire session. Software is available to help you select the elements desired.
5. Do your students keep a journal? Let them know that an illustrated history of their adventures will substitute for the journal on days they care to do so.

6. Students who are using the DartMUD IAF may be interested in seeing if they can decipher any of the secrets in the journal "Eristan! by Thaan." It is a voluntary act and shows reading interest.
7. Students who want to share their experiences, perhaps even to involve others from the class in the adventure, may make periodic reports to the class. Here is an excellent place for those old standbys: dramatization (stage or puppets), radio and TV scripts (news flash, documentary), and the like. Dialog, action, staging, sets, and costumes all reflect the student's reading comprehension, and they provide additional opportunities for expression and language building.
8. A Hint Wall may be started for the IAF users. Each may add hints at will. Should any hint be called into question, an excellent opportunity for the testing of hypothesis will have been opened.
9. You might start a convention (courtesies) list with questions such as the following and encourage the students to add to it:

- What does it mean when a character comes into the room and waves?
- What does it mean if you are talking to someone and he or she waves?
- What does it mean if you wave and that person says "uh . . . " instead of waving back?
- What does :-) mean?
- What are other common courtesies and conventions from Eristan? From your family? From the classroom?
- What are some other places that have their own conventions (courtesies) about language?

A Final Comment on Objectives

As an educator with 25 years of postdoctoral opportunity to observe human learning in many contexts, I have come to believe "we learn by doing." In fact, we learn what we do. Avid readers become good readers. Diligent students learn how to learn (how to use the resources to discover the information they seek). Nowhere in this chapter have I pretended that IAF is for students who cannot read, rather, it is for those who can but who lack facility, adeptness, and motivation. The powerful motivation of an epic adventure, lived out by the student in total response to his or her actions, brings to pass hours of authentic reading, writing, and visualization.

Planning and organizational skills improve the adventurer's lot, so he or she can begin to develop in the company of others who can suggest, answer questions, and demonstrate—every bit of which is presented through written communication and absorbed through reading. Allowing the student to participate is all that is really required, all that is really desired. The participant will read and write, guaranteeing improvement in reading and writing. The goals and objectives in Table 4.3 are meant to help you, the school personnel, to see into the medium, to see past the surface action of sword fights in the marketplace into the depths of the skills required to participate. This list of goals and objectives is introductory rather than exhaustive. I trust you to construct others for the students in your classroom as you have opportunity to observe the learning behaviors of motivated students.

Table 4.3. Lesson Plan.

Cognitive Domain

Topic: Computer Use. Given a computer with IAF access and a suitable client, the student will:

- establish a character in an IAF production, complete with logon name and password
- successfully complete remote logons to the IAF host using logon name and password
- utilize the "alias (macro)" feature of the remote IAF system
- utilize the "script" feature of the local host or of the desktop system to create small programs for completing repetitious actions (essentially a programming skill)
- student will describe the computer network used to connect to the IAF host and will include (a) the desktop unit with modem or LAN, (b) the local host, and (c) the remote host. More advanced answers will also show where the different programs, if any, are running (the macro facility, the client, the aliases, the IAF or MUD). Answers that are more advanced still will include the concept of routers, backbone, and gateways.

Topic: Reading Comprehension. Given a successful character creation, the student will create a basic map of the environs or will, alternately, demonstrate an understanding (reading comprehension) of location details by moving the character to the proper rooms for obtaining food, drink, shelter, clothing, tools, and the like.

The student will demonstrate a reading comprehension of descriptive detail by engaging nonplayer characters (NPCs) who hold promise of yielding appropriate experience and goods while refraining from encounters with those too powerful or devoid of other profit.

Table 4.3. Lesson Plan (con't.).

Given an active engagement with an NPC, the student will demonstrate the ability to read and comprehend the near-taschistoscopic scrolling text by pressing or withdrawing from the engagement, as indicated by the messages. Given that the student is hailed by another character, the student will make a response appropriate to the content and context of the message. The student constructs visual images of the material being read as evidenced by the production of pictures during the "art class."

Topic: Reading Speed. The student demonstrates the ability to selectively read by pointing out the essential elements of an engagement that is scrolling at 24 to 48 words per second (1,440 to 2,880 words per minute).

Topic: Writing (Composition). Student will demonstrate an understanding of convention by using different vocabulary in IAF than in more formal class assignments as evidenced by a comparison of samples of the two sets of output.

Topic: Organizational Strategies

Chronological Sequence of Events

- Helps a newbie by telling a summary of his own experience
- Helps a newbie by telling the sequence for putting on gloves or bracers
- Tells the proper sequence for learning to cook (or other skill)

Spatial Relations

- Finds (goes to) various places at will
- Helps a newbie by giving directions

Cause and Effect

- Cautions a newbie about watching the "concentration indicator" while engaged in certain activities
- Explains why Skull hits a player who takes the lantern from the storeroom

Conditionals

- Holds an item in the preferred hand (i.e., a tool for parry in the off hand, a tool for striking in the strike hand)
- Explains to a newbie how to determine the off hand and the strike hand or how to hold an item in the desired hand
- Sets the "allocations" for handedness
- Explains to a newbie how to set "allocations" for handedness

Affective Domain

Topic: Willingness. The student demonstrates a willingness to participate in print-based activities by voluntarily using IAF an average of three hours per week. The student will use a keyboard-based activity an average of three hours per week.

Table 4.3. Lesson Plan (con't.).

Topic: Attitude. The student attitude that reading and writing are "school subjects" will transfer to an attitude that they are "life skills" as evidenced by the student volunteering to use a computer-based methodology for solving a real-life problem.

Topic: Enjoyment. The student will demonstrate enjoyment of IAF by using it voluntarily.

Psychomotor Domain

Topic: Keyboarding. The speed at which the student generates characters at the keyboard will show steady improvement as measured by (the measure used at your school).

CONCLUSIONS AND RECOMMENDATIONS

I now compare the power of authentic engagement with the traditional attempts at producing student involvement.

Laura Robb, writing in *Reading Today* (1995), discussed the traditional methods of encouraging the reluctant writer to make the attempt. One element is the *Interview,* which reveals the student's attitudes and emotions about the writing process. It helps the traditional teacher sort out those who will not write because they cannot spell from those who claim they can think of nothing to say. The advice to other teachers is traditional. "Packed with useful clues that begin to explain negative attitudes toward writing, interviews provide vital information teachers can use during conferences and for planning interventions that can lead to change. The sixth grader who wrote 'I do not like to write because I never can think of something to write about' might risk writing with teacher support on finding topics and collecting ideas" (p. 30).

Robb offers the traditional advice on prewriting activities, saying "since reluctant writers often have difficulty getting started, the prewriting strategies that follow offer frameworks for gathering and organizing information. . . . Model the strategies with the whole class" (p. 30). The suggested strategies are sound, in the traditional sense. "Think about your topic; have a conversation with yourself. Talk about your topic with your partner. Question each other to collect additional detail. Add details to your original list. Select ideas by circling them. Read and discuss with your group" (p. 30).

Robb leaves us with this final thought, "Significant changes in attitudes and performance might take years" (p. 30). Yes, even the best of the traditional approaches, to use her words, just "nudge the student forward."

I am reminded of the story about SuperGrow Garden fertilizer. The directions for use were something to this effect: (a) Plant your seeds; (b) mix a little SuperGrow into a sprinkler of water; (c) water the seeds; and then (d) jump back! I have seen these "reluctant students" on the football field, where they roar like lions and charge like rhinos. That's the kind of motivation these students have. All they need from us is an authentic opportunity to become engaged in an interesting, print-based task.

When that has been done, jump back!

REFERENCES

Bartle, R. (1990a, November 15). *E-mail: Subject: Early MUD history.* Available at: http://Web.ccs.neu.edu/home/lpb/muds/jwadir/mud-history.

Bartle, R. (1990b). *Interactive multi-user computer games.* British Telecom plc: MUSE Ltd. Available at: ftp://parcftp.xerox.com/ pub/ MOO/papers/mudreport.txt

Breidenbach, J. (1994). *Drool.* Available at: http://Web.mit.edu:8001/afs/ athena.mit.edu/user/j/b/jbreiden/game/entry.html.

Evard, R. (1993, November) Collaborative networked communication: MUDs as systems tools. *Proceedings of the Seventh Systems Administration Conference (LISA VII)*, pp. 1-8. Available at: http://Web.ccs.neu.edu/home/remy/documents/cncmast.html.

Griffith, B. (1995, July 10). E-mail: Subject "Re: request for information on audience participation plays."

Holmes, R. (n.d.). *The Mystery of Edwin Drood.* Available at: http://Web.mit.edu:8001/activities/mtg/archives/mtg-archives.html.

Huang, M. M. (1992, March 23). E-mail: Subject: "Re: history: VMS Monster, Sceptre of Goth." Available at: http://Web.ccs.neu.edu/ home/lpb/muds/jwadir/mud-history.

Mullin, E. (1995). *Interview: Graham Nelson.* Available at: http://Web. users.interport.net/~eileen/design/xyzzy.1c.html.

Nelson, G. (1995). *The craft of the adventure* (2nd ed.). Five articles on the design of adventure games. Available via FTP at: ftp://ftp.gmd.de/if-archive/info/Craft.Of.Adventure.txt.

Portner, P. (ca 1964). *Shear madness.* Available at: http://Web.dc202. com/kendyctr.html.

Rand, A. (1968). *Night of January 16th.* New York: New American Library. (Original work published 1935.) Available at: http://Web.mtsu.edu/ ~m_c_000b/chrono.html.

Regents of the University of California. (1991). Available at: http://inls.ucsd.edu/y/OhBoy/Adventure/about.html.

Robb, L. (1995, August/September). Workshop can support reluctant writers. *Reading TODAY*, p. 30.

Smith, E., Geeslin, R.H., & Geeslin, C. (1969). *Reading development kits.* Menlo Park, CA: Addison Wesley.

SUGGESTED READINGS

Burka, L. P (1993). *The MUD archive.* Available at: http://Web.ccs.neu.edu/home/lpb/muddex.html.

Burka, L. P (1995). *The MUD line.* Available at: http://Web.ccs.neu.edu/home/lpb/mudline.html.

Geeslin, R. (1995, December). *Educational resources from educational programming.* My homepage, containing the latest information, links, and helps. Available at: http://Web.galstar.com/~rhawk/.

Gilbert, P. (1995, October). *The interactive-fiction page.* Available at: http://yallara.cs.rmit.edu.au/~s9406702/if/.

Graves, D. (1987 August). Second generation adventure games. *The Journal of Computer Game Design, 1*(2), 4-7. Available via FTP at: ftp://ftp.gmd.de/if-archive/programming/general-discussion/Graves.1.

Graves, D. (1988, December). Bringing characters to life. *The Journal of Computer Game Design, 2*(2), 10-11. Available via FTP at: ftp://ftp.gmd. de/if-archive/programming/general-discussion/Graves.2.

Graves, D. (1991, October). Plot automation. *The Journal of Computer Game Design, 5*(1), 10-12. Available via FTP at: ftp://ftp.gmd.de/if-archive/programming/general-discussion/Graves.3.

Graves, D. (n.d.). *What is IF anyway?* Available at: http://speedracer.nmsu.edu/~jholder/if/ch5-if.html.

Hoover's Handbook Database. (1995). Austin, TX: The Reference Press. Available at: http://pathfinder.com/@@TyxAMsHA8gAAQOBo/money/invest/hoover/profiles/12007.html.

Krause, D. (1995). Available at: http://Web.cis.ohio-state.edu/hypertext/faq/usenet/tv/game-shows/usa/faq.html.

Oz Project Publications. (n.d.). Available at: http://Web.cs.cmu.edu/afs/cs.cmu.edu/project/oz/web/papers.html.

Reese, G. (1995). *LPMud FAQ.* Available at: http://Web.imaginary.com/LPMud/lpmud_faq.html.

Reilly, S. (Ed.). (1994, October). *The Society for the Preservation of Adventure Games* (#3). Available at: http://Web.cs.cmu.edu/afs/cs.cmu.edu/user/wsr/Web/IF/spag.3.html.

URLS

Beowulf:
http://Web.uky.edu/~kiernan/BL/kportico.html
http://Web.georgetown.edu/labyrinth/subjects/british_isles/anglo-saxon/anglo-saxon.html.http://ucsu.colorado.edu/~anschutz/germanic.html
http://Web.ccc.nottingham.ac.uk/~aczkdc/asresource.html
http://Web.georgetown.edu/cball/oe/old_english.html

King Arthur:
http://Web.zmall.com/bmm/books-faq/arthurian.html
http://Web.hamline.edu/~jltidbal/grail_html/metafront.html
http://reality.sgi.com/employees/chris_manchester/faq.html
http://reality.sgi.com/employees/chris_manchester/guide.html

Questing the Grail:
http://calvin.stemnet.nf.ca/~djohnsto/arthur/highhist.txt
http://Web.columbia.presents.com/g/p/fk/index.html
http://marlowe.wimsey.com/rshand/streams/gnosis/grail.html
Knights of the Round Table:
http://Web.microserve.net/~rsy/
http://arachnid.cs.cf.ac.uk/User/A.M.Gimblett/arthurian/arthur.html

Merlin:
http://calvin.stemnet.nf.ca/~djohnsto/artbrit.html

Old West:
http://Web.WellsFargo.com/ftr/ftrsty/index.html

Hypertext Fiction:
http://Web.ugcs.caltech.edu/~benedett/lit/
http://cnsvax.albany.edu/~hfiction/monique.html
http://Web.duke.edu/~mshumate/original.html
http://Web.duke.edu/~mshumate/hyperfic.html
http://Web.feedmag.com/95.09guyer/95.09guyer_sample1.html

About Hypertext Fiction:
http://Web.eastgate.com/Events.html
http://jefferson.village.virginia.edu/pmc/issue.592/review-4.592
http://Web.feedmag.com/95.09guyer/95.09guyer_sample1.html

About Interactive Theater:
http://Web.rit.com/Whats_IT.html

About Interactive Fiction (Lonely Fiction):
http://Web.ecst.csuchico.edu/~gchance/Designers
http://Web.users.interport.net/~eileen/design/xyzzy.1.html
ftp://ftp.gmd.de/if-archive/Master-Index
http://Web.cdromshop.com/cdr/desc/p.045445065634.html
http://Web.cis.upenn.edu/~lwl/mudinfo.html

Mystery:
http://Web.cis.upenn.edu/~lwl/mudinfo.html

II

STUDENT PUBLISHING

5

"LOOK WHAT I PUBLISHED!": INCREASING MOTIVATION FOR WRITING BY GLOBAL ELECTRONIC PUBLISHING

Mary O'Haver and Thomas O'Haver

We developed and tested a number of projects for fourth- and fifth-grade students in which they use technological tools to produce curriculum-related educational products, including print, multimedia presentations, and electronic publications, that are targeted to and have value for people outside the classroom. Many of the projects are designed for lower grades in the school. With the introduction of computer-mediated communication (CMC) via the Internet, the target audience for student products expands to include students and classes in other schools all over the world. The World-Wide Web provides a means of publishing student writing and artwork, and electronic mail provides an avenue for readers outside the classroom to provide feedback to the students regarding their work. We have found that these projects increase students' motivation for writing and encourage them to think of themselves as producers and not just as consumers. The motivational benefits apply to the teachers as well as the students.

PROBLEM STATEMENT

The task of motivating all students to achieve and expand their potential remains one of the central problems of education. We believe, with Shneiderman (1992a, 1992b), that "the path to motivating students is the joy of creation" of substantial projects that have value and importance both to them and to people outside the classroom. We also agree that computing and communication technologies have opened up new possibilities in the educational environment by empowering students in remarkable ways. For us, the immediate problem is how to adapt this philosophy to the less technologically sophisticated, more curriculum-oriented environment of the elementary classroom.

The school where this work has been conducted is located in eastern Montgomery County, Maryland. The school is an "average" suburban public school, not a technology magnet or demonstration school. The student body of the school is very diverse ethnically and economically. The school does not have a computer teacher or other full-time staff with official technology responsibilities. Therefore, an important part of our problem is how to implement and sustain technology innovations in such an environment.

DESCRIPTION OF PROCESS

Types of Projects

The essence of our approach is that students use technological tools to produce curriculum-related educational products, including print, multimedia presentations, and electronic publications, that are targeted to people outside the classroom. Our students have created projects in a wide variety of curriculum-related topic areas, including Native American cultures, famous scientists, famous Black Americans, the Bill of Rights, biography book reports, endangered species, tessellations, geography, explorers, insects, and autobiography.

These projects have taken the form of newspapers, educational posters, pamphlets with emphasis on advertising or persuasive writing, science and alphabet books for the younger grades, multimedia presentations in the form of HyperCard Stacks and KidPix slide shows, designs for commemorative postage stamps, topical POGs (circular bottle-cap designs), and World-Wide Web pages.

In all these projects, students research their topic, using reference CD-ROMs, the World-Wide Web, and the usual library and print sources, and they use a word processor to write a paragraph or brief essay, then combine it with appropriate graphics. Graphics may be obtained from canned clip art, digitized images obtained from CD-ROM collections or from the Internet, original art work created by the students from art programs or scanned conventional media, and, in the case of the multimedia projects, digitized sound. These projects can be adapted to any subject area and revised for various grade levels. All projects have clearly stated objectives, requirements, and evaluation criteria. Several deadline dates are built in so the projects proceed at a satisfactory rate.

Student Training

The school has two computer labs: a primary lab for grades K-3 and an upper-grade lab for grades 4 through 5. The primary lab is staffed with a computer aide to help the teacher with her students. The upper-grade lab has no aide so that student training is done for the most part by the teacher or another teacher that volunteers to help out. The primary lab has regularly scheduled classes in which students are introduced to various programs. Students also get time to practice keyboarding. During the initial training in the upper-grade lab, students get a quick review of equipment and commonly used programs. After the initial training sessions, training takes place on an informal basis. The teacher instructs some students how to use the scanner, the video digitizer, and so on as the opportunity or need arises. In turn, these students become trainer to instruct students as they need to use the equipment. The same method is used when learning how to create HyperCard Stacks, digitize sound, or to get into more advanced procedures in a particular program. As the need arises, the training is done in small groups. A great deal of cooperative learning is the norm in this environment.

Staff Training

In traditional tutorial and drill-and-practice computer applications, each student typically works individually, following the on-screen instructions on a single computer program. In contrast, the creative production projects described in this chapter result in a much more active environment, with students exploring and discovering new software, moving about between special-purpose stations, asking and giving helping to each other, working together in small groups, and using a variety of different programs and equipment at one time. This environment requires a higher level of technical proficiency and comfort on the part of the teacher, who must respond to many demands at once as they attempt to keep up with fearless and enthusiastic students.

We have found that even faculty who felt comfortable with their personal use of the computer still felt uncomfortable when having to take a whole class into a lab setting. With a few teachers we tried a team-teaching approach in which the trainer would begin the class in the computer lab and little by little the regular classroom teacher would take over. This has lead to several teachers making more use of the computer lab for creative projects that empower students rather than just the tutorial programs they tended to use when their comfort level was low.

Hardware Distribution

The distribution of computers in the school is controlled by a technology committee formed of interested teachers and administrators. The committee gathers information on computer needs and recommends the distribution of computer hardware and software. On this basis, most of the computers in the school are located in lab settings for group use. Some computers are also placed in individual classrooms; a teacher who wants a computer in his or her room must state to the committee how he or she plans to use it and what type of software is required.

Lab Scheduling

The upper-grade computer lab is scheduled on a need-to-use basis. A blank three-week schedule is posted, and teachers sign up for blocks of time as they need the lab. Scheduling is flexible; students from other classes, not scheduled at a particular time, are allowed to come in and work as long as there are empty machines. This kind of scheduling allows each staff member to use the lab as it fits into their particular subject area and project plans. The primary computer lab made a compromise: Half of the time is set up for regularly scheduled classes, and the other half is left open for special projects as teachers find the need for extra time in the lab.

OUTCOMES OBTAINED

Examples of Student Projects

Figures 5.1 through 5.6 show excerpts from some of the projects created by our students. These and other projects can be viewed more fully on the school's World-Wide Web page, located at: http://www.wam.umd.edu/~toh/Fairland.html. A perspective on the problem of integrating computers into daily classroom life, from the point of view of an elementary teacher, is given in the Appendix.

Fairland Elementary School

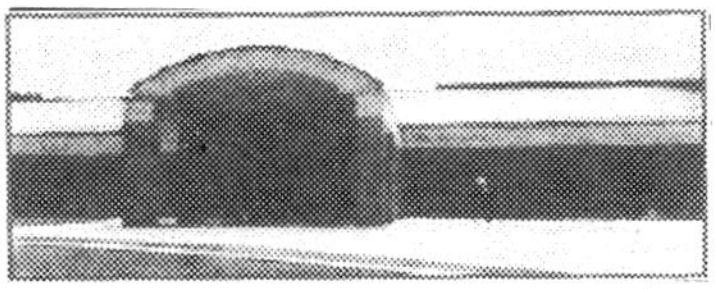

Montgomery County Public Schools, Maryland

http://www.wam.umd.edu/~toh/Fairland.html

Student-Produced Projects

- Commemorative Stamps for the Bill of Rights, 5th grade (96-97) NEW
- Tessellations Project 5th grade (95-96)
- Native American Storyteller Project 5th grade (95-96)
- Digital Village Project: Electronic Self-Portraiture 4th grade (95-96)
- Maryland POGs! 4th grade (94-95)
- Native American Commemorative Stamp Designs 5th grade (94-95)
- Famous Americans Biography Book Reports 5th grade (94-95)
- Tessellations Project 5th grade (93-95)
- Other Student Computer Projects 5th grade (92-95)

- Email we have received from our readers! NEW

About Fairland

- About Montgomery County Public Schools
- About Fairland Elementary School
- History of the school
- Computer facilities

Other Web sites

- Web sites related to our curriculum
- Electric Elementary, online magazine for kids
- Cromwell Valley Elementary (Maxine Shindel)
- Delmar Elementary (Patti Weeg)
- Other schools in Maryland
- Some of our favorite Web sites

"Fairland's students are not just using the Web; they are helping to build it."

Figure 5.1. The Fairland World-Wide Web home page. These pages are served by the host computers of the Computer Science Center of the University of Maryland at College Park, through the cooperation of the Maryland Collaborative for Teacher Preparation

Rosa Parks

By Eloise

Book report and stamp artwork by Rebecca

Rosa Parks was born in Tuskegee Alabama on February 4, 1913. Her parents were James and Leona Mc Cauley. Her father was a carpenter and her mother was a teacher. Rosa Parks was a quite, but very brave Black girl who attended the Montgomery Industrial Schools for girls. She had a younger brother named Sylvester. From her parents jobs, it seems like they where a middle class family. When Rosa Parks was real small, her family moved to a farm. Rosa Parks now lives in Chicago, Illinois.

Rosa Parks is the Mother of the Civil Rights Movement. One day in 1955, she refused to give up her bus seat to a white person. She was arrested and put in jail for not giving up her seat. Rosa Parks and other people kept protesting against the unfair rules for Black people riding the buses. Finally the United States Supreme Court made the bus company change its rules. Black people felt good about this. Rosa had made a big difference. As years went by, other unfair rules for Black people where also changed.

This stamp Commemorates Rosa Parks Rosa Parks who is now 81 years old and is known as the Mother of Civil Rights Movement. the word Rosa Parks stands for fairness because she and others worked to get fairness. Rosa's gentle looking face on the stamp shows how she was, still she wanted fairness.

Rebecca  [Recorded comments - 36K]

[Return to top of report]

[Return to Book Report Index]

Figure 5.2. One of a set of 17 illustrated book reports of biographies of famous Americans produced by Mrs. O'Haver's fifth-grade class, 1994-1995, and published on the Fairland World-Wide Web site

Student and Parent Attitudes

It is clear that the students' attitudes toward their work has changed when they become aware that their work will be read and used as a resource by others. This is an incentive to check their work carefully, to seek assistance from others for any suggestions, and to learn new techniques that may improve their presentation. Even after the work

Antelope or Chof, Kachina Doll, by Peter C.

This stamp commemorates a kachina doll named Antelope or Chof. The Hopi Indians from the Southwest made the doll. In addition, they made many other kinds of kachina dolls. The Hopi Indians made the dolls out of wood. After they finished, they would give the dolls to young Hopi girls during kachina ceremonies.

Click here to return to the Index.

Figure 5.3. One of a set of 38 Native American commemorative postage stamp designs, produced by Mrs. O'Haver's fifth-grade class, 1994-1995, and published on the Fairland World-Wide Web site

Ducks on Parade, by Sean

There are nineteen good ducks and three black and yellow goons!

Figure 5.4. One of a set of 19 tessellations drawn by Mrs. Sulik's fifth-grade class, 1994-1995, and published on the Fairland World-Wide Web site

THE MARYLAND STATE FLOWER

by Charles H.

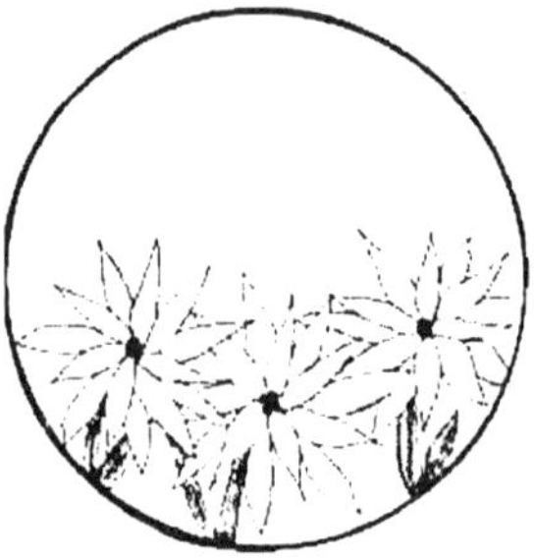

The black eyed Susan is a wild flower that grows in fields. It is related to the white daisy. Sometimes it is called the yellow daisy. The black eyed Susan is a composite plant. This means that what looks like one flower is actually is made up of many flowers. Each one of the yellow petals is a separate flower. The black eyed Susans grow in a great abundance in the whole state of Maryland. In 1918 at a meeting of the General Assembly at Annapolis, this flower was chosen to be the Maryland's state flower. It was chosen to be the state flower because it has the colors of the Marylands flag. And it has thirteen petals, and there were thirteen colonys. The black eyed Susans grows in many states in our country. In fact the black eyed Susans really started growing in the West and spread to the East. They will re-seed themselves every year. They may grow one to three feet tall.

Figure 5.5. One of a set of 22 POGs depicting official and unofficial symbols of the state of Maryland, produced by Mrs. McGrath's fourth-grade class, 1994-1995, and published on the Fairland World-Wide Web site

Figure 5.6. A card from one of three Hypercard stacks on Native American themes. Each student prepares one such card. Each card contains a brief essay, artwork, a digitized video image of the student, and a digitized sound bite recorded by the student

graded, students insist on making corrections or additions to their projects. Recently, a former student of ours, now in middle school, discovered some minor errors he had made in some of his work posted on the school's World-Wide Web site. He became very concerned that corrections be made immediately. Students appear to have a vested interest in their work even after the traditional grade is given and they have moved on to something else. Parents also are extremely enthusiastic about many of the projects the students create. They often tell their teachers that their child is now showing them how to work the computer at home or is urging them to get one if they do not have one.

Feedback from Outside the Classroom

Since the Fairland Web site was set up in January 1995, the school has received on average one e-mail message per week from someone outside the school system who has discovered the children's work and writes to comment and to complement the class or individual students on their work. These writers have included students and teachers from other schools, journalists researching topics for articles, parents of students, college professors, the state department of education, and people who work with Native American students. All such e-mail correspondence is printed out and posted in the classroom for all the children to see. Much excitement is generated in the class when a new message is received.

TECHNICAL SECTION

Computer Lab Setup

The projects described here were carried out in the upper-grade computer lab, which contains 30 student stations, two shared laser printers, two flat-bed scanner stations, a video digitizer station, and a teacher demo station with an overhead projector, all based on various Macintosh models. The selection of Macintosh computers simplifies the installation and upkeep of the lab by nontechnical personnel because these models come with built-in local-area network hardware and client software, sound support, and SCSI (Small Computer Standard Interface) ports that allow CD-ROMs, scanners, and external hard disk drives to be added without opening the computers.

Software selection. Standard software on each computer for student use includes a word processor/desktop publishing program (The Writing Center), an integrated package (Works), a drawing package (KidPix), a simple slide show program (Slide Show), a software development toolkit (HyperCard), a typing tutor, a Web browser (Netscape), and sound. Heavily used software is installed on the hard disk of each station; less commonly used software is stored on the server and remotely accessed by the stations.

In order to simplify access to the software, "aliases" to all programs that are commonly used by students are placed on the desktop of each computer. The hard disk icon remains closed during normal operation. No software protection scheme (such as At Ease) is used in the upper-grade lab so that those students will begin to develop skill with the standard file and disk manipulation tasks.

Local area networking (LAN). All of the computers in the lab are networked. One computer acts as a dedicated file and print server. The print spooler facilitates the sharing of one or more laser printers by all the stations on the Net. Installation and configuration of the server software was performed by school district computer personnel. Routine upkeep, including removing computers and adding new ones, can be performed by local nontechnical personnel without disrupting the network. When turned on, each student station automatically logs onto the network as a "guest," not requiring a password, and mounts the server volume. Guest logins do not have to write permission to the server. Teachers who know the server password can log in as administrator for the purpose of installing software on the server or changing folder permissions.

Server folder permissions. The LAN network software (AppleShare) allows read and write permissions to be set for any volume (disk) or directory (folder) by the network administrator. We set up three special folders in this way: one with read and write access as a general scratch area for temporary data and for transferring files between stations, one with read-only access for distributing templates and other electronic documents to the students, and one with write-only access for students to submit finished documents. Aliases to those three folders are on the desktops of each student station.

Templates. Rather than require that the students create their project entirely from "scratch," we provided templates that serve as example projects and frameworks around which the student can build their work. In the case of Hypercard and Web page projects, these templates also contain certain required "scripting" language that students need not understand completely. The students need only type their text into the designated areas in the template (or, more likely, copy and paste from their word processor) and then link the previously created graphics and sound elements by specifying the file names under which they have been stored.

Internet access. Currently only one computer in the upper-grade computer lab has Internet access. A standard voice-grade telephone line, with a sufficient speed modem (14.4 KB or faster), is used to provide access to the nearby College Park campus of the University of Maryland, which provides UNIX shell accounts to teachers in Maryland schools. Students do not have their own individual e-mail accounts; all e-mail communication to and from the class goes through the teacher. Graphical access is made possible through the use of a SLIP emulator. This allows teachers and students to use the Web and other network client programs to search for and access information on the Internet. The network does not have a router to allow simultaneous Internet access from all the computers on the local area network.

Local Web. The Web browser we used has the capability of displaying Web pages that are resident on the local file system or on a LAN file server. Thus it is possible to create a "local" Web site that is accessible only on a local network. For this reason we have installed this software on each student station in the lab. These stations cannot access the Internet in real time, but they can access any Web pages that are stored on the file server. Because the LAN connections are much faster than a telephone connection using a voice-grade telephone line and modem, the Web pages and graphics appear much faster, even when many stations are accessing the same page at the same time.

MULTIMEDIA ELEMENTS

Graphics

Graphics to illustrate student documents are obtained in several ways, all of them simple enough that the children themselves do all the work, after appropriate training.

Scanner. The lab has two flat-bed scanners, one color and one greyscale, both using the software that comes with them. These are used to scan student artwork and photographs. The scanners attach to a SCSI port and can be installed easily without opening up the computer to which it is attached. The scanner saves files in a format that many software packages consider standard (e.g., PICT).

Video capture. The capture of still images from a video source (e.g., a live picture from a video camera or from a running video tape) is accomplished by using either an add-in video digitizing card (e.g., VideoSpigot) or a computer that has a built-in video digitizer. Both of these options come with the required software, which saves captured images in a standard format. Video cameras and VCRs are not uncommon in schools and can often be borrowed from the media center (library). We use this method to capture portraits of the children to be used with their reports and newsletters and to capture scenes from videotapes taken on film trips or other activities away from the classroom.

Electronic camera. We also used electronic cameras (such as Apple QuickTake and Connectix QuickCam) that attach to the computer's modem (serial) port. Some electronic cameras are battery-operated and portable and take color pictures that are stored in the camera's memory until downloaded to the computer. Some cameras are available in greyscale and color models, must be connected to the computer in order to work, and are the least expensive of all the electronic camera devices. Many cameras have fixed-focus lenses with no zoom or close-up capabilities. But almost all cameras save files in standard formats.

Computer drawing program. Various drawing programs (e.g., KidPix, the drawing module in Works) and the low-cost commercial drawing program (e.g., Expert Color Paint) can be used by students to draw color illustrations. These programs are saved in standard formats.

Capture from Internet. Web browsers (such as Netscape) make it easy to capture and save graphics that appear on its pages; often the user just clicks and holds the mouse button down over the desired graphic. A pop-up menu appears that allows the graphic to be saved or copied to the clipboard. The graphics are usually saved in their original formats, that is, either in GIF (Graphics Interchange Format) or JPG (Joint Photographic Expert Group) formats.

Graphic file formats. Note that most of these means for creating or capturing graphic images result in PICT files. Fortunately, most of the software used by the students accept graphics in PICT format. This makes it straightforward to open a graphic created in one program within a different program. For example, the children can open a scanned image in KidPix or another drawing program in order to erase or add features, add text labels, and so on. They can include captured, scanned, or computer-drawn images in Writing Center documents, using the same Get Graphics command that is used to insert clip art. (It is important for students and teachers to understand that the selection of clip art to illustrate documents is not limited to the set of pictures that comes with the program when it is purchased; you can "make your own clip art" by any of the means described earlier.) For display on Web pages, however, graphic files must be converted into GIF or JPG formats; this can be easily done with any of several freeware or shareware graphics programs, such as Graphic Converter.

Sound

Sound clips can be added easily, using the small microphone that comes with many sound cards or with multimedia computer systems. Sound recording/playback is a standard feature of multimedia systems. For adding sound to Web pages, the shareware program SoundMachine 2.1 provides both record and playback functions.

Video

Small "postage stamp" video clips of moderate quality can also be digitized using the same equipment used to digitize video stills, from live action or from videotape. These small movies can be displayed using various software depending on the computer system and on Web pages (with the appropriate helper application). Digitized video clips take a lot of memory and disk space so it is most effective to keep them small and short (like a TV commercial).

APPENDIX: A TEACHER'S PERSPECTIVE

If you're a teacher who is new to all this technology stuff, you may be thinking, "Sure, you make it sound like it's easy to do, but I know it's not that easy." It is true that integrating the computer so completely into the curriculum is not something you can do immediately. You surely do not go from having little experience with this technology to creating complex multimedia productions and World-Wide Web pages overnight.

I have an advantage because I have been using computers at home and in my classroom since the late 1970s and have learned new things as they crop up. So experience, knowledge, and most of all comfort have been developed over a long period of time. I have had the luxury of having time to play and having help at home when problems crop up. But do not let this discourage you from getting started. When you decide to get started you will be surprised how many support systems are available to you. If your school district does not provide adequate support, try getting help from parents, your students, local high school students, and local businesses

To start off, you must realize that you have already done the hard part. By that I mean that you already know the curriculum and how to deliver it in a differentiated way to accommodate the diverse population in your room. You have developed a system that maintains an atmosphere in which the love of learning can take place. You have behavior management under control. You help students grow academically, socially, and emotionally. You do all this and more during the course of a day. This is really the hard part and the basis of what makes a good teacher. The technology is just a new tool to add to your bag of tools you use everyday.

This new tool can do many things, but you should first start with the simple things. When I got my bread machine I started making the prepackaged mixes first. Then I tried using some of the simple recipes they suggested. I am still at that stage. I have not ventured on my own but I know I will. Do the same with your computer. Start with simple word processing. You may want your students to simply type, spell-check, save, and print their material. That is what I did for a while. I even called it "multimedia" because I had them draw a picture and type a story to accompany their artwork. We are just adding a new tool to help students create and display their final product. As you become comfortable with one aspect of this new tool, try another and another. Before you know it, your repertoire will expand. What is the worst that can happen, that it does not pan out like you planned? Well, all of us have had that happen without the help of computers. We just pick ourselves up, look for the positives from the experience, and try again.

There may be times when you will ask yourself why you ever got started with this because, you could have done it faster and easier another way. But we are not always looking for the easy way out. Do not despair. You will be surprised how you and your students will be motivated by this new tool. The computer is a tool that empowers the user. The user is in control with the limiting factor being the perseverance and imagination of the user.—Mary O'Haver, Fifth-grade teacher

REFERENCES

Shneiderman, B. (1992a). Education by engagement and construction: A strategic education initiative for a multimedia renewal of American education, In Barrett (Ed.), *Sociomedia: Hypermedia, multimedia and the social creation of knowledge* (pp. 13-26). Cambridge, MA: MIT Press.

Shneiderman, B. (1992b). Engagement and construction: Educational strategies for the post-TV era. In I. Tomek (Ed.), *Computers and learning, Proceedings of the International Conference on Computers and Learning* (pp. 39-45). New York: Springer-Verlag. (Reprinted in the Journal of Computing in Higher Education, 2(4), Spring 1993, 106-116.

6

USING AN ONLINE JOURNAL TO TEACH STUDENTS ABOUT SCIENCE

Patrick L. Fullick

In the United Kingdom the media designated 1995 as the year of the Internet. During these 12 months, it was impossible to watch television or read the newspapers for more than two weeks without coming across an article on the "information superhighway." Initially these articles were enthusiastic—about the possibilities offered by the new technologies and how new ways of working would result. As time went by, the articles became more apocalyptic in tone, predicting the undermining of the moral welfare of the young and the breakdown of society through the flood of pornography and other information to which the young would now have access through the new communication medium. I believe that there are real benefits in Internet use for U.K. science teachers and their students. And so, amid the hype and the horror, I began to think what might be done to bring the Internet into school science.

In this chapter I describe why I believe the Internet can be used as a practical medium for publishing students' work done in the course of their school science lessons. I suggest that this process can enhance students' attitudes toward their science studies, that it can increase students' understanding of science concepts, and that, if used appropriately, it may increase students' understanding of the nature of scientific inquiry. I also share some of the lessons that I have learned along the way, as I have worked with teachers, IT support services, and administrators.

STARTING OUT

Models for Successful Curriculum Innovation

Few teachers in U.K. schools have access to the Internet in the mid-1990s, although no official figures are available. (My own estimate, based on a search through URLs, is that certainly no more than 100 U.K. schools were active users of the Internet at the end of 1995, if one defines an active school as one with established Web pages, with evidence of active Internet use given in those pages.) Some teachers were enthusiastic enough to get their own, private, Internet connections set up from home, using one of the Internet providers that sprang up so rapidly in the United Kingdom throughout the mid-1990s. There were, of course, some pioneering schools who established themselves on the Internet early on, but by and large the general attitude toward using the Internet as a tool in schools was at best neutral and in some cases downright negative. During the year, one senior administrator remarked to me that he thought there were many teachers in schools who still wished that "the whole Information Technology business would just go away."

At this stage I already had the idea that the Internet could offer teachers of science and their pupils enormous opportunities, although I was unsure how to go about convincing the teachers of this. I decided to approach the situation by involving teachers right from the start, seeking to bring about classroom change with the practitioners' consent. Fullan (1991) suggests that successful change at school level has six themes:

1. Leadership and vision—where do we want to go and how are we going to get there?
2. Evolutionary planning—the willingness to adapt plans as we go along.
3. Initiative taking and empowerment—developing collaborative power structures
4. Staff development and assistance—helping people to learn new ways of doing and thinking
5. Monitoring/problem coping—controlling the process of change through evaluation and monitoring
6. Restructuring—social changes necessary for the change to become deeply rooted.

Rather than simply saying to teachers—"You really should be using the Internet in your science teaching, and here's how you should be doing it"—I have attempted to involve teachers as closely as possible with the project. In doing so, the teachers and I implicitly address Fullan's themes together, articulating a shared Vision of what we want to do and how we might try to get there, Planning what needs to be done and reviewing these plans as we go along, encouraging and supporting individual Initiatives (by teachers and their students). Staff Development has formed part of our plan, and we have strategies for Monitoring how things are going and responding to difficulties. I return to Fullan's sixth theme, Restructuring, at the end of this chapter.

Finding a Shared Vision

On first exposure to the Internet, most of us go through a phase of exploring to see what is available, using the Internet as an end in itself rather than as a means to an end. Wanting to move teachers and their students to serious Internet users rather than just Internet surfers, my first step was to identify a group of enthusiastic local science teachers. For me, finding such teachers was reasonably straightforward as I am involved in both preservice and inservice teacher education as part of my work at the university. A natural extension of such work is to involve teachers in the local community in my research, which is part of the role of the education academic.

At our first meeting, the teachers and I discussed how we might use the Internet to enhance young people's experience of school science. Although most of the teachers in the group had only a sketchy idea of exactly what the Internet actually is, they realized from the start that it could offer them and their students new insights. As we talked, teachers told stories about the way that many students find communicating by using computers very motivating. Common accounts included students typing messages to each other across the school's computer network after lessons before proceeding to walk home together. Elsewhere in the United Kingdom, Wright (1993) reported similar enthusiasm among students for computer-mediated communication (CMC). If such enthusiasm was to be harnessed in science classes, we decided that students communicating science to each other over the Internet had to play a big part in it.

As a routine part of practical work in school science, students write up their laboratory and field work, as required by the National Curriculum (DFE, 1995). This writing is often assessed in some way, and sometimes the work is displayed on the walls of classrooms and corridors for other students to see. Often students are encouraged to present their accounts to each other, describing what they did and how they accounted for their results. Yet it is very rarely that students get the chance to do this on anything other than the smallest scale, because traditional technologies make publishing work a cumbersome process, with long time lags built in. Just think about sending your students' paper-based accounts of their science investigations to students at the school just down the road, and then establishing a postal correspondence about the work and you will see what I mean.

In contrast to traditional publishing methods, the Internet provides a way to publish students' work quickly and simply. It can make that work available for other students around the world to read, and it can carry correspondence from those students as well. The combination of rapid publication and wide availability immediately attracted us to this idea of publishing students' work. We therefore decided to produce an electronic journal for science students, calling it *ScI-Journal*. The capitalization of the journal title is deliberately ambiguous, so that it reads as Sci (for "Science") and as Sc1 (for "Science 1"—the Attainment Target in the National Curriculum for science [DFE, 1995] which relates to experimental and investigative science).

We also made a decision to limit the target age range of the journal to secondary school students aged 11 to 16. This decision was based partly on the teachers' own institutions (all were from such secondary schools) and partly on my concern to provide a manageable focus for the journal. At this stage we were especially concerned that students should be able to find articles that would interest them and that would be appropriate for them to read. Restricting the journal to a limited age range seemed an appropriate way of doing this.

POSSIBLE OUTCOMES: WHO GAINS WHAT?

Student Attitudes

Our initial planning for *ScI-Journal* was based on the idea that students would find the use of computer-mediated communication as part of their science studies intrinsically motivating. As a result, we reasoned, students would approach their science lessons with a more positive attitude, showing an affective gain (Bloom, Krathwohl, & Masia, 1964). For the teachers, this was of course an attractive proposition—after all, who could be against the idea of producing more willing, enthusiastic, and cheerful students?

Much more importantly, we thought that such changes in attitude might benefit students too, making science a more positive experience for them. Head (1985) makes the point that adolescence is a time in which virtually all students have a very strong need to develop a personal identity, and he suggests that in many cases the individual's personal response to science and science teaching is influenced by a particular view of science as objective, instrumental, and emotionally neutral. Strategies that Head puts forward to counter such influences are rooted in the idea of making science meaningful for the individual—these include a tactic that Head calls "reformulation." Essentially reformulation is a process in which students explain their ideas using their own words to the teacher and to other members of the class, a process that is immediately identifiable in writing for a student science journal.

Students Learning Science

Although affective gain on its own provides a good reason for pursuing the idea of publishing students' work, the constructivist view of knowledge suggests that there are likely to be benefits in the cognitive domain (Bloom, Engelhart, Furst, Hill, & Krathwohl, 1956) that may be of equal or even greater importance. Driver (1989) wrote:

> If learning science is essentially a process of culturation into the ideas and models of conventional science, the danger from the point of view of learners is that they accept what they are presented with through books, teacher talk and guided experimental work because of its authoritative status. This can and does get in the way of students making sense of the ideas for themselves and results in the 'real world' and 'school science' being kept as distinct systems. (p. 103)

The work done by Driver and others in the constructivist field shows that an essential part of learning science involves the personal construction of knowledge, through social interactions with peers, older students, and teachers.

Discussions, poster presentations and so on obviously provide scope for such interactions between individuals inside the classroom, but my teacher colleagues and I could see that the scope of these interactions can be widened enormously through electronic publication of students' work. Not only can students discuss their work with an audience that is potentially of magnitude greater than that in their own institution, but the presentation of ideas to that audience involves a process that has a very different quality to the presentation to fellow students in the same class. In writing for *SciJournal*, students must think carefully about their investigative work. They must present their findings in a logical, ordered way, and they must seek to explain them in the context of the scientific knowledge that they have. In putting forward explanations, they must seek to convince their readers; they must therefore have a sense of the audience for whom they are writing.

Sutton (1994) argues that the object of the interpretation of practical work in school science should be not the experiment itself, but what someone has said about the experiment, in other words: "Science lessons should be the study of systems of meaning which human beings have built up" (p. 63). Writing, publishing, and reading material about students' practical science work provides an important way of doing just this. By getting our students to write about what they did, and why they think they saw whatever it was that they say they saw, we can get them to concentrate on the systems of meaning that they are developing and to think about the ideas behind the words. The outcome of all this, we reasoned, must be cognitive gain—students who can understand science better.

Students Learning About Science

Although those who study the way scientists work, whether as philosophers or sociologists, far from agree about the nature of the scientific method, there is widespread agreement that the production of scientific knowledge is a process that involves the negotiation of meaning between members of the community of scientists (see, e.g., Chalmers, 1982; Collins & Pinch, 1993; Kuhn, 1962; Ziman, 1978—a position commonly referred to as social constructivism.

In discussing the interpretation of their practical work with their peers, students are also involved in the social construction of knowledge—seeking to negotiate a system of meaning that is acceptable not only to them but also to the other parties in the discussion. This social construction of meaning is a process that is commonly hidden from our students, many of whom see science as a process in which scientists reveal the truth about nature (Aikenhead, 1987). In constructing their own meaning through using *Sci-Journal*, it seems possible to us that students can be helped to understand that this process is common to all inquiry and will gain a better understanding of the nature of science itself.

Common Goals

It is worth making the point that the possible outcomes I have set out here have emerged over the course of about 12 months, during a process of considerable discussion. Although our goals have not always coincided, the process of negotiation has nearly always produced something with which we all feel reasonably comfortable. And at all times we have genuinely tried to put the benefit of students first, thinking at all times of improving the quality of the science education they receive.

GETTING THERE

As well as setting out our vision for *ScI-Journal*, the first stage of the project also involved planning how we might attain that vision. Inevitably, this process involved much evolutionary planning (Fullan's second theme).

Initial Plans

At the beginning of the project, my initial plans for the way the journal would work were simple and as follows:

1. Students carry out a science investigation and produce a report of their work using information technology to produce text and graphics. This report includes a statement of the aims of their investigation or the hypothesis being tested, and it gives enough detail to ensure that students in another school can repeat some or all the work if they so wish. Students give the results of their work and draw conclusions in which they try to explain their results using science that they have met.
2. All reports include the name(s) of the author(s), together with the name of their school and an electronic mail address at which they may be contacted.
3. The report is sent electronically to Southampton University by FTP or by e-mail, including the report as an attachment.
4. Once received at the university, the report is turned into an HTML document. It is then mounted on the World-Wide Web as part of the next edition of the journal. (For this task I set aside about a week in order to learn some HTML.)
5. Following publication, correspondence about articles can be directed to the letters page of the journal if it is appropriate for a wide readership, or it can be sent directly to the school concerned using the e-mail address published with each article.

I always knew that this was an ideal, although I thought little of how far from the realization of the journal it was likely to be.

Modified Plans

One major reason for modifying my initial plans for the operation of *ScI-Journal* was technical. For historical reasons concerned with centralized curriculum planning, many schools in the United Kingdom use a type of computer that is almost unique to the U.K. education sector—in the area local to Southampton University, schools using such machines are in the majority. These machines use a proprietary operating system, and only the later versions of the operating system are able to read and write PC-formatted disks. Although PC-based software and hardware packages for Internet connection became widely available and reasonably priced in the United Kingdom during the mid-1990s, such packages were not readily and cheaply available for the computers commonly found in schools, limiting the ability of schools even to begin to sample what was available on the Internet. When this is put in the context of a continuing government squeeze on education spending, the picture for Internet access in schools can be seen to be difficult.

In order to get networked access to *ScI-Journal*, we modified my initial plan, making use of a network to which all schools in the county (Hampshire) are connected for the purpose of school administration. This network is a text-only service for which schools pay only a small annual fee. As well as being carried on the Web (to give access to schools outside Hampshire), *ScI-Journal* is also carried on this text-only service, enabling schools to gain access to it using existing technology. This still has some problems, some of which are technical, others of which are very different.

Technical Difficulties

The local, text-only computer network made it difficult to take students' work and transmit it electronically to the university because of the incompatibility of the machines used on the network with those found in classrooms. In response to this, students and teachers have generally resorted to producing their work on disk and sending it to me by mail—far from what I first had in mind.

The text-only system is also far from ideal from the standpoints of presentation and ease of use. Most students wish to include diagrams in their work. The text-only system cannot handle these, and so accounts of experiments must be limited to descriptions. And instead of the familiar hot links or hotspots found on Web pages, the system uses the function keys on the computer keyboard, which students find much harder to use than the mouse click.

The other technical issues that have needed to be addressed concerned training teachers to use the local system and translating the journal from HTML into the text-only format. In both of these I was fortunate in enlisting the help of Kate, an IT specialist working in the IT Services department of the Local County Authority. My experience suggests very strongly that a contact like Kate is essential when working in a technical area that requires expertise outside one's own area. Although I was happy to provide help and guidance about any aspect of Internet work, the Hampshire network was well outside my knowledge, and on more than one occasion I had cause to bless Kate and her help.

Although all these difficulties are reasonable small, when they are combined with the institutional problems described later they present a considerable set of challenges to be met when introducing our science students to the Internet. Before leaving the subject of technical difficulties, however, it is worth looking briefly at the issues concerned with producing the Web page edition of the journal. These issues are generally applicable to Web page authoring for U.K. schools and may apply to an even wider audience.

Being reasonably computer literate, I had little difficulty learning HTML. Instead, the principal difficulty in producing Web pages for *SciJournal* has been writing HTML that shows what I want it to show. This is particularly true in the case of producing simple chemical or mathematical equations, in which the most common need is for subscripts (e.g., for the formula of calcium carbonate), superscripts, and fractions. My experience suggests that you can nearly always find a way around this, if necessary, by getting what you want on the screen of your word processor, using a program with the facility for screen capture, making a graphic image of it, and putting this in the Web document.

However, including huge amounts of graphic images is less than ideal for two reasons. First, anyone using a text only browser will be unable to see what you have put in. Second, graphic images take time to load, especially across a telephone line.

It is therefore better to use text if you can and to rely on the formatting capabilities of the Web browsing software the reader is using. Doing this needs care, however, because you cannot be sure that your readers have the latest all-singing, all-dancing version of whatever browser software you are using, especially if they are in a school. This is especially true for U.K. schools who are running browsers on proprietary machines, which can have capabilities very different to browsers on PC- or Mac-based systems. For this reason I try to keep the HTML I write as simple as possible and run several different browsers with different levels of technical sophistication—if it does not display correctly in my most basic browser, I do not use it.

Nontechnical Difficulties

The text-based system in Hampshire schools began primarily as an administrative tool, for schools to exchange data with the central office of the Local Education Authority. As the system developed it was also used as a medium for distributing career education, but the provision of computers in schools for accessing the local network has remained primarily in the administrative areas of schools. Access to computers in such areas has perhaps posed the greatest problem of all for teachers in the project, given the reluctance of administrators and managers in schools to allow students access to such areas and allow students and teachers access to what is seen as an administrative tool for the purposes of education.

IN CONCLUSION

So far we have not learned as much as I had hoped about the effect of publishing students' work on the Internet. The reason for this is simply that it has taken much longer to establish this project than I had ever imagined at the start. However, we have learned quite a lot about attempting to introduce the Internet into school science classrooms, as I explain later.

Outcomes Thus Far—For Students and Teachers

As I write this, we have one edition of *ScI-Journal* produced, with another well on its way. Schools working on the project have responded to the challenges magnificently, and students have been enthusiastic. The comments of one year 9 girl are typical: "The idea of someone in Australia, reading something I've written and then writing back to me, is great—I'd really like the chance to use something like this to make contacts in other countries to exchange ideas about diet and health for the work we're doing in science at the moment." Such enthusiasm is reinforced as students get e-mail correspondence from other students from around the globe reading their work.

Teachers are enthusiastic too, sending material that their students have produced and are keen to see published. Offers of students' work are beginning to come from around the world, and I was delighted to find an article written by an 11-year-old student, which he had managed to upload to our FTP server with the help of his mother.

We thus have some evidence for affective gain in students who have articles published in the journal, but we have as yet no evidence for the cognitive gain that we believe the use of *ScI-Journal* will produce. Acquiring evidence in respect of these beliefs will take time and will be one of our priorities once we feel that we have the journal working well, with an active readership of students corresponding about their work.

Outcomes Thus Far—The Process of Change

In seeking to set up an electronic journal for students, I wanted managers, teachers, and their students to change their perception of Information Technology (IT) in a substantial way. Instead of seeing IT as an occasional tool in classroom science, I wanted them to see (and use) it as a means of communicating science with others around the world—to seize the power of the medium and use it to enhance students' education.

The experience of planning the *ScI-Journal* shows that the process of bringing the Internet into classrooms in a school that is not already using the Internet as an educational tool requires substantive structural changes, that is, changes in such things as organizational arrangements, roles, and finance (Fullan, 1991). In this sense it is not much different from any other major curriculum innovation, except for the technical dimension. To see the implications of this, we can look at the three groups within a school who were involved in the process of change in introducing *ScI-Journal*.

Students. Being generally accustomed to the use of IT in their work in science classes, students appeared to take writing accounts for *ScI-Journal* in their stride. Greater problems would doubtless have been encountered had we asked students to provide accounts in HTML rather than as text files. Evidence such as the accounts earlier on in this chapter in which students are described communicating with each other using IT support the notion that students are able to adapt quite flexibly to new practices involving computers.

Teachers. Those involved in the project needed to make changes to their practice, to incorporate planned use of *ScI-Journal* into their teaching. Familiarity with the methods needed to use and write for the journal was also needed. Such changed behavior was part of the "price of change," which such teachers calculated on signing up for the project and as such presented little in the way of a barrier to change. For these individuals, the greatest challenge lay in finding time to implement the changes and in convincing colleagues at all levels of their possible benefits. In other words, teachers became agents of institutional change as well as people who were engaged in changing their own practice.

Planning for the *ScI-Journal* project took account of the need to build a shared vision with these two groups and had involved lengthy discussions with teachers who were able to feed in the ideas of their students. The planning process did not, however, involve the third group—school managers.

School Managers. One of the functions of members of this group is to consider the deployment of resources by the school. The notion of students engaging in active use of a resource using it to generate and review ideas with others outside the institution, is a radical departure from the traditional use of school resources, and as such required a significant change in the perceptions of members of this group.

In seeking to introduce Internet use by change involving teachers and their students alone, no attempt was made to enlist the support of managers directly, relying instead on teachers to convince their senior colleagues that participation in the project was desirable for the school as a whole. This course of action was an attempt to minimize the structural change needed in schools and was supported by adapting existing resources (the "administrative" network).

McGreal in Volume 1 of this series points out that technical competence is not an asset for education managers, meaning that solutions to technical problems within schools need to be sought carefully, and that such solutions may need careful explanation to managers. Senior managers saw our suggested use of "administration" computers by teachers and pupils as undesirable, not fully understanding that the login IDs used by students and teachers would bar access to the sensitive information available to managers and administrators.

This strategy of minimal structural change relied on teachers being able to convince managers that participating in the project was desirable. Faced with managers who were convinced that there were technical reasons for being at least very cautious, this strategy has had to be rethought, and managers have since become involved in discussions about the project, its curriculum aims, and its technical dimensions as a way of addressing the issue of structural change directly.

ADVICE TO OTHERS

In applying to other projects what has been learned from the experience of setting up *ScI-Journal*, I suggest that any development that involves the introduction of the Internet to a school that has had no previous Internet experience needs to consider the need for structural change right from the outset. The extent of this change should not be underestimated, and the need to support managers with technical information to help them make decisions about resource allocation should also be recognized.

Changes come slowly. In a recent article, Schofield (1996) wrote:

> Perhaps the Internet has arrived too quickly for teachers to have worked out a view. Computers, for example, were recognized as the coming thing for 20 years before the first micros appeared in 1975, and it was almost a decade before they were widely used in schools. However, the World-Wide Web, which is driving the use of the Internet, didn't really exist until 1993, and even a year ago, it wasn't considered important. (p. 8)

It may take time, but the experience with *ScI-Journal* shows that publishing students' work on the Internet may pay great rewards.

REFERENCES

Aikenhead, G.S. (1987). High-school graduates' beliefs about science-technology-society. III. Characteristics and limitations of scientific knowledge. *Science Education, 71*(4), 459-487.

Bloom, B.S., Engelhart, M.D., Furst, E.J., Hill, W.H., & Krathwohl, D.R. (1956). *Taxonomy of educational objectives: The classification of educational goals. Handbook I: Cognitive domain.* New York: David McKay.

Bloom, B.S., Krathwohl, D.R., & Masia, B.B. (1964). *Taxonomy of educational objectives: The classification of educational goals. Handbook II: Affective domain.* New York: David McKay.

Chalmers, A.F. (1982). *What is this thing called science?* Milton Keynes: Open University Press.

Collins, H.M, & Pinch, T. (1993). *The Golem: What everyone should know about science.* Cambridge: Cambridge University Press.

Department for Education (DFE). (1995). *Science in the national curriculum.* London: HMSO.

Driver, R. (1989). The construction of scientific knowledge in school classrooms. In R. Millar (Ed.), *Doing science: Images of science in science education* (pp. 83-106). Lewes, UK: Falmer Press.

Fullan, M.G. (1991). *The new meaning of educational change.* New York: Teachers College Press.

Head, J. (1985). *The personal response to science.* Cambridge: Cambridge University Press.

Kuhn, T.S. (1962). *The structure of scientific revolutions.* Chicago: University of Chicago Press.

Schofield, J. (1996, January). You can BETT on the Net, but can you bank on the teachers? *The Guardian Online,* 1-13.

Sutton, C. (1994). Well, Mary, what are they saying here? In R. Levinson (Ed.), *Teaching science* (pp. 61-75). London: Routledge.

Wright, B. (1993). Desert Storm simulation. *Computer Education, 73,* 2-5.

Ziman, J. (1978). *Reliable knowledge.* Cambridge: University of Cambridge Press.

III

ONLINE CORRESPONDENCE PROJECTS

7

KEY PALS: THE GOODWILL AMBASSADORS OF THE 1990S

Annette Christy

E-mail has become a common form of communication for persons having online access to the Internet or to a local network (LAN). How to use these services to augment classroom instruction or as a resource for service learning projects becomes another option for the teacher to introduce.

Many studies have confirmed that by using e-mail student writing skills greatly improve (Burrall, 1992; Crowley, 1989; Potter, 1992). Although students use the same skills online as on paper, the magic of being able to use a computer keeps their interest peaked. Getting started with a telecommunications project is not difficult. The instructor will have to set aside some additional time for identifying these items: (a) what the guidelines should be, (b) during what part of the school day this will occur, (c) design specific goals, and (d) the plan for a closure activity to this project.

GETTING STARTED

A telecommunications project does require some specific equipment. The classroom, computer lab, or media center must have a separate phone line. The computer must have an internal or external modem connected to this phone line. It is best to have a modem that has a speed of 33.6 bits per second (bps) or faster because this increases the speed at which a text can be uploaded or downloaded to the host computer. The computer must have a telecommunications software package loaded on its hard drive. Choose software that is easy to use with simple instructions on how to add phone numbers to its address book. Ask colleagues or your school district's computer technician which ones they use and recommend.

If your building does not have an Internet connection, selecting an online service is the next step in the process. The major online services will gladly send a free preview kit consisting of a disk and literature. Look for very recent articles that compare the online services because these services are constantly upgrading their offerings to be more competitive, and online features change from month to month. Costs will be another factor to consider. Some online services offer specially designed packages only for schools, whereas others may provide a flat rate on hourly access. Choose a service that has a local phone number or an 800 number to dial into its service. Costs will quickly escalate if a phone number is not within your immediate calling area.

Another important item to consider is the type of online support each service offers. Is help available online? Can the technical service department be reached by a toll-free number? In other words, how user friendly is the service? Finally, consider what kinds of safeguards the service provides. Chat rooms and bulletin boards can be open invitations for undesirable participants or inappropriate discussions. Two major services now monitor these areas with personnel trained to intercede in case online conversations take on questionable subjects or use abusive, objectionable language (Eisler, 1995).

Once the hardware and software are in place for telecommunications, the next step is to train the staff. They must feel comfortable with this new curriculum offering before they will commit their students to using it. Lever (1991) stated that in order for staff training to be successful, several guidelines should be followed: (a) schedule this training at a convenient time for the staff; (b) team them up with partners; (c) train them in small groups; (d) secure the enthusiastic support of the building principal for this project; and (e) consider offering some type of incentive or a reward to the participants. Once the staff understands the concept of telecommunications, they will help in supporting this key pal project.

Before the students actually start transmitting messages, go into their classes and explain to them some basic concepts about e-mail, the specific program they will use, what they can expect from the service, and approximately how often they will be online. If at all possible, print from off-the-screen the various menus they will use. Enlarge these menus and make them into transparencies to use as a teaching device for these classes. In this way they will be prepared and more confident for their first encounter with the new program. Explain to students that because of the very nature of e-mail, it will never be a private correspondence between the immediate key pals. They must know that because this is a school-sanctioned project, they will adhere to certain standards, netiquette, and guidelines. A code of ethics statement should be signed by all participating students. These statements can then be placed in their individual folders, along with copies of their online correspondence (see Schrum & Day, Vol. 1, this series).

Before the project actually starts, arrange ahead of time when these key pals will be online. For some online services, it is best to reach them during off-peak hours when businesses or industry are not as likely to monopolize all the access lines. For other services this is not a consideration. Experience will be the best guide for these situations. A very important strategy to consider is emphasizing to the classroom teacher what specific number of students can be accommodated at one time. It will be very frustrating to the telecommunications teacher and to those students if only a few can be at the online work stations while the others are waiting with nothing to do.

POSSIBLE KEY PAL PROJECTS

Possible key pal projects do not have to encompass the entire globe. It would be best to start with a neighboring school and work out any little kinks in the delivery service. Then, once all the problems have been resolved, try taking on a project using more students or for a greater time period.

A beginning project could be one of helping students make transitions from one school to another. For example, middle school key pals could send welcoming messages to in-coming primary students. These messages might convey tips on how to deal with coming to a new school, dispel needless fears of being picked on by older students, and assure them that the middle school teachers are just as kind and friendly as those in the primary school. The welcoming messages should also add some personal thoughts. The middle school students might mention how well they remember their own fears and uncertainties a short time ago as they were leaving the primary school.

A visit by the primary students to tour their new school would also help in this process. If a school tour can be arranged, having the key pals available to meet their younger counterparts would also be helpful. It is also a good idea to have students wear name tags for this event. The middle school students could act as tour guides answering questions and helping to instill confidence among these younger students.

The same could be done with a key pal project linking eighth grade students to high school students. Many eighth grade students often experience anxiety and stress during the final months of middle school. Frequently these students have spent several years at one school. Leaving the security of this school and its very familiar scheduling, classroom locations, friends and teachers seems to produce some trauma. This situation is perfect for introducing key pal correspondence between the two schools. The high school students could send the first welcoming messages. These messages could convey the same types of assurances as those messages from the middle school key pals. Again, a tour of the high school should be arranged, with the high school key pals acting as tour guides. Perhaps having a "Meet Your Key Pal" social before the tour started would help the younger students feel welcome and less reluctant to end their middle school careers. Having a high school admissions counselor or even the principal come and welcome them would also be a good public relations strategy.

Other possible key pal projects could involve using online services to share science projects or results of experiments, conduct joint experiments, critique favorite authors or books, and discuss historical events that occurred within that locale. Another possible area would be that of career awareness, linking up student career interests to those persons already in that particular field. Many high schools have business or industry internships for their seniors; therefore, these seniors could become mentors and advisors for younger students interested in similar careers. These seniors could become positive role models who advise the younger students to stay in school and keep focusing on their studies.

All these projects will provide the participants with a feeling of self-esteem and self-worth. For many students, these feelings are absent in their daily lives. Giving them the opportunity to become a key pal is a worthwhile learning experience and will instill a feeling of confidence and the knowledge that they have shared in another person's learning.

Making the Key Pal Project a Success

Key pals seem to work more efficiently if they have a partner when they are at the work station. The partner's duty is to help the typist with spelling, punctuation, and spacing. Younger students become so involved in the mechanics of typing, they frequently forget to check the screen for any kinds of typing errors. Have them take turns being the typist or the spell checker. In that way no one will feel as if one partner is always criticizing the other.

Time is a critical factor for these projects. Some online services only allow a specified time for usage, or a particular project must be finished within a short time frame. Always allow additional time for a telecommunications project. Unexpected events may interfere with the best of plans. These interruptions could range from the online service being inaccessible for a few hours to a few days, equipment problems, scheduling conflicts, or no phone service due to severe weather or service lines being cut by area construction crews. Test the online service before a class comes to use it. Sometimes a few extra minutes used to test the service will be enough to insure that the key pal session will proceed smoothly, without any surprises.

All key pal participants should have individual folders to keep their printed out correspondence, their signed ethics statement, a time management chart of how many messages they have sent and received, and a signed parental consent letter. The parental consent letter is very important. It not only keeps parents informed of what their child is accomplishing, but also gives permission for their child's participation in these projects. It is a good public relations instrument and also acts as a safeguard for the instructor. If the ethics statement and the permission form are printed on two different colored papers, they become easily recognizable in the folder. The instructor should not allow a student to participate in these telecommunications projects until both of these documents are signed and in that student's folder.

Students like to have copies of the messages they have received online. It is also a good idea to print out the messages they are going to transmit. In this way, the teacher has a record of how many times online messages have been sent and received. This can be especially helpful when a key pal at either end is not cooperating. On these hard copy messages, use a highlighter pen to mark the sender's and receiver's name. So often the names are hidden in lengthy destination codes. Thus a highlighted name can be easily found within this coding and the message quickly placed in the proper folder or given to the intended student.

Most online services have the capacity to retain the addresses of persons or organizations that will be used often. Address books can be very useful. Enter in them the complete address of anyone who will be contacted often. Then choose a nickname or shortened form of this address. Post these shortened addresses on the telecommunications work station. For example, "Writing to Wren High School? Use this address: Mary." Setting up the address form in this way will help students correctly address their e-mail and also drastically reduce the number of returned messages because of faulty address forms.

Another way to get an online project started quickly and without glitches is to fax class rosters to the participating schools, so key pals can be easily lined up with one another. Consider exchanging photos of the key pals or a videotape with the students briefly introducing themselves. These activities help to overcome feelings of shyness and awkwardness when writing to a stranger for the first time.

Network among teaching colleagues or friends for possible key pal sources. Whenever educators meet, project ideas just seem to flow. Post a message on a bulletin board service (BBS) or through a key pal service for potential links. One such source is iecc-request@stolaf.edu. Here projects, surveys, discussions, and classroom partnerships can be listed, and potential online hookups can take place.

CLOSURE ACTIVITIES

It is important to bring these projects to a definite close. Some of the online activities will be extremely short, whereas others will last for many months. Students need some kind of ending event. The closure activities can be very simple such as a farewell message or as elaborate as a field trip. If at all possible, having the key pals meet one another is a very effective way to bring this project to a close. Another way is to exchange a final video with the key pals expressing how much they enjoyed the experience and learned from it. Having students complete surveys is another method of evaluating just how successful and valuable the project was. A comment section on the survey also can be an excellent indication of how much students gained from this experience. If teachers were part of the online project, have them also complete a survey on how worthwhile they thought the project was for them and for their classes. The feedback from these surveys will help an instructor plan for future online projects. They can be useful in making adjustments for any problems that may have occurred or help focus on which past experiences may need some fine-tuning. These surveys and comments also can aid in avoiding potential scheduling or equipment difficulties.

The rewards are extensive. Small problems that may appear can be easily overcome through persistence, patience, and cooperation. Telecommunications offer boundless opportunities for students to expand their horizons and broaden their knowledge. This chapter has only touched the surface on ways to bring students and teachers together online. The possibilities are endless. Educators are known for their creativity and resourcefulness. Therefore, in planning these online projects, they will only limited by their imaginations.

REFERENCES

Burrall, B. (1992, October). Telecommunications = motivation. *The Computing Teacher*, pp. 27-28.

Crowley, M. (1989, April). Organizing for electronic messaging in the schools. *The Computing Teacher*, pp. 23-26.

Eisler, M. (1995, September 5). Policing the Net. *USA Today*, p. A1.

Lever, J. (1991, November). *Strategies for empowering educators with technology.* Paper presented at the Annual Conference for the League for Innovation, Miami, FL.

Potter, R.L. (1992). *Using telecommunications in middle school reading.* Bloomington, IN: Phi Delta Kappa Educational Foundation.

8

USING CMC TO BRING REAL-WORLD EXPERIENCES INTO THE CLASSROOM: THE ELECTRONIC "PEN-PAL" PROJECT

Thomas Brush

School systems around the country are struggling to integrate new instructional strategies into their curriculum while maintaining the general structure of their classrooms. Two of these strategies—(a) providing students with experiences that demonstrate the real-world applicability of the curricular content, and (b) providing students with a variety of perspectives and viewpoints on issues discussed in the classroom—are receiving a great deal of support in the research literature (Brown, Collins, & Duguid, 1989; Cognition and Technology Group at Vanderbilt, 1992; Resnick, 1987). The research states that by structuring learning tasks in real-world contexts, and by providing multiple perspectives to instructional content, students obtain a deeper understanding of the application of the content in a wide variety of relevant situations.

Implementing these strategies in the classroom can prove difficult, however. Somehow, a connection needs to be established between "real-world" activities occurring outside the walls of the classroom and the curricular content being delivered inside those walls. Computer-mediated communication (CMC) had been used in other situations to provide students with access to outside knowledge bases such as information resources at universities and has been used as a connection between multiple individuals for purposes of discussing issues from a variety of viewpoints (e.g., Brush, Knapczyk, & Hubbard, 1994; Pugh, 1993). Based on these past implementations, a CMC project was developed at a midwestern school district to attempt to provide an electronic community-school connection. The project involved linking computers at centers scattered throughout the community to the school district's electronic network. Elementary students were encouraged to have electronic "pen pals," that is, senior citizens who would correspond with students electronically and share their vast wealth of knowledge. Using the network, students were able to share written information, academic problems, pictures, drawings, and school projects with the senior citizens. By linking with these individuals in the community, students had the opportunity to discuss issues with a population of individuals with whom they would not normally interact, thus receiving a wider array of viewpoints on current events and other issues.

POPULATION SERVED/TARGETED

The setting for this project was a K-5 elementary school located in a small urban community in a Midwestern state. Enrollment at the elementary school was approximately 650 students. Approximately 70% of the students enrolled in the school were Caucasian, 25% African-American, and 5% Hispanic or Asian-American.

This project targeted fifth-grade students in two classes at the elementary school. All students in the classes participated, thus there were varying degrees of ability, socioeconomic status, and computer knowledge. Because the elementary school for these students used an inclusion model, approximately 10% of the students participating in this project received some form of special education services. Approximately 50 students participated in the project.

In addition to the students, older adults were recruited from the community and asked to participate in the project. Approximately 30 individuals volunteered to participate in the project. The volunteers ranged in age from 50 to 70, and many were involved in an introductory computer class sponsored by the school district's adult education program.

OUTCOMES HOPED FOR

Through the implementation of this project, several outcomes were expected from both students and the senior citizen participants. These outcomes are described as follows:

1. Students would acquire a better understanding of past events and issues through their interactions with individuals who lived through those events.
2. Students would acquire an appreciation for the knowledge possessed by a segment of the population with which they generally did not interact.
3. All participants would obtain a working knowledge of an electronic mail system and be able to compose, send, and receive electronic messages.
4. All participants would acquire an understanding of the issues and concerns that are important to a very different segment of the population.

DESCRIPTION OF PROCESS

Prior to the beginning of the school year, three to five computers and printers were set up in three locations: (a) the classrooms to which the students participating were assigned, (b) a large room in the basement of the community center where some adult education classes are delivered, and (c) a room in the district's adult education building. Telephone lines were installed in these locations, and each computer was connected to the phone lines via high-speed modems. Word processing, communications, and electronic mail software was also installed on each of the computers.

During the first week of school, the project facilitator met with the classroom teachers and the instructor for the "older learner" introductory computer class in order to receive lists of participants. During discussions with the classroom teachers, they voiced some concern regarding the writing abilities of some of the students receiving special education services. It was decided that some of the better writers in the class would be asked to team with their peers who had writing difficulties, and that they would jointly write and respond to their pen pals.

After receiving the lists of participants, the project facilitator established computer accounts for each individual and randomly matched a student with a senior volunteer. Due to the differences in numbers between student and senior volunteers, some of the seniors were asked to correspond with two students. Once the matching was complete, the project facilitator provided the classroom teachers and computer class instructor with a list of the pen-pal pairings.

In separate sessions, the project facilitator then provided the teachers, students, and senior pen pals with training on the use of the computers and electronic mail software. He discussed and demonstrated how to access their electronic mail computer accounts; compose, send, and receive electronic messages; store messages in electronic folders for future reference; and print messages. At the end of each of the training sessions, the teachers handed out pen-pal user names to each of the participants.

Once training was completed, the classroom teachers began assigning "projects" to the students. Initially the projects assigned were fact finding; in other words, because the students had never actually met their pen-pals, they were asked to find out as much as they could about them. The first few letters students sent to their pen pals included information about themselves, their families, and their interests and hobbies. In these letters they asked their pen pals to respond with similar information. After two or three general correspondences in which the pen pals became more acquainted with one another, the teachers asked the students to use their pen pals' knowledge and experiences to help them learn more about history, politics, and other content areas. Through electronic question-and-answer sessions, students learned about recent historical and political issues from individuals who were firsthand observers. Some of the topics discussed between the pen pals included:

- life during the great depression
- changes in industry throughout the years (particularly the automobile industry)
- impressions of past presidents (Roosevelt, Truman, Eisenhower)
- perspectives of World War II from the home front and from the battlefield
- changes in the local community through the years
- the evolution of technology
- advances in medicine (e.g., polio).

Throughout these correspondences, the teachers would monitor the discussions and assist students with researching topics for their pen pals. The teachers would also guide students toward asking questions that were relevant to topics being discussed in class. In this way, students were receiving information related to curricular content from an entirely different perspective.

Students continued corresponding with their pen pals for a period of 15 weeks. At the end of the project, a debriefing session was scheduled where students and their pen pals were able to meet face to face. During the debriefing, all the participants discussed the benefits of the project and provided feedback to the project facilitator regarding improvements that could be made for the next implementation of the project.

OUTCOMES ATTAINED

Interviews were conducted with the participating teachers immediately following the completion of the project. In addition, both students and senior volunteers were asked to complete a short written survey during the debriefing session. These data were used to determine whether the outcomes proposed for the project were met. The following conclusions can be drawn from these data.

Participation in the project enhanced students' knowledge and understanding of recent historical events. Both the teachers (through interviews) and the students (through the survey) stated that they felt classroom discussions of historical and political events were enhanced through their correspondences with pen pals. In addition, the teachers stated that they believed students had a better understanding of issues discussed in class if they had the opportunity to discuss them with their pen pals first.

Participation in the project gave all participants the opportunity to "talk" to individuals with whom they generally did not interact. In the surveys, both students and senior citizens overwhelmingly responded that they enjoyed corresponding with their pen pals and looked forward to reading their messages.

Nearly all participants gained expertise in the use of the electronic mail software used in this project. Although there were some technical problems, a majority of the participants stated that they felt comfortable with electronic mail and would like to use it again if given the opportunity.

CONCERNS AND WORDS OF ADVICE

Although, based on the outcomes defined, this was a very successful project for all participants, there were several areas that caused some problems and should be addressed should this type of project be replicated.

Problems with Telecommunications

The project facilitator received numerous complaints that the telecommunications hardware and software used for the project was not user friendly or reliable. On numerous occasions students and their pen pals stated that their messages did not get through on the first try, and they needed to resend them. In addition, the participants had some difficulty grasping the different steps they needed to complete before they could log in to their e-mail accounts (e.g., starting up the computer, establishing the telecommunications connection via modem, logging into their accounts). The project facilitator needed to provide ongoing technical support to the participants in order for the project to run smoothly. If the telecommunications aspect of the project could somehow be bypassed (that is, if all of the computers used in the project were networked together so that modems and phone lines were not necessary), then the technical problems encountered in this project would have been greatly reduced.

Problems with Correspondences

Although a vast majority of the senior citizens who volunteered to be pen pals enjoyed the experience thoroughly and responded to students on a regular basis, there were a few participants who did not correspond on a regular basis. Thus, some students received substantially fewer messages than other students, and the messages they did receive contained less informative content than the responses sent by other pen pals. This inequity in pen-pal responses led some students to feel apathetic toward their assignments and damaged the self-esteem of some students who were not receiving regular messages from their assigned pen-pals. The teachers and project facilitator monitored the number of messages received by students and reminded the senior volunteers that they needed to correspond regularly. In future implementations of this type of project, however, the need to correspond regularly and provide thoughtful, informative responses should be stressed to participants (particularly the adult participants) frequently.

Access to the Technology

Due to the limited funds available for this project, student and senior access to their electronic mail accounts was somewhat limited. Students had five computers in one of their classes connected to the school's network for e-mail use, and seniors had two locations in the community (with three to four computers) where they could access their e-mail. Although this proved to be somewhat of an inconvenience to the participants, computer time was scheduled throughout the day, and only participants in the pen-pal project were allowed to use the computers. These factors helped keep access problems to a minimum. Still, if more computers were available to the participants (such as a networked lab), there may have been an increase in the number of messages composed and sent by the participants.

It should also be noted that with any project involving older adults, contingencies should be made for unforeseen problems that may take place throughout the project. Absences due to personal or family illness can occur fairly regularly with this segment of the population, and teachers should inform students of these possibilities. Sadly, one of the student's pen-pals became seriously ill during the project and could not continue corresponding with the student. In this case, another senior volunteered to write to this student in addition to her assigned pen pal. She was even able to take copies of the student's messages to the senior who was ill and provide medical updates to the student. This led to an interesting discussion of new and old medical practices, aging, death and dying, and other fairly lofty philosophical issues. However, these types of occurrences stress the importance of having plans for circumstances that could disrupt the interactions between students and their pen pals.

DISCUSSION AND CONCLUSION

Why CMC?

In the project I have described, CMC provided the means for information transfer and interaction between students and community members. Nevertheless, it could be argued that this type of project could have been implemented without the use of CMC. Students could have written letters using pencil and paper, and these letters could have been sent to the senior volunteers via regular mail. Teachers could have also scheduled for senior volunteers to visit their classrooms and discuss issues with students face to face. However, there are some problems inherent in using either one of these alternatives for this type of project.

Traditional pen-pal projects in which individuals correspond using conventional mail generally occur over long periods of time. Replies to letters most often take days or weeks to be received. With a project such as the one discussed here, in which the correspondences were tied into the content being delivered in the classroom, time is much more of a factor. Students needed to receive replies from their pen pals fairly quickly and frequently if the information was to be used in class. If students received messages containing information relevant to content covered in class a week ago, then it was likely that the information was not useful to the current class discussion.

In addition, if some types of face-to-face discussion groups could have been formed between students and members of the community, it is doubtful that these groups would have had the kinds of discussions that were taking place via CMC. Time constraints inherently placed on face-to-face meetings, access to large numbers of individuals, and the inherent awkwardness of face-to-face discussions between students and adults would have hindered the discussions and most likely posed limits on the interactions. The richness of the interactions and discussions found through electronic communications may not have occurred if those discussions took place without the use of CMC. Thus, creating an environment in which community members and students could interact and share ideas and information would have been extremely difficult, if not impossible, without the use of CMC.

Summary

This project demonstrated the power of CMC in an instructional setting. Through CMC, two important instructional strategies were implemented. First, real-world activities were integrated with classroom activities. Students were able to receive firsthand knowledge of the applicability of the concepts and issues they were discussing in school to the problems being faced by citizens in their community. Second, a wider array of perspectives and viewpoints were brought into the classroom via students' electronic discussions with their pen pals. Students were able to hear about history, politics, and a variety of other topics from individuals with whom they would not normally interact. Thus, through asynchronous CMC, experience and expertise scattered throughout the community was brought into the classroom and linked to the school's curricular content.

TECHNICAL SECTION

Hardware

There were several different pieces of hardware used to connect the students and senior volunteers via electronic mail. First, computer accounts for all the participants were kept on an IBM Model 95 file server running Novell 3.12. Students accessed their accounts using Macintosh LC550s. Seniors accessed their accounts using a variety of different PC-compatible computers. All computers used for the project were connected to telephone lines using 14.4 bps modems. The file server was connected to the district's Ethernet network; also connected to the network was a Shiva LanRover. This piece of hardware allowed up to eight remote computers to connect to the district's network (and file server) at one time via normal telephone lines.

Software

The electronic mail software used for the project was PegasusMail. This software is available free of charge via the Internet and runs on any file server using Novell server software. There are versions of PegasusMail for the Macintosh, Windows, and DOS platforms. In addition to PegasusMail software, each computer used for the project had ClarisWorks version 2.0 (or 1.0 for Windows) installed. This provided participants with the ability to compose letters using the ClarisWorks word processor, then "cut" and "paste" their letters into PegasusMail.

Students connected to the e-mail file server through the Shiva LanRover using Appletalk Remote Access version 1.0, then they were able to run the Macintosh version of the PegasusMail software. Seniors using the PC-compatible computers connected to the e-mail file server using software called CITRIX (from Citrix corporation). This software allowed remote PC-compatible computers to dial in to a Novell file server and establish a high-speed connection over telephone lines (up to 57.6 bps). Once the seniors connected to the e-mail file server, they ran the DOS or Windows version of PegasusMail.

REFERENCES

Brown, J. S., Collins, A., & Duguid, P. (1989). Situated cognition and the culture of learning. *Educational Researcher, 18*, 32-41.

Brush, T., Knapczyk, D., & Hubbard, L. (1994). Incorporating technology into the field-based preparation of teachers. *Journal of Technology and Teacher Education, 2*(1), 91-102.

Cognition and Technology Group at Vanderbilt. (1992). The Jasper experiment: An exploration of issues in learning and instructional design. *Educational Technology Research and Development, 40*, 65-80.

Pugh, S. L. (1993). Using case studies and collaborative computer-assisted communication to support conceptual learning in a teacher-education course on critical reading. *Educational Technology, 33*(11), 30-38.

Resnick, L. B. (1987). The 1987 presidential address: Learning in school and out. *Educational Researcher, 4*, 13-20.

9

CONNECTING TO A MEANINGFUL LIFE: A CASE STUDY

MaryAnn Tille and Bob Hall

"COOL!" Getting teenagers to use this four letter word to describe anything educational is the challenge of being an English teacher of high school seniors.

However, by incorporating e-mail into a final senior research project, I heard this word many times. The theme of my English class project was "Searching": searching for self and career, searching for love through family and friends, searching for heroes, and, finally, searching for a meaningful life. The culminating project was an essay explaining a personal definition of a meaningful life (see Appendix A). Besides utilizing literary and current event resources, I wanted the student essays to reflect the impact of increasing global communication. Because e-mail seemed the perfect tool to gather this information, I began a project incorporating the advantages of computer-mediated communications (CMC).

Goals and Objectives

There were several specific goals and objectives for this project. First, I wanted to introduce the students to the concept of e-mail as a communication tool and a skill that would carry from the classroom into the world outside of the classroom. Wishnietsky (1991) notes that schools must prepare students for the electronic environments that they will encounter as adults, and I observed that many colleges and businesses supported and used various forms of online communications. I reasoned that if my students could acquire these skills in high school, they would have confidence in using these methods of communication and feel more comfortable in electronic, online environments. This project, therefore, was a link of educational goals to technologies that are being used in the academic, business, and professional fields.

Second, technology offers students in rural and isolated environments the opportunity to widen their perspectives and viewpoints. I wanted my students to see a world beyond the small, rural community in which they reside. This project was viewed as a nonthreatening introduction to computer-mediated communication and a starting point to broader applications in their personal lives and careers.

Third, the project provided an excellent opportunity to involve the local community in an exciting and cutting-edge effort. It is sometimes difficult for community members to feel part of their school system they financially support. This project provided them the opportunity to be part of the curriculum, share their opinions and values, and interact with the student population.

Finally, finding something that this video-oriented, Sesame Street-entertained generation considers exciting is a constant problem for the classroom teacher. This is especially true when the class is composed of students of varied intellectual capabilities. The senior students of this project were such a group, a heterogeneous class that combined students with varying levels of academic ability. Introduction to e-mail provided the spark that motivated these students to actively participate in the project and the class.

Preliminary Activities

The Ayersville Local School District is a member of the Northwest Ohio Computer Association (NWOCA). NWOCA is a data acquisition site of the Ohio Educational Computing Network (OECN) and supports 28 member school districts with administrative and academic computing services. Although the students in this project had previously used online resources through the monitored student-access Gopher provided by NWOCA, they had always logged on under the immediate supervision of a teacher or librarian. I was apprehensive about the broad use of individual student accounts because our high school did not have an official user agreement for internet and e-mail access (see Schrum & Day, this series, Vol. I, for examples). The liability factor was a major concern so the first step in the CMC project was to develop an official agreement. With the leadership of the school district technology co-director, an acceptable use policy (AUP) was formulated based on the NWOCA standard. This locally developed policy was submitted and approved by the Ayersville Board of Education (see Appendix B). Even though this was a time-consuming effort that delayed the start of the project, establishing an AUP was critical in clarifying acceptable online behavior, detailing student responsibilities and expectations, and providing a measure of liability relief.

The second step in the CMC project was obtaining student account numbers. These were secured from NWOCA following a request by the school district superintendent. A total of 48 seniors requested account numbers. Finding e-mail addresses for the students to contact was the third step in the project. Through the recommendation of specialists at NWOCA, I selected and subscribed to a number of listservs. Listservs can be described as computer programs that manage mailing lists (Wheeler, 1992). These listservs are found on mainframe computers at various locations throughout the world and serve as mail distribution systems for people with common interests. A message posted to a listserv is sent to all subscribers on the list, enabling people to carry on discussions about specific topics of common interest.

I created a special mail message folder to store listserv information and directions because it is vital to save instructions regarding subscribing (becoming a member of the mailing list), unsubscribing (removing your address from the mailing list), and other special features. My mailbox has been overflowing ever since. Some days I received as many as 140 mail messages. This became such a time-management problem that I had to start coming to school earlier and earlier to handle the volume. My experience mirrored that of Hawisher and Moran (1993), who noted that the teacher leading an e-mail project will find it impossible to keep up with the volume of messages and will need to turn authority over to students as quickly as possible.

Through trial and error I weeded my listserv subscriptions to those that provided the best potential addresses for my students to use in their e-mail correspondence. Listservs at the addresses noted in Appendix C supplied the best information usable contacts for the needs of this project. I posted messages to these Listservs asking for key pals and searched the lists for addresses. When I saw an address of an individual or another high school class that I thought was appropriate for the students, I printed a copy and put this copy in a folder.

At the same time a notice was placed in a school newsletter that was mailed to all community members. In this notice I shared my e-mail address and encouraged community members to contact me for a potential exchange of ideas with the students. As expected, I received replies from adults. However, replies were also received from former students who were away at college but wanted to participate. A similar response has also been reported by Baer (1994), who found that past students are eager to maintain contact with their former teachers and peers via e-mail.

I divided incoming messages into three categories: high school and college students (individuals), requests from entire classrooms, and adults (individuals). I eventually accumulated more than 150 addresses. The English students were then required to choose and contact two or three of the addresses (see Appendix D). The assignment of students to addresses was not entirely random. I tried to match interests and other commonalities. For example, a student from New Jersey who wanted to correspond with athletes planning to attend college on athletic scholarships was matched with one of our prospective college athletes. A yearbook editor from Harlem was matched with a student on our yearbook staff. I also encouraged my students to choose one adult and one student in order to vary the viewpoint and reaction to the project questions.

Teaching Activities

Smith, Kim, and Bernstein (1993) stated that incorporating CMC into a course may require a term of preparation, and experience with this project proved that teaching students to use e-mail can be a time-consuming task. The training was accomplished through a combination of one-on-one instruction and handouts. Topics covered included use of communications software, file capture and saving, and e-mail etiquette. Once the students had demonstrated an understanding of the basic procedures, each pupil completed a practice e-mail session that included composing and sending a message to me. I replied to each message. Although this involved much teacher time, it was an excellent instructional tool and instant demonstration of the power and capabilities of CMC.

An unexpected occurrence was the leadership that the students themselves assumed. Once students became familiar with the process, they eagerly taught their peers. This not only saved teacher time, but also spread enthusiasm for the project. Poling (1994) notes that e-mail projects can foster cohesiveness of the class as a whole, and my experience readily supports this position. As some students began to receive their first messages, other students wanted to log on. Afghanistan, Tasmania, Australia, and England became common topics of conversation. With the exception of an e-mail address mix-up and nonresponses to some messages, the procedure went smoothly. The students saved their messages to their disks and then printed them to use as notes to be used in the culminating essay.

Problems and Concerns

On the negative side, a project such as this will create a few anxious moments for the teacher. Once I had helped the students get online, the outgoing and incoming discourse was out of my direct control. Being out of control but yet responsible for project outcomes is not for the weak-hearted teacher, especially when mass media sources daily proclaim the dangers of the Internet. Fortunately, no serious problems emerged. Several students received forwarded chain letters, which were a nuisance. We simply deleted them.

Time management played a critical role in the organization of this project. First, sources of potential addresses had to be located and collected. I found that listservs provided the greatest number of usable addresses. However, these listservs had to be discovered, subscribed to, and queried. Sometimes subscribing was difficult because the listserv address might have changed or the address had been incorrectly noted by a secondary source. Fortunately, when the address of a listserv changes, a forwarding address is often provided. Second, each listserv had to be evaluated for its ability to provide meaningful content. If a listserv provided usable addresses and information for the project, the subscription was continued. Otherwise, it was necessary to unsubscribe and discontinue membership. All this required a great amount of teacher time.

Access to terminals is often a problem and limiting factor for participants (Johnson, 1992; Shedletsky, 1992). In this project there were only three terminals for 48 students, and pupils were frustrated when they wanted to send a message but were unable to find an available system. I would recommend beginning with a more workable student-terminal ratio if at all possible. Another frustration for the students occurred when they had sent a message but received no response. I warned the students of this possibility in advance; however, it was still discouraging to them when it happened. In these cases I had the effected students select another address from the stacks. Because the students had saved their previous letters to disk, all they had to do was copy and paste them to the new address.

Although most students enthusiastically embraced the CMC project, it must be noted that such feelings were not universal. Two students in the senior class felt that using e-mail was against their personal religious convictions. Out of respect for their private beliefs, I did not insist that they participate with the e-mail portion of the project. For this reason, it is important for the teacher to have an alternative assignment prepared in advance and available for use.

OUTCOMES

A major outcome of this CMC project was the students' realization that writing is a viable and expressive communication tool. Completed essays indicated that student attitudes about the components of a meaningful life had apparently changed as a result of their interaction with others from outside of their usual circle of contacts. For example, none of the Ayersville students initially mentioned personal security as an element of a meaningful life. After correspondence with several European key pals who listed security as a key issue, Ayersville students began to consider the importance of personal safety. Following the Oklahoma City bombing, these students suddenly empathized with their key pals; several individuals included security as a priority in a meaningful life.

For the first time students saw that writing could be the basis for making personal judgments. It was humorous to hear students draw conclusions about key pals based on their messages. Suddenly, the question "Who cares about grammar?" was answered as the seniors scurried to the thesaurus or writing handbook. They criticized misspelled words and poor sentence structure in the messages they received. Needless to say, my students increased their use of the spelling and grammar checker because they did not want to be similarly judged. Marcus (1995) and Hall and Hall (1991) have also reported this type of student reaction in their CMC projects, which indicates that e-mail assignments can have a positive effect on the development of writing skills and self-critique.

Another positive outcome of this CMC project was the link between community, school, and curriculum. Community members and former students provided their definitions of a meaningful life. In this way, all groups gained an understanding of each others' viewpoints and a link was forged between classroom and community. Since completion of the project, several community members have asked if they would again be invited to take part in future efforts. Any school project would welcome this response.

Personally, an added bonus of all these messages was the knowledge I gained from the interaction with dedicated teachers and technology directors worldwide. The KIDSPHERE service especially provided information about a variety of technological issues that related to the project. Information such as how to cut and paste into e-mail from a word processing program, excellent software suggestions, and numerous descriptions of innovative Internet projects was available.

DISCUSSION AND RECOMMENDATIONS

After completing this CMC project, there are several recommendations that must be emphasized and extended for future efforts. Although I did not experience problems or difficulties with student behavior online, I will increase the emphasis on the acceptable use policy, for I sensed that some students did not fully understand the serious nature and consequences of inappropriate actions. In addition to the common problems of obscenity and unsuitable material, I was also afraid that the students did not realize how easily cultural standards could be violated through innocent but improper statements, comments, or attempted use of humor. In the future I plan to incorporate a checklist covering all major points of the AUP. Participants will initial each category as an indication of understanding. To provide documentation in the event of problems, I will administer a test covering key points of the agreement; participation in the CMC project will be dependent on satisfactory performance on this quiz. I will also cover the major points of the AUP during regular parent-teacher conferences. This will give parents an opportunity to ask questions and acknowledge their child's responsibilities within the project. I strongly suggest that those interested in developing acceptable use policies read the chapter in Volume I entitled "The Internet and Acceptable Use Policies: What Schools Need to Know," by Lynne Schrum and Kay Day. It provides an excellent overview of issues and recommendations relating to student access of the Internet. Two additional suggestions involve e-mail orientation and training. First, the teaching of basic e-mail procedures should be separate from the English class. This will ease course-of-study conflicts and the competition for time required by other class requirements. Second, the procedures should be taught early in the year. Students suffered from information overload as they tried to master e-mail at the same time they were organizing a major essay. Basic procedures can be incorporated into smaller e-mail projects during which students correspond to fellow classmates for practice. This activity could be incorporated into the English curriculum by focusing correspondence on a specific novel, short story, or essay. The printed messages would then form the basis of a writing journal. Familiarity with e-mail procedures and protocols prior to the start of the English class would free the students to concentrate on the correspondence and content of the major project.

A CMC project should not become an end in itself, but must be linked to curriculum goals (Johnson, 1992). The teaching of online communication skills should not be conducted in isolation; rather, these skills must be integrated into an authentic learning situation. The students involved in this CMC project received hands-on experience using technology as a communication tool while completing a project that had clearly defined instructional goals and objectives.

CONCLUSION

Without question, online communications will play an increasingly important role in the future. Students who acquire experience and expertise through classroom projects will possess confidence and skills that readily transfer to college and career. This project demonstrated that computer-mediated communication is a means of extending the boundaries of an environment, regardless of actual physical location.

Work with a CMC project is self-motivating; students who were reluctant to participate in other class activities were challenged and intrigued by the vastness of the e-mail audience. Kids like to talk. When talking and technology are linked, a dynamic combination is produced. Curiosity is also a motivating factor. First-hand correspondence with people from other countries enables students to form their own unique conclusions about other cultures instead of relying on textbooks and the media.

Our future may depend on how well we can interact with people who are culturally different as well those nearby in the local community. The students who participated in the Meaningful Life project used technology to gather information from local and global sources in order to form new and unique personal perspectives. They also learned that technology and the communication that it provides may contribute to expanded viewpoints of life. This generation may be the first to realize that due to cyberspace the distance between individuals of the world is very small indeed.

"COOL!"

APPENDIX A: SEARCHING FOR A MEANINGFUL LIFE

This year Senior English has been a search. First, we looked for self and career. Remember how Beowulf traveled across the sea to find meaning in his life? The next nine weeks we looked for love through family and friends. Do you have the compassion of Chaucer's plowman? Then we searched for heroes. Who could forget the suffering of Paul in All Quiet on the Western Front? Finally, this last nine weeks we've been searching for clues to a meaningful life. Did you admire Macduff's loyalty to his country? Boxer's diligence in Animal Farm?

By this time, you're probably mumbling to yourself, I'm tired of looking at life; I'm ready to get out of here and live it! Unfortunately (or fortunately depending on your state of mind for the day), we still have some time to go. This leads to a concluding assignment. . . .

Write your personal definition of a meaningful life. What will be a priority in your life? What do you not want in your life? Did you renounce the evil of Grendel? Why? Search for support among all the reading you've done in four years of high school as well as current event topics.

1. The paper is to be three pages in length, double-spaced. Creative development of the whole paper will be emphasized.
2. Conduct two interviews of people who would be knowledgeable about your definition. If you were issued an e-mail account number, replace the face-to-face interviews with e-mail correspondence. You could also do a combination of interview and e-mail.
3. Follow-up thank you notes are required. They are due a minimum of two school days prior to the papers due date. For those of you doing e-mail correspondence, be sure you print your follow-up thank you notes.
4. Research people and information related to your topic by reading magazine and/or newspaper articles, biographies, autobiographies, etc. the Internet will be available for additional research sources.
5. Bibliography cards, note cards, outline, rough draft, and interview questions and answers will be submitted with the final paper.
6. The paper will include a title page and three pages of text with MLA citation. A minimum of three different types of sources must be cited.
7. This will be your only assignment for this period of time. All unsatisfactory papers (D or F) must be redone until satisfactory or an incomplete will be given.

Remember, as Marcus Aurelius said way back in the second century, "Our life is what our thoughts make it."

APPENDIX B: SYSTEM USER AGREEMENT

The Northwest Ohio Computer Association and Ayersville Local Schools

Welcome to the Information Superhighway!

The Superhighway known as the Internet is an exciting and quick method of accessing vast, diverse and unique amounts of information. The Internet is a worldwide computer network that was established in 1969 by the U.S. Department of Defense. It originally served as a means of sharing information that was vital to national defense. The Internet can be compared to the interstate highway system developed in the 1960s and 1970s. Instead of providing a means of transporting goods and people, this information network provides a means of transporting information and allows for global communication. The Internet is an electronic highway connecting thousands of computers all over the world and millions of individual subscribers.

Internet access is available to all users of the Northwest Ohio Computer Association (NWOCA) communications network. As a member of NWOCA, Ayersville School is able to provide access to the Internet for the staff and for students. This access is being offered as part of a collaborative effort involving the Ohio Department of Education, the state-licensed regional data processing centers known as the Ohio Education Computer Network (OECN), and the National Science Foundation.

Through the local connection to the Internet, Ayersville students will be able to utilize electronic mail (e-mail) and remote login. Using e-mail, students will be able to share information and exchange messages with other users around the state, around the country, and around the world. Remote login allows a user to log onto a computer system in a distant location. Ayersville students will be able to access the computer systems of many public and university libraries and the databases established by a variety of educational and government agencies.

The goal in providing access to the Internet is to promote educational excellence in the school districts participating in NWOCA. The smooth operation of the network relies on the proper conduct of the end-users, who must adhere to strict guidelines. The use of this network requires ethical and legal utilization of the network resources. If a user violates any of these provisions, his or her account with NWOCA will be terminated and future access will be denied. The signature(s) at the end of this document is/are legally binding and indicate(s) that the individual(s) who signed has/have read the terms and conditions carefully and understand their significance.

Guidelines for Acceptable Use

This is a legally binding document. Read carefully before signing. Guidelines must be followed to insure the integrity of the Internet. Use of the system will be monitored by the NWOCA staff and the Ayersville School staff. Anyone caught abusing the system will lose user privileges indefinitely.

1. The use of the NWOCA network is a privilege, not a right. Inappropriate use will result in a cancellation of this privilege.

2. Security on any computer system is a high priority, especially when the system involves many users. Individuals who are aware of a security problem have an obligation to notify the system administrators at the earliest possible time. Any user identified as a security risk or having a history of problems with other computer systems may be denied access. Attempts to log onto the system as any other user will result in cancellation of user privileges.
3. All users are expected to abide by generally accepted rules of network etiquette which include the following:
   a. Do not use abusive language, vulgarities, obscenities, etc. in messages.
   b. Illegal activities are forbidden. Transmission of any material in violation of any U.S. or state regulation is prohibited. Such activities will be reported to the appropriate authorities and will result in the loss of privileges on the network and may result in criminal prosecution.
   c. Do not reveal personal addresses or phone numbers. E-mail is not guaranteed to be private since system administrators can access accounts and the mail system software may misdirect messages.
   d. Any use of the network that disrupts other users or seriously degrades performance is unacceptable.
   e. All information accessible via the network is private property. No reposting of such information is allowed without prior consent of the author.
   f. All correspondence via e-mail is to be written in English.
4. The Internet provides access to the unique resources of many other organizations. Use of other organization's networks or computing resources must comply with rules appropriate for that network.
5. Ayersville School, NWOCA, and the OECN make no warranties of any kind for the service being provided and deny any responsibility for the accuracy or quality of information obtained through network services.
6. Vandalism will result in cancellation of privileges. Vandalism is defined as a malicious attempt to alter or destroy or reduce the usability of data.
7. NWOCA may require new registration and/or account information from users in order to continue network services. Users need to notify NWOCA of any changes in their account information.
8. Currently, there are no individual user fees for this service.
9. The NWOCA system administrators reserve the right to limit or suspend access to the OECN and/or the Internet or to supersede

portions of this agreement as may be deemed necessary for the safety or security of the NWOCA member districts or the OECN.

10. All terms and conditions as stated in this document are applicable to NWOCA and the OECN. These terms and conditions reflect the entire agreement of the parties and supersedes all prior oral or written agreements and understandings of the parties. These terms and conditions shall be governed and interpreted in accordance with the laws of the State of Ohio.

Please read, sign, detach and return the bottom portion.

USER: I understand and will abide by the guidelines given for using the Internet. I further understand that violation of these guidelines is unethical and may constitute a criminal offense.

User Signature: ______________________________

Date: ____________________

PARENT/GUARDIAN: (Required if user is under the age of 18.)
I have read this document and understand that the Internet access is designed for educational purposes and will hold harmless Ayersville School, NWOCA, the OECN and other organizations on the Internet for materials acquired by the above user from the network. I accept full responsibility for supervision of the user if and when usage is not within a school setting. I give my permission to issue the account and certify that the information contained on this form is correct.

Printed Parent/Guardian Name: ____________________

Signature: ______________________________

Date: ____________________

TEACHER: I have read this document and agree to instruct the student on acceptable use of the Internet.

Signature: ____________________

Date: ____________________

APPENDIX C: LISTSERVS

The following listservs proved the best information and contacts for the Meaningful Life project. These listservs and addresses are accurate as of publication. However, it is important to note that listservs and their addresses are subject to change.

1. KIDSNET
   Global network for teachers and students in grades K-12
   To subscribe, address an e-mail message in the following manner:
   TO: kidsnet-request@vms.cis.pitt.edu
   SUBJECT: (LISTSERV ignores this)
   MESSAGE: Subscribe KIDSNET <first name> <last name>

2. KIDSPHERE
   Global network for K-12 children and teachers
   To subscribe, address an e-mail message in the following manner:
   TO: kidsphere-request@vms.cis.pitt.edu
   SUBJECT: (LISTSERV ignores this)
   MESSAGE: Subscribe KIDSPHERE <first name> <last name>

3. IECC—INTERNATIONAL E-MAIL CLASSROOM CONNECTIONS
   You must subscribe to each of the following lists separately.
   IECC@STOLAF.EDU
   Intercultural E-mail Classroom Connections. "IECC" is intended for teachers seeking partner classrooms for international and cross-cultural electronic mail exchanges. This list is not for discussion or for people seeking individual pen pals.
   To subscribe, address an e-mail message in the following manner:
   TO: iecc-request@stolaf.edu
   SUBJECT: (LISTSERV ignores this)
   MESSAGE: subscribe iecc<first name> <last name>
   IECC-PROJECTS@STOLAF.EDU
   IECC Project Announcements. "IECC-PROJECTS" is an electronic mailing list in which people may announce or request help with specific projects that involve e-mail, internationally or cross-culturally.
   To subscribe, address an e-mail message in the following manner:
   TO: iecc-projects-request@stolaf.edu
   SUBJECT: (LISTSERV ignores this)
   MESSAGE: subscribe iecc-projects <first name> <last name>
   IECC-DISCUSSION@STOLAF.EDU
   "IECC-DISCUSSION" is intended for general discussion about questions, issues, observations, etc. in the Intercultural E-mail Classroom Connections.

To subscribe, address an e-mail message in the following manner:
TO: iecc-discussion-request@stolaf.edu
SUBJECT: (LISTSERV ignores this)
MESSAGE: subscribe <first name> <last name>

4. K12-EURO-TEACHERS
Connect with classrooms looking to start e-mail projects with people from other nations
To subscribe, address an e-mail message in the following manner:
TO: Majordomo@Lists.eunet.fi
SUBJECT: (LISTSERV ignores this)
MESSAGE: subscribe K12-EURO-TEACHERS<first name> <last name>

5. KIDLINK
Global dialog among 10- 15-year olds.
To subscribe, address an e-mail message in the following manner:
TO: LISTSERV@VM1.NODAK.EDU
(or LISTSERV@NDSUVM1.BITNET)
SUBJECT: (LISTSERV ignores this)
MESSAGE: SUB KIDLINK <first name> <last name>

6. HILITES
A service of the GLOBAL SCHOOLNET FOUNDATION, source for classroom collaborative learning projects
To subscribe, address an e-mail message in the following manner:
TO: Majordomo@gsn.org
SUBJECT: (LISTSERV ignores this)
MESSAGE: subscribe hilites <first name> <last name>

APPENDIX D: MEANINGFUL LIFE E-MAIL PROCESS

1. Select two addresses. Write on the sign-up sheet which two you have selected.
2. Re-read your handouts on sending e-mail.
3. To save online time, prepare your message in advance. Keep it brief and courteous. Be sure to include my e-mail address. I have included a sample below. If you decide not to send your message, press the clear key located above the 7 on the numerical keyboard followed by the letter K on the main keyboard.
4. Be sure to enclose the address: IN%"   "

5. Print your message to include with your notes. (Just press Command-P to print what is on the screen or capture to file under session to save it to your disk and then print.)
6. Check for messages daily. Print all messages you receive. I would also suggest you capture to file to maintain addresses and information.
7. At the conclusion of your e-mail exchange, be sure to send a final thank you message.

Sample message:

Dear Mrs. Jones,

My senior English teacher Mrs. Tille (AYR_ACA_MT@NWOCA.OHIO.GOV) is having us research the qualities of a meaningful life. I would appreciate it if you would answer these questions for me:

1. What do you think is most important to have in life?
2. Why do you think so?
3. Can you tell me a story that shows this is true?

If you do not have the time to respond at this time, would you please reply telling me so I can contact someone else. Thank you in advance.

Bill Smith, Defiance, Ohio,
AYR_000099@NWOCA.OHIO.GOV

REFERENCES

Baer, K. (1994). Staying connected to graduates. *English Journal, 83*(4), 77-78.

Hall, S. & Hall, P. (1991). *Between schools: Inter-classroom collaboration.* Old Westbury, NY: Conference on Computers and English. (ERIC Document Reproduction Service No. ED 333 481)

Hawisher, G.E. & Moran, C. (1993). Electronic mail and the writing instructor. *College English, 55*(6), 627-643.

Johnson, V.L. (1992). *Towards a global classroom: Using computer-mediated communications at UAA.* Anchorage: University of Alaska, Vocational Teacher Education Research Project. (ERIC Document Reproduction Service No. ED 356 759).

Marcus, S. (1995). Emailiorating student writing. *Electronic Learning, 14*(4), 18-19.

Poling, D.J. (1994). Email as an effective teaching supplement. *Educational Technology, 34*(5), 53-55.

Shedletsky, L. (1992). *Computer-mediated communication to facilitate seminar participation and active thinking.* Boise, ID: Western States Communication Association. (ERIC Document Reproduction Service No. ED 347 582)

Smith, C., Kim, H., & Bernstein, J. (1993). Computer-mediated communication and strategies for teaching. *Journalism Educator, 48*(1), 80-83.

Wheeler, D.D. (1992). *KIDLINK in war and peace.* San Francisco, CA: American Educational Research Association. (ERIC Document Reproduction Service No. ED 350 985).

Wishnietsky, D. H. (1991). *Using electronic mail in an educational setting* (Fastback No. 316). Bloomington, IN: Phi Delta Kappan Educational Foundation.

10

CHARACTERS ONLINE: 4TH AND 12TH GRADERS' EXCHANGE LETTERS

Patricia R. Grimes and Miriam Owens

What valuable lessons can elementary teachers introduce to fourth graders in the month of May? What lessons will high school seniors in Advanced Placement (AP) literature classes even consider once the AP testing has been completed? No matter the grade level, every teacher faces this end-of-the-year dilemma: which lesson can the teacher choose to provide a challenging and rejuvenating learning experience for students as well as the teacher, all of whom are almost burned out? Miriam Owens and I faced this dilemma. We sought a solution. Thus, we found an online letter exchange to be one possible answer.

BACKGROUND

How did our student online communication begin? In the spring of 1994, Prince William County Instructional Team member John Munnell, a technology specialist, called teachers together to suggest they consider some form of intergrade communication via network. Although Miriam Owens and I had never met before, we began to talk. We found we were both interested in three areas of the Prince William

County Curriculum: (a) historical content—especially American history; (b) purposeful research; and (c) writing for different audiences. As the meeting ended, Miriam and I made plans to continue to talk.

Shortly afterward, I talked with Mary Ann Hardebeck, Reading Specialist at Woodbridge High School. She mentioned she had read about a student-to-student letter exchange via network. I shared this with Miriam. Almost immediately we agreed the letter format would work well with our students considering their age differences. What we did not know was whether a network exchange was possible. Along with stepping into the unknown, Miriam and I had additional concerns: Why were we doing this? What type of technology would this letter exchange require? How would we evaluate student performance? Even with all these questions, we decided to move forward, to seek an answer to our questions. Little did we know what type of journey we were embarking on.

GOALS

Once again, our primary goal was to find a challenging end of the year learning experience for our students. More specifically, Miriam and I wanted to piece together content, process, and product. First, we decided on content. We would have the students focus on fiction as well as nonfiction figures from the Revolutionary and Civil War eras. We decided elementary students would research historical figures using texts in their library. Meanwhile, the seniors would research primary sources about the historical figures using online database services. All students would then exchange information via network. But in what form would this exchange of information take place? Because letter writing was indeed representative of the eras we had chosen, our letter writing format seemed a perfect match for the last piece of our puzzle. As Miriam and I finished planning, we quickly realized we had hours and hours of work in front of us. You see, we knew many of our students would first need instruction in conducting research whether it was in the library or online, in using the word processing programs on the school computers, and in writing letters—a rarely used form of expression today.

CONTENT

As Miriam and I chose historical figures, we had to consider the availability of information as well as the figure's link to Virginia. Thus, our students chose from the following list of nonfiction historical figures:

George Washington
James Monroe
George Wythe
Benjamin Banneker
Patrick Henry
Martha Washington
James Lafayette
John Paul Jones
George Mason
Dolly Madison
James Madison
Thomas Jefferson
James Monroe
Henry Clay
William Henry Harrison
John Marshall
Robert E. Lee
Lighthorse Harry Lee
Meriwether Lewis
William Clark
John Tyler
Cyrus McCormick
Harriet Tubman
Stonewall Jackson
Clara Barton

After picking an historical figure of their choice, the 25 fourth graders examined two reference sources—an encyclopedia and one additional text—about their historical figure.

When fourth graders started the second part of the letter exchange, they examined the historical fiction figures from the following texts:

Alphin, Elaine Marie. (1991). *Ghost Cadet*. New York: Scholastic. Characters: Benjy/Hugh

Beatty, Patricia. (1987). *Charley Skedaddle*. New York: Troll Associates. Characters: Charley, Granny Jerusha

Brady, Ester Wood. (1976). *Toliver's Secret*. New York: Bullseye Books/Random House. Character: Ellen

Clark, Margaret Guff. (1980). *Freedom Crossing*. New York: Scholastic. Characters: Laura/Martin

Collier, James, & Collier, Christopher. (1974). *My Brother Sam is Dead*. New York: Scholastic. Character: Tim

Collier, James, & Collier, Christopher. (1978). *The Winter Hero*. New York: Scholastic. Characters: Justin/ Peter

Forbes, Ester. (1943). *Johnny Tremain*. New York: Dell. Character: Johnny Tremain

Fritz, Jean. (1987). *Early Thunder*. New York: Puffin Books. Character: Daniel West

Gauch, Patricia Lee. (1991). *Thunder at Gettysburg*. New York: Bantam. Character: Tillie

Reeder, Carolyn. (1989). *Shades of Gray*. New York: Avon Camelot. Character: Will

Reit, Seymour. (1988). *Behind Rebel Lines*. San Diego: Harcourt, Brace Jovanovich. Character: Emma

After the first year of borrowing copies of the paperbacks listed here from elementary schools all over the county, the next year Miriam and I wrote a grant for the *Washington Post* requesting money to purchase enough paperbacks in order for all our students to have copies. The grant was approved. Thus, we continued with our project the following year.

Meanwhile, at the high school, the 75 seniors, working in pairs, researched primary sources regarding the historical figure they had chosen as well as the time periods. Their research would help them in answering the elementary students' letters, whether the letter was about the historical figure or a historical fiction character. Sandy Munnell, Technology Specialist at Woodbridge Senior High School, helped students start their online searches.

Some of the online services students found helpful are as follows:

www.upress.virginia.edu. (George Washington's diaries)

http://worcester.lm.com/women/resources/promwom.html

http://www.cc.rochester.edu.sba

http://www.wvlc.wvnet.edu/history/historyw.html (WVA history)

http://www.virginia.edu/~history/home.html

http://www.yahoo.com/test/Social_Science/History/Journals/
www.loc.gov (American Memorials Project/Library of Congress)

http://www.si.edu/ (Smithsonian)

cobweb.utcc.utk.edu/hoemann/warweb.html (Civil War sources at the University of Tennessee)

www.augustana.edu/library/specch.html (Civil War memoirs at Augustana College)

http://jefferson.village.virginia.edu/vshadow2/ (Civil War)

http://www.cvc.lsu.edu/civlink.htm (Civil War)

www.arts.gla.ac.uk/www/ctich/histlinks.html (resources for history/Search SOSIG)

http://www.georgetown.edu/crossroads/crossroads.html (American studies resources)

American Historical Documents (Gopher: University of Minnesota consultant.micro.umn,edu search Libraries/electronic books/title/historical)

Telnet: ukanaix.cc.ukans.edu (American History Topics)

Yahoo searches via Humanities, History, American History, Social Science, Society and Culture

http://leo.vsla.edu/public/public.html (the Library of Virginia Publications Program)

In addition, students examined texts in the library. Because Woodbridge Senior High School has its card catalogue online, seniors began their in-school search with a keyword combination of "the historical figure's name" and "primary source." Next students examined atlases, financial charts, speeches (from the *Annals of America*. William Benton, Editor. Chicago: Encyclopedia Britannica, 1986), primary sources (in Frazier, Thomas. *Voices of America. Readings in American History*. Boston: Houghton Mifflin, 1985), letters, and other sources.

PROCESS OF WRITING

For the first part of the project, fourth graders used their notes from their two sources and wrote a first draft of their research paper. They carefully placed the two resources they had used in a bibliography. Next they met in the computer lab and drafted a letter to their assigned historical figure. Once they had completed their letter, they saved the letter as an ASCII (or text only) file. The use of a text file was critical in order to send the message via network. The elementary school librarian later downloaded the students' letters onto her computer. Then she sent the letters via e-mail through the Prince William County Schools' network to the high school. (In the second year of our letter exchange, the librarian sent the letters via a state network. The change provided a quicker exchange of letters.)

Once the letters arrived, the seniors headed to the school computer lab. The seniors downloaded the fourth graders' letters. Then, with primary source material in hand, they began their replies. In all replies the seniors answered the fourth graders' questions as well as provided the fourth graders with new information. For example, the seniors would share information about an historical figure's childhood. They might include a map (from a primary source) and ask the fourth grader to compute the distance from one locale to another. They might ask a fourth grader to add figures or to comment on different aspects of the historical figure's lifestyle. Once seniors finished the first draft of their letters, they met in revision groups. Here they checked for authenticity of the styles of the eras. They also checked for the appropriateness of their letters for their fourth-grade audience.

Revision groups discussed the letter format: address (usually the name of the historical figure's home) and the date of the era; the salutations—My Dear Friend, To George Washington, From Monticello; and the closings—Cordially, Your Most Humble Servant, Stay Strong. Revision groups then discussed the importance of including information and questions about that historical figure in the body of the letter. Seniors checked for information that would require the elementary student to check his or her research or reading. For example, in a letter from George Washington, one senior discussed the misconceptions that exist concerning Washington's teeth: "You see, those are just myths about my wooden teeth after all. What do you think?"

Sample letters are as follows:

(fourth grader)

Dear Martha Washington,

Why were you worried abut becoming the First Lady? Martha, I'm sorry your two infants died. Where did you grow up?

Sincerely,

____

(senior)

Mount Vernon, Virginia

Dear ________________,

It is nice to hear from you. It brings me much pleasure to know that you are interested in my life. It seems as if so many people are interested in the life of the First Lady. That is understandable considering I was the "first" First Lady. I was worried about becoming First Lady because I would be so much in the eyes of the country. I was not greatly interested in being the center of attention. I dressed plainly; people often mistook me for the family maid. Nevertheless, I managed the President's home with dignity and grace.

I appreciate your regrets about the children's death. At that time, it was not uncommon for children to die soon after birth.

After reading your letter, it appears as if you are interested in my upbringing. I was raised near Williamsburg, Virginia, in New Kent County. I've enclosed a map for you. Will you color in my county and tell me the nearest city to it? After I moved to Mt. Vernon, however, I never returned to my home, not even after my beloved George died.

As I sit here telling you about my life, I remember many wonderful stories I would like to share. Would you like to know about my pets? I hope to hear from you soon.

Your friend,

Martha Washington

(fourth grader)

John F. Pattie Elementary
1i6125 Dumfries Rd.
Dumfries, VA 22026

May 20, 1780

Dear Captain John Paul Jones,

Sir, I have been honored to hear from you. How did you like Russia? Did you learn the language? And did you think you were a good Admiral in the Russian Navy? I realize that this is a personal question, but is it true that you were in love with Dorothea Dandridge? And what was John Read like?

Sincerely,

____

(senior)

Paris, England

May 26, 1792

Dear ________________,

I am glad to have received your letter. It gets lonely sometimes as my crew and I spend months at sea. Your questions concerning my time in Russia made me recall good and bad memories of my tenure in the Royal Russian Navy. You may wonder how a Scottish sailor goes from fighting in the Revolutionary War for the Americans to fighting in the Turkish War for the Russians. The truth is that Empress Catherine heard of my success as a raider for the rebels' cause. She requested my naval expertise to help her forces defeat the Turks in the Black Sea. Can you find the Black Sea on the map I enclosed? Please color it in and send it back. She promised me the rank of rear admiral. Of course, I love adventure and accepted readily. I dedicated myself to this campaign almost as much as I did to the Revolutionary War. Not because I felt moral and emotional ties, but because I wanted to again prove my fighting ability and cunning on the high seas. I know that my actions helped to protect the Crimea. However, even when I won battles, others tried to steal my honors from me. It is this willingness to dishonor a fellow service member that eventually motivated my return to . . .

Students repeated the process in the second part of the project, except this time students focused on the historical fiction texts. Also the seniors asked the fourth graders specific text questions whereby the younger students had to go back to their historical fiction texts in order to reply. Note the following letters:

(fourth grader)

Dear Solomon Butcher,

Hi! I'm back and I have more questions to ask you. Did you like being a photographer? Mr. Butcher, how did you feel when the negative was burnt? What was the land around the sod houses like?

Sincerely,

____

(senior)

Solomon Butcher
near Mason City
Custer County, Nebraska

Dear ________________,

I am glad you have more questions for me. I am happy to answer them. I really like being a photographer. In fact, I like it so much that I have made it my life's work. Do you ever take pictures? I have a special reason for taking so many pictures of Custer County. Do you remember why?

When that negative was burnt, I felt sick to my stomach. But then I had a bright idea and decided to paint something over the hole so no one would notice. Do you remember what I painted?

The area where we live is flat. Occasionally, you'll see a tree or two, but only if there's water nearby. Do you know why? Yes, we have wildflowers and types of grasses out here. You would be amazed at all the animals. Which ones did you notice in my story?

I'm on my way to visit Uncle Swain and Aunt Sarah. Do you remember my story about Uncle Swain and the snow? Let me know.

Write soon.

Your friend,

Solomon Butcher

(fourth grader)

Dear Master Daniel West,

I sit in my room now writing this letter, and I want to ask you many a question. Why did you name your boat the Libera? . . .

(senior)

Salem, Massachusetts

May 25, 1775

Dear Master ____________,

Before I address the matter of your inquiry, I must note that your writing skills are quite sophisticated for a lad of your age.

When the Footes gave me their boat, I was reluctant to change the name. Though it would preserve the memory of my friendship with my dear friend's family, Mr. Foote insisted that I change the name to reflect my own sentiments. Do you remember when I studied Latin? Well, I chose a name which was a word I thought would be a fitting title for the boat of an American. Why do you think I chose that word? And why would that be important in this book? . . .

I remain your friend with hopes for Peace and Liberty,

Daniel West

PRODUCT

The letters alone did not constitute the product. Miriam posted all letters—from the elementary and high school students—in an end-of-the-year elementary school fair. The county made a video in which they interviewed student participants from both grades as well as Miriam and me. Most importantly, Miriam and I noticed other quantitative as well as qualitative results.

For quantitative results, Miriam saw her fourth graders' letters jumping from half a page or less (approximately 125 words) to a full page or longer (250-750 words). With both parts of the project, students exchanged letters twice: a total of 400 letters. Quite honestly, in reevaluating the letter exchange, we know there would be even more growth if we continued the exchange for a longer period of time. However, keep in mind that we were using this assignment to solve an end-of-the-year problem.

With the qualitative results, Miriam and I still shake our heads in amazement. The fourth graders grew excited about spending time in the computer lab; they begged to go each day. They surrounded Miriam when she came to class with the downloaded letters from the seniors. Other fourth graders grew jealous of the class "talking" to historical figures.

Some 15 miles away, the seniors never missed a day of school. They came to class excited. They could not get over how much the fourth graders knew. They sweated as they searched the library trying to find an answer to a fourth grader's difficult question. They laughed at their own misconceptions of history. And they sympathetically reacted when one fourth grader started his letter, "Dear Thomas Jefferson, I have no friends, except you."

CONCLUSION

When Miriam and I look back at our first attempt, we laugh. All that could go wrong did. We could not find enough historical fiction texts, our electronic transmissions often were frozen at an intermediary transmission site, students forgot to save files as ASCII text files, and students (both at the elementary and high school levels) sometimes did not receive letters and therefore sat sadly by others at work who had. Yet, by the second year, things ran more smoothly. As always, there were glitches, but none of the dimensions of the first year. Miriam and I are already talking about next spring. Already, we know there will be differences. Miriam will now be working with fifth graders. Thus, our history focus must change. We will be using fiction and nonfiction historical figures from the 1940s. But, you see, the grade levels and time periods really do not matter. What does matter is content, process, and product. Yes, in Prince William County, Virginia, that end-of-the-year dilemma has been solved. We are excitedly exchanging letters: Characters Online!

IV

FOREIGN LANGUAGE LEARNING

11

USING COMPUTER-MEDIATED COMMUNICATION AS A RESOURCE FOR FOREIGN LANGUAGE INSTRUCTION IN K-12 SCHOOLS

Jeri H. Dies

The world is out there for exploration, communication, and interaction. A computer with a modem or networked access to the Internet permits worldwide communication possibilities. Computer-mediated communication (CMC) has the potential to revolutionize the learning and teaching of foreign languages. As a teacher of foreign languages, I must find ways to interact with the speakers, reading materials, and culture of the foreign language that I teach. It is a requirement for me as well as my students to be en route to a higher level of language proficiency and cultural awareness.

Using CMC for K-12 foreign language teaching has had until recently major obstacles. K-12 foreign language teachers have lacked computer hardware, software, and the connectivity vital to access the Internet. How do K-12 teachers get Internet access in order to use CMC for themselves and their students? Many K-12 teachers choose to pay their own way onto the Internet via a commercial Internet provider (America Online, CompuServe, Prodigy) in order to have the necessary access. Alternative ways of Internet access include becoming a member of a community-sponsored Freenet (Tallahassee, Rio Grande, Cleveland) or a state-sponsored network such as TENET (the Texas Education Network) or FIRN (Florida Information Resource Network).

Once access becomes available, CMC can prove invaluable as a teaching and learning tool for both foreign language teachers and foreign language students. CMC provides the means for engaging foreign languages and their cultures without physically having to cross a border.

THE K-12 FOREIGN LANGUAGE TEACHER

CMC is becoming increasingly important for preservice and inservice K-12 foreign language teachers. Foreign language teachers keep seeking opportunities for augmenting and maintaining their own language skills. At the same time they seek opportunities for increasing their knowledge about language teaching methods. The Internet allows for meaningful communication and interaction among teachers both inside and outside of the United States on a continuing basis.

Teacher-to-Teacher CMC via Discussion Lists

A primary discussion list (see Collins this volume for description of lists) for foreign language teachers is FLTEACH (LeLoup & Ponterio, 1995). FLTEACH provides foreign language teachers extensive opportunities for professional discussion with peers about many issues and concerns of the foreign/second language teacher. It is an open forum for discussing all subjects related to language teaching and learning. Recent messages to FLTEACH have included questions about technology, interesting Web sites of interest to language teachers, questions about block scheduling of classes, teachers' proficiency levels, and employment opportunities. FLTEACH currently has over a thousand subscribers. The average number of messages for this list is about 20 to 25 message per day during the academic year.

Jean LeLoup who co-founded FLTEACH with Robert Ponterio believes that FLTEACH fulfills a need for professional communication among foreign language educators at all educational levels. She explained that "[FLTEACH] is one way teachers can interact with colleagues all over . . . to improve themselves and their teaching" (Jean LeLoup, personal communication, August 9, 1995).

I have been a subscriber to FLTEACH for about two years. From the discussions on this list I really sense the need for foreign language teachers to escape from the isolation of their classrooms. If FLTEACH does not last as a means of conquering this isolation, I truly believe another forum would take its place because once professional conversations begin, I doubt that anyone will accept having the door closed again.

Nevertheless, some caveats are advised for teachers not accustomed to dealing with large quantities of e-mail messages arriving via a discussion list or group. Finding time to read and manage all the information available is one gargantuan task that must be addressed in the age of CMC. At times the overwhelming mountain of information may seem untenable. I find the acquisition of technology skills commensurate with the acquisition of foreign language proficiency. Learning any skill requires creative, meaningful, and extended interaction in order to obtain higher levels of proficiency. So, if I want to be competent at using CMC, I will want to engage with the technology on almost a daily basis in order to become optimally proficient.

Therefore, subscribing to a discussion list such as FLTEACH gives me as a beginning user of CMC the opportunity to learn to interact with and manage the mail that arrives daily. Most e-mail programs allow me to delete messages by reading only the list of subject headings for messages. If I have no interest in that particular subject, I may simply delete it without taking time to read the entire message. On the other hand, if I see a subject that interests me, I may read and reply to that message to get more information or to make a comment about the subject to the entire discussion list or simply to the individual who sent the original message.

Another discussion list for foreign language teachers who want to increase the use of technology for teaching languages is Language Learning Technology International (LLTI). This discussion list is definitely geared toward the application of technology for foreign language learning. For example, recent postings have included information about updating language laboratories, sources for foreign language software, and conference announcements relating to technology and language teaching. There are several participants on this list who manage foreign language learning laboratories. In addition, most are also language instructors who actively use technology for teaching (see References).

For myself I have found it beneficial to subscribe to a few more generalized mailing lists. For example, Newjour is a list devoted to recently discovered Web sites that may be of interest to teachers. From this list I have gotten several resources including foreign language newspapers and magazines that provide me with the latest news from those countries. Again, because I subscribe to many mailing lists, I know that I must check and deal with my e-mail messages at least two times per day. Discarding all the e-mail that does not seem relevant to my current needs is a must. I know that I must not get to the point that the messages will overwhelm me and my e-mail mailbox.

Additional CMC Resources For Language Teachers

The International Association for Learning Laboratories (IALL) publishes the *IALL Journal of Language Learning Technologies*. It is sent to members of the IALL. It is a very good resource for increasing knowledge about all aspects of applying technology for teaching languages. Each issue has a column called Network Update that features some of the latest resources found on the Internet. In a recent issue, teachers were provided information about finding key pals (the electronic version of pen pals) for their students and subscribing to a discussion list for teachers interested in using the Internet for teaching (Backer, 1995).

The Web Page as Teacher Resource

I have recently created my own home page on the Web. My rationale for creating a web page was to catalogue and organize the many resources for foreign language learning available on the Internet. In addition, I plan to add information specifically related to the classes I teach (Dies, 1995a). Many individuals in foreign language teaching and research have created Web pages. For example, not only is FLTEACH one of the premier discussion lists, the moderators have constructed a Web page with numerous links to resources for teaching and learning about a variety of foreign languages and their cultures.

I feel that I have a professional duty to continue the search for useful CMC resources for teaching and learning foreign languages. It takes many people to find the new Web sites that appear almost daily. As I began this chapter, I decided to do an Internet search. Using my preferred web browser (the medium for exploring the Web) Netscape, I conducted a search of the Internet. I simply typed in "K12 foreign language" as the topic for the search. Several Web sites on the Internet were delivered in a list to me for exploring. Some were secondary schools with their own Web pages. I contacted the Webmaster (person in charge of the Web page) identified for each Web page via e-mail. All replies from the Webmasters indicated that they were on the verge of using CMC for increasing foreign language learning opportunities. One school in Georgia hopes to interact with some of the many international visitors who will be attending and/or participating in the Olympic Games held in Atlanta. Later when the international visitors return to their countries, they hope for a continuing connection via the Internet.

A superb source for authentic materials from many Spanish-speaking countries may be found via the Latin American Network Information Center at the University of Texas at Austin (UT-LANIC). I have benefited from being able to incorporate news for my Spanish classes from *La Nación*, Costa Rica's leading daily newspaper, via the Internet. There are extensive resources found at the UT-LANIC site that provide all kinds of geographical, cultural, governmental, and various kinds of statistical information about all the countries of Central and South America (see References).

Many K-12 classroom teachers use their three-month summer "vacation" to upgrade knowledge and skills. In the past most foreign language teachers opted for summer study to improve their target language skills. Most recently K-12 teachers have chosen to attend summer seminars about the application of technology in the foreign language classroom. The acquisition of technological skills can reveal many new avenues for expanding the K-12 foreign language teacher's list of resources.

CMC PROJECTS FOR THE K-12 FOREIGN LANGUAGE STUDENT

Recently I profiled a project using electronic mail for my university-level Spanish classes (Dies, 1995b). It gave my students increased opportunities of interacting with me as well as interacting with each other. In addition I had them explore the many possibilities on the Web for gathering information about many Spanish-speaking countries.

K-12 foreign language students need opportunities to discover that learning a foreign language is both achievable and relevant for a future in a global society. Fortunately, the Web permits authentic interactions among foreign language students, native speakers of the language they study, and interaction with the everyday culture of the country where the language is spoken, without needing to purchase an airline ticket.

A Sampling of K-12 Teachers' CMC Projects

Many K-12 teachers are eager to put CMC to use in their classrooms. There are many ongoing projects throughout the United States. I "met" two teachers via FLTEACH. Michele Whaley teaches Russian in Alaska, and Ingrid Berdahl teaches French in Virginia. Michele and Ingrid first met each other during the summer of 1994 while attending a summer institute at the K-12 Foreign Language Resource Center at Iowa State University. As a final project they co-authored a report highlighting a variety of Internet resources for language teachers (Whaley & Berdahl, 1995).

After reading this project report, I wanted to follow up to see what classroom projects they had undertaken since attending the summer institute in Iowa. I wrote e-mail messages to both authors requesting an update. I was delighted to hear that they are both continuing their pursuit of CMC possibilities for their foreign language students.

Ingrid Berdahl teaches French at Wakefield High School in Arlington, VA. One of Ingrid's classes sent a jointly composed e-mail message as well as individual student e-mail messages to a French class in Russia. In another class students exchanged greetings with French students in an Oregon school. Her plans for the coming school year include collaborating with a colleague who teaches French at the same high school in order to find students in France who might be willing to undertake cross-cultural CMC activities. She plans to subscribe to the discussion list International E-mail Classroom Connections (IECC), which helps teachers obtain key pal opportunities for students around the world (Ingrid Berdahl, personal communication, August 17, 1995).

Michele Whaley teaches Russian at East High School in Anchorage, AK. Michele has been using e-mail as the means of communicating with high school classes in Russia. She is aware that the connectivity problems from her side of the equation are much different when compared to the severe lack of connectivity at partner schools in Russia. She is determined to continue exploring the possibilities of finding and creating more resources for students who study Russian language and culture. She notes that some of her best successes have been in encouraging other teachers to learn about and explore CMC resources.

Michele's current goals involve an interdisciplinary project with a teacher of social studies at her school. Presently, she is considering the creation a Web page to illustrate the final results of this collaboration.

Looking at the future Michele expects to continue expanding the uses of CMC via ongoing e-mail projects. At the same time she wants to use her knowledge of authoring tools for addressing differences in her students' levels of achievement. Finally, Michele would like to interweave all the CMC possibilities seamlessly together in order to achieve the best overall learning outcomes for her students (Michele Whaley, personal communication, August 20, 1995).

Betty Clough teaches French at McCallum High School in Austin, TX. I first met Betty when I was a supervisor of foreign language student teachers at the University of Texas. At that time she was determined to incorporate CMC as a resource for her language classes. She had received some support for using Minitel as a source for authentic language materials from France. Minitel began several years ago in France as an online telephone directory. It has since become an online, interactive system for many services including banking, airline reservations, online chat groups, and commercial advertising in French. A large drawback for American teachers to use Minitel for their classes has been the hourly service charges for connecting to Minitel.

Recently, Betty told me that she had been so busy that it was difficult to keep up with responding to her e-mail messages. She still uses the Minitel connection for her classes. At beginning levels she wants her students to explore and understand what Minitel is and what services it has available. In more advanced classes, she has students research several different French-speaking countries by using Minitel as a kind of online encyclopedia.

One discussion list that Betty uses is the *CGF* (*Classe Globale Francophone*). The participants are French students from a variety of countries. She wants to continue researching possibilities with other teachers as well. She knows that her quest for incorporating CMC into her French classes will not end (Betty Clough, personal communication, September 2, 1995).

E-mail proficiency is the first skill that a K-12 teacher will want to explore and conquer before moving on to other CMC platforms. The next logical step would be the use of web browsers for including the possibilities of the Web for teaching and learning.

The Web Page as a Learning and Teaching Resource

Many projects are being developed and shepherded by groups with similar goals for creating and maintaining Web pages. I describe next one of many Web page projects.

La Clase Mágica is a Web page dedicated to bilingual/bicultural students and their families. The information contained on this Web page details a project that has been created especially for bilingual Spanish/English children from ages 6 to 12 in an afterschool setting. The Web page is a collaboration among bilingual children, the children's parents, and a research group from the University of California at San Diego (including university students who act as mentors to the children while receiving college credit for their participation). The children are given the opportunity of playing interactive computer games that are designed around a central figure called *El Maga* (the Wizard).

In addition there is a parents' home page as well as guidelines for creating a similar resource locally. Links to other Hispanic resources are available to individuals who would like to know more about *El Mundo Latino* [The Spanish-speaking World] (Vásquez, James, & Chambers, 1995).

This particular project helps to illustrate all the possibilities for using a well-constructed Web page as a teaching and learning resource. A Web page planned and constructed especially for a teacher's class content area and students should give students the opportunity to have a personal place on the Internet to call their own.

THE FUTURE: NO PASSPORT REQUIRED

The potential for using CMC as a teaching tool for foreign language instruction is limited only by imagination. Real-time, synchronous communication with video via the Web will soon become the ultimate authentic communication venue for language instruction.

Foreign language teachers are constantly challenged to simulate real interactions between their students and the target language. It is always hoped that these simulations will lead to understanding and the ability to communicate in the foreign language. With CMC increasingly available as a resource for teaching, classroom simulations can readily begin to approximate more and more real communicative interactions.

In fact, a most exciting possibility is that students may have the opportunity of "meeting" native speakers and/or other learners of the same target language via the Internet. With audio and video possibilities increasing for CMC, students learning a foreign language should be able to interact with pen pals who can be seen and heard. Perhaps most exciting of all, the individuals who are linked by CMC will have decided which subjects they want to discuss via these long distance, face-to-face encounters. When classroom simulation becomes communicative reality, both foreign language teachers and students will have truly been successful.

REFERENCES

Backer, J.E. (1995). Network update. *IALL Journal of Language Learning Technologies, 28*(1), 95-103.

Dies, J.H. (1995a). *Jeri Dies Home page*. Available at: http://www.fit.edu/~jdies.

Dies, J.H. (1995b). Español con technología: E-mail in beginning Spanish classes. In M. Warschauer (Ed.), *Virtual Connections: Online activities and projects for networking language learners.* Honolulu: University of Hawaii, Second Language Teaching and Curriculum Center.

International Email Classroom Connections (IECC). [Web page]. Available at: http://www.stolaf.edu/network/iecc/.

Language Learning Technology International (LLTI). [Web page]. Available at: http://eleazar.dartmouth.edu/IALL/.

Latin American Network Information Center (UT-LANIC). [Web page]. Available at: http://lanic.utexas.edu.

LeLoup, J., & Ponterio, R. (1995). Networking with foreign language colleagues: Professional development on the internet. *Northeast Conference on the Teaching of Foreign Languages Newsletter, 37*, 6-10. Available at: http://www.cortland.edu/www_root/flteach/networking.html.

Vásquez, O., James, Y., & Chambers, E. (1995). *La Clase Magica* [Web page]. Available at: http://communication.ucsd.edu/LCHC/LCM/index.html.

Whaley, M., & Berdahl, I. (1995). *Exploration of the Internet*. Unpublished manuscript.

12

CMC IN THE FRENCH LANGUAGE CLASSROOM

Robert Longpré

The study and learning of French as a second language is undergoing a process of change in Saskatchewan and Canada. In Saskatchewan, change is guided by the Department of Education as instruction moves away from teacher-centered models toward learner-centered models using a communicative approach. The model upon which curriculum development is based finds its roots in the National Core French Study Report of 1990. A number of other change factors put added stress on the educational system other than just curriculum reform. Budget reductions, lack of trained subject specialists, rural isolation, and declining student enrollments affect curriculum offerings within smaller rural schools.

In an attempt to cope with these changes, French programs are either abandoned outright or offered using distance education formats. Change is a painful reality affecting not only school programming; change is affecting the communities in which these schools are located. As many of our rural communities get smaller and smaller, all too frequently school and community survival becomes the principle issue. Course offerings become a secondary issue. Distance education then becomes the only way to access a French program. The lack of a face-to-face conversational paradigm for learning the second language leaves the second language learner at a disadvantage that seeks resolution.

CONTEXT OF THE STUDY

Rural schools in Saskatchewan have experienced declining enrollments causing many schools to close their doors. This has been an ongoing problem that has plagued the province for a number of years. Even with the bussing of students to central schools within their school divisions, student enrollments for French and other courses are too low for a number of schools to justify the offering of those courses. This results in a disparity in the postsecondary preparedness between students from larger urban centers and those from rural settings.

Exacerbating the financial dilemma faced by the schools that survive the rural-urban migration are requirements that have expanded the number of compulsory and optional courses (students must complete 24 credit classes in comparison to a previous standard of 21) to be completed in order to receive a secondary school diploma. These changes in course requirements, as well as the development of new curricula reflecting the advances in instructional design based on learning theory, necessitate the staffing of schools with capable teachers who have the requisite training in order to effectively present those courses. As a result, many schools in rural Saskatchewan cannot now hope to offer a full range of courses. This results in a core instructional program with few options, a situation encouraging yet more migration to larger centers as parents attempt to provide full educational opportunity for their children.

The use of technology can enable schools to provide an expanded curriculum, including French, in a way that allows small schools to remain open and students to have more choice in their selection of optional courses. Some use of technology has long been a part of French as a Second Language (FSL) courses such as the use of video, audiocassettes, and electronic visual aids. Computer technology has also made a positive presence in the FSL classroom. Computers can provide extended language skills practice in a consistent and interactive manner.

Part of the technological revolution that has just begun to have an impact on education, and FSL in particular, is the use of the Internet. The K-12 educational system has recently been introduced to the Internet. Like previous introductions of new media technology, using the computer for human-to-human interactions is receiving mixed reviews.

With the growth of the Internet, a sizable number of second-language instructors and learners have begun to experience a new dimension in second language learning such as the French conversational experiences on Internet groups such as CAUSERIE and JASETTE. The interactive nature of computer-mediated communication

(CMC) requires that the learner take charge of his or her own participation and learning. The learner decides with whom, when, where, why, and even how to dialogue using the French language. The Internet provides the learner with an opportunity for authentic conversation in French in a number of ways that add to the depth of the second-language learning experience. The use of CMC can provide for some of those language experiences that are missing in Saskatchewan rural schools, in distance education settings, and within the traditional second-language classroom.

A BRIEF LEXICON

Throughout this chapter reference is made to a number of terms that bear some explanation for the reader. I present in the following a brief explanation of those words as I understand them. For a more complete understanding, I recommend the reading of the documents mentioned at the end of this chapter.

The C/E Model

This acronym represents the communicative/experiential model for second-language instruction that grew out of a national project studying French second-language instruction and learning.

CAUSERIE

Causerie is a French discussion forum that has an international audience. The group meets for casual conversation on the Internet on a listserv. The host of the French conversation is located at the Université de Québec. The participants are a blend of francophones and francophiles. Many are teachers and professors of the language, others are students with more advanced "conversational" skills.

IECC (Intercultural E-mail Classroom Connections)

This listserv group allows a teacher to place a request for a partner classroom for his or her students. Provision is also made for participation in project and surveys. Teachers are provided with a discussion channel to debate the problems and successes of the classroom connections.

JASETTE

This is a forum for university students, senior high school students, and French language instructors. The participants meet for French conversation, which is hosted from Georgia. The forum allows students to practice their conversation skills in a relatively risk-free environment. The level of language use ranges from beginner to expert. Care is taken to ensure that the level of language usage remains at a level that encourages the students to participate.

NCFS—The National Core French Study

This study was sponsored by the Canadian Second Language Teachers Association during the 1980s. Their final report, which proposed a model for curriculum design, was published in 1990. More about the NCFS is explained later.

WHY USE CMC?

The idea for the study of second languages through acts of communication, rather than through the study of language forms and semantic structures, has been the central focus of teachers and program developers for about 20 years. The communicative approach of language instruction tries to include form, function, and use of language into a total package that teachers bring to the second-language classroom.

In the process of providing courses for second-language learning, there has been a tendency to build programs that plan for structured, linear, and additive functions, a process inconsistent with the reality of learning a second language. The natural way to learn languages (a process that is evidenced by children who quickly learn a second language in immersion settings) requires learners to be in situations in which language is learned through language use in natural settings or simulated settings.

In 1984, the Canadian Association of Second-Language Teachers sponsored a study investigating second-language instruction. The study included the piloting of two experimental units at differing grade levels: "Initiation au voyage" piloted in the spring of 1987, of which the author was a piloting teacher; and "Se lancer en affaires," piloted in the spring of 1989. These units were constructed using a C/E focus, a holistic design paradigm for second-language instruction.

To create a C/E learning environment, learning activities need to be learner-centered, goal-oriented, and meaningful, providing learners the opportunity to use their existing knowledge of communication. This C/E model has been adopted by the province of Saskatchewan as a model for curriculum design as well as the preferred method of instruction. For the rural school in Saskatchewan, however, the lack of teacher specialists trained to instruct using the C/E model, and the lack of resources due to fiscal restraints, often leads administrators and instructors to retreat to textbook study and patterned exercises.

Trying to engage in meaningful dialogue while taking a second-language course is difficult within isolated rural classrooms or through study by distance education means (correspondence courses) with its time delays for postal exchanges, the frustration of attempting synchronized telephone conversations, and the nonreactive nature of audio and video cassettes. How, then, can the needs of these second-language learners be met? Interactivity is needed in order to provide for and true communicative activity for second-language learning. Dialogue provides the interactivity necessary for learning a second language.

The advances in communication technology have now made possible the designing of a C/E second-language component for rural and distance education. In the CMC environment learners can participate with presence; that is, their interactions are personal, allowing the learners to become part of a social group in a conversation, and allowing them to feel that they are "heard," that they are present in authentic dialogue. The experience of CMC, as an interactive media, "approximates genuine human interaction" as it gives the learner more control over learning and more "collaborative" learning experiences (Schwier, Brown, Misanchuk, & Proctor, 1992).

CMC provides learners with an audience as well as a voice, two prerequisites for genuine dialogue and authentic communication. The bridging of distance and feelings of isolation (even within the context of the classroom) are part of the benefits in giving learners a voice. The resulting collaboration to solve real problems using their experiences of life and communication results in a sense of community for learning, an environment in which the teacher becomes the facilitator of learning rather than the arbitrator of knowledge.

The interactivity of communication has an "oral" nature as discussed by Phillips (1994) during online dialogues, especially when experienced in talk or chat modes, or on unmoderated discussion lists. Dr. Phillips attributes this oral nature to the "rapid turnaround" of messages on interactive lists. This oral aspect to online dialogue lends itself well to the needs of second-language learners in search of an audience for authentic communication.

Also present in CMC dialogue, however, are road blocks to communication such as the issue of nonresponse and lurking. It is difficult to maintain a sense of presence and community when online dialogue disappears into silence, unlike face-to-face environments that accept nonverbal listening as part of the communication link. Regardless of road blocks, CMC can provide the necessary bridges for conversation when the face-to-face model is not practical or possible.

CMC provides opportunities for collaborative learning, working in groups across distance, time, and even culture, while they converse in the target, second language (Mathiesen, 1993). The extended audience of CMC includes peers who are native speakers of the target language, instructors of language, and peers who, like themselves, need a chance to express themselves in authentic dialogue using the second language. CMC gives second-language learners an opportunity for conversation in a nonthreatening environment (Mathiesen, 1993; Sayers, 1995) as learners have time to compose their messages. This encourages the typically silent student to become an active participant in conversation (Coombs, 1993). Finally, CMC provides second-language learners with motivation to engage in dialogue (Longpré, 1994). Motivation comes through a sense of achievement as learners realize that their communicative efforts result in authentic dialogue making the learning of a second language relevant to their lives.

INTERNET EXPERIENCES

The following section describes the Internet experiences using CMC within the second-language program in my classes. I must point out that our school is located in a small rural Saskatchewan town with a population of 1,400. The community has German and Ukrainian roots. We do not have a francophone presence in or near the communities from which our high school draws its students. There is no access to French television except through the cable services provider. For these students, French is indeed a foreign language, not a second language.

The First Stage

The initial impulse that led to a class of 14 French students being connected via the Internet with another class of students studying French came about by chance. While engaged in dialogue on CAUSERIE, there arose an opportunity to initiate a link between my French 20 class (level IV French) and another class in New Hampshire, a French IV class of five students, during the months of November 1993 and January 1994 (Longpré, 1994). French was the language used between the two sets of students even though English was their native language.

The only means of communication via the Internet was through the use of both teachers' personal Internet accounts. Due to the unequal numbers, the dialogue between the classes was in the form of class newsletters. Working in groups of five, the students prepared descriptive articles as a means of introducing themselves, their communities (both schools serve several small communities), and their school. The articles were then forwarded to the partner class. Messages from the partner class, as well as those composed by my students, were posted in a print version on a classroom wall. Over the two and a half months of the class-to-class dialogue, the students engaged in a series of five message exchanges. With the approaching end of the French 20 course, the class engaged in a general discussion regarding the activity.

As many of the students were to continue study at the French 30 level (level V), the following semester there was a general request to continue the interclass dialogue. The students affirmed their interest in maintaining the link with the students in New Hampshire. They also asked about the possibility of acquiring individual pen pals as they were excited about the speed of the exchanges. The students agreed that using the Internet as a means of conversing with others in order to practice and develop their skills was an exciting activity. They also suggested that it might be a good activity to offer other students of French. Taking their enthusiasm as a catalyst, there was a deliberate attempt to formally introduce CMC into the core French program for the period of time between February 1994 and May 1994.

The Second Stage

The second pilot program had 27 participants taking French 30, 19 students at the French 20 level, and 42 students studying French 9. The French 10 class was engaged with letter correspondence and pen pals. Partners for these classes were found through a request placed on another listserv called IECC (Intercultural E-mail Classroom Connections). In a matter of weeks, partners were found in New York, Nebraska, and a school in North York, Ontario. Communications were also maintained with the class from New Hampshire. Attempts to connect with students who were native speakers of the French language met with little success at this time.

The students were encouraged to write to their partner classes and key pals as frequently as possible. Classroom time was provided for group activity in order to construct group messages. Messages were sent as they were constructed with no editing done by the author. Students keyed in their letters into computers located in either one of the school computer labs (one lab with Macintosh computers, the other with PC computers) during nonclass hours or at home on their personal computers. No restriction was set on the students with regard to the type of word processing software. Students used both Macintosh and PC computers for keying in their messages. I then combined the letters into a single larger file as ASCII text. This larger file was forwarded to the appropriate e-mail address. The transfer of messages was performed outside the regular class activity, so it was not perceived as a hindrance by the students. The students retained their focus on the messages that were being sent and received.

The messages took various forms. The initial format of group-to-group communications was structured to take on the form of a biweekly newsletter. The messages were, for the most part, informative rather than dialogue based. However, dialogue was established in the situations in which students were able to send personal introductions to another class (such was the case with the connections with Nebraska, New York, and, for a brief time, Belgium). Some of the responses to these individual letters were from a group of distant students, and a number of responses came from individuals. The volume of message exchanges was high. With the flood of messages, there was a corresponding increase in enthusiasm among the students.

As the semester approached its conclusion, the students were asked to complete a questionnaire concerning their activities and opinions regarding the use of CMC in the second-language classroom. Their responses were considered carefully as plans were made to incorporate CMC into the official curriculum of the French program.

Student Opinions

Sixty-three students took part in a follow-up questionnaire analyzing the CMC activity. Students were first asked which format they preferred for Internet communications. Their first choice was the use of key-pal letters with the sending of classroom newsletters and surveys being chosen second and third. The idea of posting messages to a bulletin board for others to read was the least favored.

When asked about the volume of messages both sent and received, the students felt that they wrote and sent a decent amount of mail, however, they did not receive as much mail back as they would have liked. The problem of nonresponse from some of their contacts and limited response from others did not dampen their enthusiasm to continue using this medium for communication in French. When asked if they would consider continuing the contacts with their partners, they responded affirmatively.

The students were then asked if they perceived any improvement in their second-language skills with the following results. They thought that their knowledge of grammar usage increased the most. The next highest rated perception was the ability to converse (exchange ideas with others). Many saw an improvement in their vocabulary; they used and recognized more words. Following the language analysis, they responded to a question regarding the issue of sending edited versus nonedited messages. There was a definite opinion expressed in favor of sending nonedited messages. They presented the following reasons for their choice: the communication was more realistic, and they felt that they learned from their mistakes.

The students then provided data about their feelings regarding the process. They felt strongly that using CMC for French conversation provided a cooperative situation in which they worked together for successful communication, and that CMC provided a better way to practice French as they engaged in real communication with real people. The cooperative nature of the message building enabled the students to find other ways to express their ideas and also helped to share the work load in a positive way. They felt strong enough about the process to recommend the continuation of the use of CMC as part of the second-language program

The final part of the questionnaire asked the students to indicate which aspects of the use of CMC they found positive and which aspects they felt caused them problems. They were given the opportunity to suggest improvements and to express their overall opinions regarding the use of computers for the practice of communication in French. The most positive features in their minds were the chance to "meet new people from new places," "learn more while having fun," and "it's real." The problems they encountered using e-mail were technology oriented. They found it frustrating not to be able to send and receive messages with accent marks (a problem that is solved if both sender and receiver encode their messages using Mime as is available using Eudora), and that they did not have good keyboarding skills. Another problem they noted was the lack of time to write their messages. Due to the volume of mail received, many of the students had to key in their responses during their lunch hours and after classes.

In a final statement about their CMC experiences, they readily stated that the process was fun and interesting, that they learned more French while learning about other people their own age.

REFLECTIONS

Chasing the idea of using computers for conversation in the French classroom began as a light-hearted experience that seemed to take on a life of its own when the students became partner participants in the dialogues. Having tried many "experientially" based communicative classroom activities, I have been able to watch students as they attempt to find meaning in the various activities. Their enjoyment while learning using the "communicative" approaches to second-language learning has been genuine, and the rate of learning (and the retention of the students within the second-language program) has increased due to their enjoying their learning experiences. With the use of CMC, the students appeared to have invested themselves in the learning process. Learning French seemed to change status from being a "school" idea to being a "real-world" idea. For example, when students wrote to partners in Sweden, they found out that English was not a first language for the other students, that the only way that they could communicate with their new friends was through the use of French. This was repeated with key pals in Italy, Denmark, and Finland. Ethnocentric ideas began to crumble as the conversations continued.

The contact with others using the second language has been used in the past with pen pal letters, through student and class exchanges, and educational excursions to francophone parts of the world with good motivational success. What then is different about using CMC? My students commented that the speed with which the messages got exchanged made the people seem closer and more "real." Because many of the messages sent were shorter than the pen pal letters with which they also had experience, the messages were more conversational in tone. Their classmates shared in these dialogues, especially when humor was attempted, offering suggestions and ideas. This sharing within the class added a face-to-face dimension not envisioned for the CMC experiment.

Not all was positive as the students noted in their questionnaires. Many messages went unanswered with no reason being given. The issue of nonresponse that concerned my students were reflected by other teachers using CMC in a forum called IECC-DISCUSSION. After a series of postings, the moderator of the list posted a summary of nonresponse concerns (Roberts, 1994). The summary pointed out a need for the classroom teacher to be committed to the CMC activity, committed in a manner that had the CMC activity become part of the "regular" classroom/course. Advisement was given for the teacher to maintain contact with partner teachers throughout the period of time that a connection is maintained between partner classrooms. Teachers were encouraged to discuss the possibility of nonresponse with the students before the commencement of any CMC activity. Such discussion would allow the students to understand nonresponse as a natural phenomena rather than as a personal affront.

Noting that the interest in using CMC by the students had not flagged, and noting that there appeared to be increased interest by the students directed toward the expansion of vocabulary, as well as having students ask for grammatical explanations that would allow them to communicate their ideas (not a frequent occurrence in my classrooms prior to using CMC), I received the official blessing of the school division authorities to continue using CMC in the French classroom. So, the process of learning about CMC in the second-language classroom continues as students once again engage in French conversations using the Internet.

CONCLUSION

Using computers to open up the communication channels for learners of second languages, to provide them with someone to talk with whole allaying the natural reticence and shyness shared by many who attempt second languages, allows the learner to find a voice that might otherwise stay long silent. For those who find that the study of a second language is only possible through the use of correspondence courses or other methods of distance education, the use of CMC adds a "conversational" element. CMC does not replace the face-to-face model of conversation, it only provides another avenue for conversation to occur, especially when the face-to-face model is geographically next to impossible.

With the growing use of computers in business and industry, the use of CMC within the classroom also serves to prepare our students for its use outside of the classroom, a use that already spans the globe and crosses many language groups. Looking into the future, it is impossible to predict the importance and the value of CMC in the classroom. However, for the present, CMC does offer students such as mine, who are removed by geography from the main body of the world's populace, an opportunity to bridge the distance even using a language-in-the-learning.

INTERNET ADDRESSES

Discussion Lists

CAUSERIE—for teachers who would like to engage in French conversation
LISTSERVER@UQUEBEC.CA

IECC—for teachers seeking K-12 classroom partnerships
IECC-REQUEST@STOLAF.EDU

JASETTE—for teachers and students wanting to practice French
LISTSERV@VM1.ULAVAL.CA

FLTEACH—for teachers who would like to share teaching ideas for foreign language instruction
LISTSERV@UBVM.CC.BUFFALO.EDU

FRENCHTALK—for French conversation among adults
LISTPROC@LIST.CREN.NET

K12-EURO-TEACHERS—for contact and discussion with teachers from Europe
MAJORDOMO@LISTS.EUNET.FI

Newsgroups

K12lang.francais—French messaging for teachers and students
can.francais—Bilingual messaging on a variety of topics

Web Sites

AIDE FRANCAIS (for studying French): http://www.eduq.risq.net/DRD/Aide/Fr.html#debut

CMC Magazine—monthly magazine discussing CMC issues and activities: http://sunsite.unc.edu/cmc/mag/current/toc.html

Comment dit-on en francais... ?—Lexical guide for those needing French translations: http://www.culture.fr/culture/dglf/lexis.htm

French Links—Robert Peckam's master page pointing to French Web sites around the world: http://www.utm.edu/departments/french/french.html

FRENCHTALK—French language discussion forum access: http://mousa.dcs.gla.ac.uk/~ft/

IECC—access to the services offered by IECC and its archives: http://www.stolaf.edu/network/iecc/

JCMC—Journal of Computer-Mediated Communication: http://www.usc.edu/dept/annenberg/journal.html or http://shum.huji.ac.il/jcmc/jcmc.html

PLUMES—giving young people a voice using French: http://www.culture.fr/culture/dglf/plum_0.htm

REFERENCES

Coombs, N. (1993). CMC: The medium and the message. *EJC/REC, 3*(2) [Mailing list]. Available via e-mail: comserve@vm.its.rpi.edu.

Longpré, R.G. (1994). Distance education and computer-mediated communication: Tools for education reform. In R.A. Schwier (Ed.), *Educational technology and educational reform in Saskatchewan.* Unpublished manuscript, University of Saskatchewan, Saskatoon, Saskatchewan, Canada.

Mathiesen, A.B. (1993). Electronic communication media and second language learning. *Call, 7*(3).

Roberts, B. (1994, March 1). *Non-response summary.* IECC-DISCUSSION [Mailing list]. Available at: HTTP://www.stolaf.edu.80/network/iecc/iecc-discussion.html.

Sayers, D. (1995). Language choices and global learning networks: The pitfalls of "lingua Franca" approaches to classroom telecomputing. *Education Policy Analysis Archives, 3*(10). [Mailing list]. Available via e-mail: listserv@asu.edu.

Schwier, R., Brown, F.B., Misanchuk, E., & Proctor, L. (1992). *Interactive media and distance education for Saskatchewan schools* (Res. Centre Rep. No. 92-06). Regina, SK: Saskatchewan School Trustees Association.

SUGGESTED READINGS

American Psychological Association. (1994). *Publication manual of the American Psychological Association* (4th Ed.). Washington, DC: Author.

Harley, B., & d'Anglejan, A. (1987). *Report on the piloting of "Initiation au voyage": An experimental teaching unit designed for grade 8 Core French classes.* Calgary: National Core French Study, Canadian Association of Second Language Teachers.

Harley, B., d'Anglejan, A., & Shapson, S. (1990). *National Core French study: The evaluation syllabus.* Ottawa: Canadian Association of Second Language Teachers.

Hébert, Y. (1990). *Etude nationale sur les programmes de français de base: Le syllabus de formation langagière générale* [National Core French study: The general language syllabus]. Ottawa: Association Canadienne des Professeurs de Langues Secondes [Canadian Association of Second Language Teachers].

LeBlanc, R. (1990). *National Core French study: A synthesis.* Ottawa: Canadian Association of Second Language Teachers.

LeBlanc, C., Courtel, C., & Trescases, P. (1990). *Étude nationale sur les programmes de français de base: Le syllabus culture* [National Core French study: The culture syllabus].

Painchaud, G. (1990). *Étude nationale sur les programmes de français de base: Le syllabus langue* [National Core French study: The language syllabus]. Ottawa: association Canadienne des Professeurs de Langues Secondes [Canadian Association of Second Language Teachers].

Phillips, G.M. (1994, April 16). *Communities & interactivity.* IPCT-L LOG9404C [Mailing list]. Available via e-mail: listserv@listserv.georgetown.edu.

Schwier, R.A. (Ed.). (1994). *Educational technology and educational reform in Saskatchewan.* Unpublished manuscript, University of Saskatchewan, Saskatoon, Saskatchewan, Canada.

Tremblay, R., Duplantie, M., & Huot, D. (1990). *National Core French study: The communicative/experiential syllabus.* Ottawa: Canadian Association of Second Language Teachers.

Tremblay, R., Painchaud, G., LeBlanc, R., & Comeau, M. (1989). *Se lancer en affaires Avec un jeu: Unité intégrée d'enseignement pour la dixième année* [Going into business with a game: An integrated unit for grade ten]. Calgary: National Core French Study, Canadian Association of Second Language Teachers.

13

USING E-MAIL CORRESPONDENCE TO FACILITATE THE ACQUISITION OF JAPANESE LANGUAGE

Jun Ohashi

The main proposal of this chapter is to recognize the movement from computer-aided instruction (CAI) to computer-mediated communication (CMC) along the line of second language acquisition models, and to discuss the practical application of e-mail correspondence while evaluating a pilot e-mail correspondence project between Stirling and Tsukuba universities. Initially, this experimental project aimed at (a) helping students learning Japanese at Stirling University, and (b) providing teachers of Japanese in training at Tsukuba University with the opportunity to correct compositions written by learners of Japanese. This project was, without doubt, beneficial for both ends. For the students, it increased their opportunities to use Japanese and to have their compositions corrected. For the teacher trainees it provided opportunities to know what learners of Japanese outside Japan find difficult and to improve their skills in correcting errors made by the learners.

METHOD[1]

Four Stirling students were involved in this project from the postbeginners' level. They were instructed to write their self-introductions, their image of Japan and its people. They were also given tasks that required them to write a polite letter and a job application (Maruyama, 1995). They stored the assignments in their own files in the computer allocated to them. Whenever they finished each task, the person who was in charge (he was invited from Tsukuba University to coordinate the project) copied their compositions onto a floppy disc and sent them to Tsukuba University via e-mail. The teacher trainees corrected and sent them back. Compositions for the e-mail exchange were not integrated with the syllabus of the Japanese language program of Stirling University, thus they were not assessed or evaluated.

EVALUATION

There are a number of criteria for examining this project, such as management, syllabus, technology, and so forth, but I focus on the actual activities with which the learners and the teacher trainees were involved. In the following sections, I illustrate what exactly the learners and the teacher trainees experienced in the e-mail exchange and, on the basis of that, reconsider the use of e-mail correspondence, which could facilitate the learner's second language acquisition in a wider context.

Looking at data of learners' compositions and trainees' corrections, I first point out some characteristics of the activities. The students' compositions were returned after having been corrected; mistakes were identified and numbered, with as many as 35 to 40 for a short piece. Then explanations followed for those mistakes the teacher trainees thought required explanation, and comments on the students' compositions were added at the closing of the mail. Although the method of the correction was standardized, the kinds of corrections varied depending on the level of the students and how the trainees assessed the students' competence.

The pilot project was successful in the narrow sense that the initial objectives were more or less accomplished, but there are points that need to be reconsidered in terms of the activities implemented; in relation to what could have been achieved with the use of e-mail and the actual activities and experiences at both ends. In the former

[1]The computers used for this project at Stirling were Macintoshes , and the software used for word processing in Japanese was Nisus Version 3.0.1, whereas that used for E-mail was Eudora-J Version. 1.3.3.J7.

category, it is necessary to reconsider the potential application of e-mail to facilitate the learner's second language acquisition in pedagogical context. In the latter category, there are three points to be considered: (a) the topics of the composition tasks, (b) the roles assigned at both ends (Stirling and Tsukuba), and (c) correction methods.

FUTURE DEVELOPMENT

This pilot project suggested that the use of the e-mail can provide the learner with an appropriate environment and opportunities to use or learn the language communicatively, and that e-mail correspondence can be one useful source for facilitating their second-language acquisition. It is therefore important to investigate what can be achieved with the use of e-mail and how it can be best used. To do this, let us first identify e-mail as a property of computer-mediated communication (CMC) and in comparison to computer-aided instruction (CAI) and then extend the discussion into the second-language acquisition to explore the theoretical rationale of second language acquisition model in order to consider the use of e-mail in a wider second-language acquisition pedagogical context.

THEORETICAL DISCUSSION

Computer-Aided Instruction to Computer-Mediated Communication

Restricting the use of e-mail by the conventional view of language teaching can diminish the possibilities of further development of both language teaching and learning and the application of e-mail use. Recognizing CMC as "computer application for direct human-to-human communication," Santoro in Volume 1 of this series widens those possibilities. CAI affords drill and practice in segments or discrete points of one aspect of language such as grammar and Kanji. CMC can actually provide the second-language learner with opportunities to communicate with second language native speakers or other learners using the target language. The former focuses on end products, for example, the mastery of lexical items or grammatical items; the latter focuses on the processes of language learning. One can look at CAI and CMC as a dichotomy of language acquisition that is product-oriented and process oriented in nature.

Comprehensible Input versus Comprehended Input

If we reconsider the use of e-mail to facilitate the learner's second language acquisition, it is important that the new methods reflect the mechanisms by which second language is acquired: what works and what does not. In Krashen's (1982) "input hypothesis," he attempts to explain how second language is acquired by a learner. Krashen claims that "comprehensible input" which a learner manages to understand is essential in second language acquisition and that the "comprehensible input" should contain linguistic input data which is one step beyond the current learner's stage. In his input hypothesis, the learner needs this "comprehensible input" to accomplish second-language acquisition. This implies that the person providing the input controls its quality.

Gass (1988), on the other hand, proposes the notion of comprehended input stating: "whereas comprehended input is learner-controlled, that is, it is the learner who is doing the 'work' to understand as opposed to the person providing the language data" (p. 204). What Gass argues for the new inventory in the second-language acquisition model is to highlight the learner's role in second-language acquisition and give him or her more responsibility to handle any input data. Gass thinks this is indispensable for the learner's development of an internalized set of rules or grammar. The notion of comprehensible input allows only two possible analyses in which "input" is either comprehensible or not; but the notion of comprehended input, Gass argues, "presents a continuum of possibilities ranging from semantics to detailed structural analyses" (p. 204). Together with the notion of learner-controlled "input," this multistaged nature of comprehension widens the scope for second-language teaching perspectives.

Applying the notion of comprehended input to e-mail correspondence. My argument for highlighting CMC is based on Gass's hypothesis. All the efforts the learner makes to grasp "input data," or to get meaning across, and the efforts to analyze the data for internalization work positively for the learner's second-language acquisition. If so, the teacher must encourage the activities. Rapid development of CAI may provide such an ideal environment for second language acquisition. There are areas of language learning that require instruction: close-ended activities such as drilling, depending on the learner's needs, in which CAI can play a substantial role. However, as human-to-human communication is the essential nature of language, it might be suitable to look at CMC and develop effective use of this resource, rather than rely solely on CAI software that often aims at native speaker-like language manipulation, ignoring the context and quality of discourse.

Identifying the Nature of E-mail Correspondence

Identifying the nature of e-mail correspondence is important in order to identify its possible application to second language teaching and learning. Such a fundamental question as to whether the mode of the e-mail exchange is written or spoken has to be investigated based on actual discourse in communication via e-mail. In the following discussion I consider the mode of the language as a continuum, of which Nunan (1991) wrote: "spoken and written language exist as a continuum, a mode continuum, depending on the extent to which it exhibits the characteristics of the different forms. Some spoken texts will be more like written texts than others" (p. 84).

Although the use of e-mail implies a written mode and aims at improving the learner's writing skills, it also implies the more general development of communicative competence. Because e-mail enables us to have human-to-human communication across the globe, its applications can be infinite. What used to be impossible has become feasible. Real time communication is not impossible if problems such as time differences and semester timing of both institutions can be overcome. If the students' computers are networked, they can send the mail directly to their communication partners. These handy features may influence the mode of the language. As the communication develops, students can accumulate shared knowledge and information, and this growing common ground also influences the manner of their communication. Research looking at discourse in the e-mail exchange is also important to define effective task types for the e-mail correspondence.

Task Types and the Learner's Experience

According to research looking at the effects of task type on learners' performance, what the learners experience with a task largely depends on what type of task they are engaged in (Duff, 1986; Long, 1981; Nunan, 1991). If one possesses all the information and the other seeks the information, the activity correspondents engage in will be one-way communication. If, however, there are needs from both sides and both are able to fill the others' requirements, the communication will become essential and meaningful, and simultaneously process oriented CMC will be engaged.

Tasks should therefore be designed to engage the students in a meaning-focused, two-way communication. The effective use of e-mail is largely dependent on the teacher's efforts in designing tasks. These tasks should provide the students with a process in which they accomplish their objectives defined by their needs and the pedagogical rationale. This whole experience should be one source of facilitating their second language acquisition.

Bearing this in mind, I look at the pilot project again and reconsider several points raised earlier in order to design tasks for the e-mail correspondence that work efficaciously for the learner's second-language acquisition as well as for the teacher training. Focusing on activities in which e-mail could extend the opportunity of learning, I now define the objectives of the students' learning the language and the trainees' being trained, which reflects the benefit of the activities of e-mail correspondence.

The Students and Teacher Trainees' Objectives

I also reconsider what the benefits of the use of e-mail for both the students and the teacher trainees are, in relation to aims and objectives of both parties in the correspondence. Figure 13.1 is a list of possible examples of objectives that could be made mutually beneficial by means of e-mail.

Students	Trainees
Developing target language skills, internalized set of rules of the language	Providing the learners with an appropriate level of the language and its use
Second-language cultural awareness Second-language discourse awareness	Knowing and dealing with: • the learner • the learner's first language culture • the learner's difficulty • the learner's errors
Developing strategic competence	

Figure 13.1. Mutually beneficial features

Reconsidering the Pilot Project

Based on the earlier discussion, I look at the following points: (a) the topics of the composition tasks, (b) the roles assigned at both ends (Stirling and Tsukuba), and (c) the correction methods.

Creating communicative needs at both ends. Topics selected for e-mail correspondence tasks must reflect the objectives of both ends and must create needs to exchange information and opinions. For the practical examples see later discussion.

Reestablishing the roles of the learners and the teacher trainees. In the experimental project, there was not enough room for both the learners of Japanese in the United Kingdom and the teacher trainees in Japan to negotiate with each other and find out and establish their roles in the activities. The fact that the learners had the role of students and the trainees the role of teachers meant that genuine two-way communication did not take place. The students wrote compositions, and the teacher trainees corrected them. Both participants inevitably focused on linguistic forms rather than meaning.

Developing the relationship between students and teacher trainees is significant for creating an environment that encourages the students' second-language acquisition. In the pilot project, however, there was little common ground developed; the students had not known to whom they were writing until their corrected compositions were returned, and each student was corrected by a different trainee every time. It is important to maintain the relationship, once paired, for some time rather than changing it frequently. Teacher and student need to get to know one another. The "teachers" need to deal with their student's learning, and the students need correction by somebody they are familiar with, in a sympathetic and cooperative atmosphere. Only with such an atmosphere can the learner experiment with the target language. Thus it is important for the learners to know to whom they are sending their messages and to keep the same partner.

Correction Methods

For the most part the teacher trainees corrected the students' compositions, thus drawing their attention to unacceptable usage, and gave them correct or alternative lexical items and structures. This kind of information can be useful, helping the learner to adjust or refine a hypothesis that has proven to be wrong or partly wrong or to speed up the learning process. However, some corrections took no account of the learner's current second-language ability, and some were ambiguous. This inefficiency stemmed partly from the short-term partnership of the pair and the consequent faulty assessment of the learner's competence. In this correction method, concern for linguistic accuracy on the part of both student and trainee shifts the focus from intended meaning to grammar. What is needed is a way of indicating the students' errors and providing well-formed versions to them, which allows both student and the trainee to focus on meaning. Consideration should also be given to the timing as well as the method of correction; to the appropriate time for overt correction, for covert correction, and for no correction at all. The choice of correction method will depend on the pedagogical context, but covert correction tends to encourage the learner's second-language acquisition because the focus is on meaning; the negotiation of meaning is encouraged but the intention to communicate is not frustrated. Trainee teachers must learn to correct in such a way so as not to impede the communication of meaning.

PRACTICAL EXAMPLES OF TASKS FOR E-MAIL CORRESPONDENCE

Project-Based Learning

After students have read and discussed some issues of Japanese society in class, the students could seek further information via e-mail. For example, "blood types" are frequently referred to in Japanese society as a way to identify the personality of self as well as others. The students read about and discuss this from various aspects. They could then gather more information about it via e-mail, if the timing of this topic coincides with the very beginning of the mailing. When exchanging self-introductions, information about blood types can be incorporated. Gathering all students' information received from their Japanese partners, the teacher could have the students organize a survey to find out, for example, what proportion of Japanese people really believe in the correlation of personalities and blood types, and so on. Heated discussions could follow without much effort from the teacher. The students can report the results of the discussion to their partners. In this whole process, the students inevitably learn a lot of vocabulary and expressions describing personalities that focus on the meaning.

Journal Writing

Making the most of the fact that the teacher trainees are the students' partners on e-mail, we can create a support system for the students. The learners, being self-reflective, can ask or express anything that has to do with their learning the Japanese language, their problems, and so forth whenever necessary. What the learners potentially experience with this activity is that they clarify issues or ideas about learning.

This retrospection is important in various ways. First, it will get the learners to recognize the language learning consciously, and it will give the learners an opportunity to evaluate their own progress and eventually raise their awareness of learning strategies. Second, in terms of the learners' second language acquisition, it will give the learners more chances to use or experiment with linguistic materials studied in class in meaningful and less-threatening settings, in that they can revise the materials and test their hypothesis. It is also a great benefit for the learners to have someone other than the teacher who can advise them on their learning process because there is no assessment involved; they can write whatever they want. For the teacher trainees, this activity is a great opportunity to observe what is happening in the learners' learning processes, and it would give them a lot of insight on teaching, which they cannot experience in the training program. They can discover the learners' difficulty, patterns of errors, and extent of cultural awareness.

CONCLUSION

The use of e-mail can be tailored according to the needs and objectives of those who are participating. This use has great possibilities in many ways and can be regarded not only as a resource available for the learner's autonomous study but also as an integrated part of syllabus design. I would like to again raise the awareness of the unique nature of e-mail correspondence in natural settings and advocate more empirical research on discourse analysis of e-mail in order to examine its uses in second language teaching and learning. It is also up to the teachers to continue research on the activities via e-mail to find out what is happening and what the learners are experiencing in order to improve its use.

REFERENCES

Duff, P. (1986). Another look at interlanguage talk: taking task to task. In R. Day (Ed.), *Talking to learn* (pp. 147-181). Rowley, MA: Newbury House.

Gass, S. M. (1988). Integrating research areas: A framework for second language studies. *Applied Linguistics, 9*(2), 198-217.

Krashen, S. (1982). *Principles and practice in second language acquisition.* Oxford: Pergamon.

Long, M. H. (1981). Questions in foreigner talk discourse. *Language Learning, 31*(1), 135-157.

Maruyama, D. (1995). *How students learn Japanese.* An unpublished report on an e-mail project carried out at the University of Stirling.

Nunan, D. (1991). *Language teaching methodology: A textbook for teachers.* Hemel Hempstead: Prentice-Hall International.

14

SURVEY PROJECT: AN EXAMPLE OF COMPUTER-MEDIATED COMMUNICATION IN A FOREIGN LANGUAGE CLASSROOM

Junko K. Ady

In this chapter, I state the reasons for the use of computer-mediated communication (CMC) in a foreign language classroom. This is followed by a description of the actual use of CMC in my classroom. Finally, I discuss the potential for future CMC.

PROBLEMS IN TRADITIONAL CLASSROOMS

The importance of language teaching to promote students' communicative proficiency in actual contexts has long been advocated in foreign language pedagogy (Brown, 1987; Ommagio; 1986, Oxford, 1990; Widdowson, 1978). When we pursue this goal in traditional classroom settings, various instructional problems occur. I point out next five problems that are significant.

First, the quality and amount of language input to students are important. Ommagio (1986) emphasizes the use of authentic input in instruction. The large amount of language input is necessary for students' language acquisition (Sanaoui & Lapkin, 1992). However, when students learn a foreign language outside of the target country, the amount of authentic language input and students' language use is most likely limited to the classroom. The various contexts of language use are lacking in a traditional classroom.

Second, because a language reflects its culture, it is necessary to include culture in a foreign language classroom (Cononelos & Oliva, 1993, Davis & Ye-Ling, 1994; Ommagio, 1986). Yet, because of limited time, it is difficult to incorporate culture in a traditional classroom.

Third, when students actually use the foreign language in the target country or with a native speaker, they have to be able to use everything they know to communicate. Therefore, it is important to emphasize the task based holistic use of the language instruction approach instead of traditional cumulative instruction in order to prepare students for the real world (Cummins & Sayers, 1990; Kroonenberg, 1994).

Fourth, the importance of language learning strategies (Oxford, 1990) is not often emphasized in the traditional classroom. As Oxford (1990) states, it is important for teachers to promote language learning strategies among students to make them more effective learners. Learning strategies can also be applied to other subjects (Oxford, 1990).

Fifth, the lack of time and the large number of students force teachers to use teacher-centered instruction. Such passive learning does not prepare students for the real world (Cummins & Sayers, 1990). Yet, in learner-centered instruction, students are more motivated because their learning is relevant to themselves (Cononelos & Oliva, 1993).

SOME SOLUTIONS

Proponents of the use of CMC argue that the use of CMC overcomes these problems (Beauvois, 1992; Beazley, 1989; Cohen & Miyake, 1986; Crookall & Wilkenfeld, 1985; Cummins & Sayers, 1990; Davis & Ye-Ling, 1994; Kelm, 1992; Kroonenberg, 1994; Reynolds, 1992; Riel, 1987; Sanaoui & Lapkin, 1992; Sayers & Brown, 1987; Shires, 1992; Soh and Soon, 1991, Southworth, 1986; Wollstein, 1986).

However, more is needed than CMC capability in the classroom. According to Riel and Levin (1990), successful students' networking projects are marked by having a group structure, a well specified task, and a coordinator to facilitate group planning.

Considering the previously mentioned problems and limitation I had, I created a lesson plan using CMC in my classroom. The limitation was that there was no computer available for sending and receiving Japanese characters in school, and I was the only one who had an e-mail account and Japanese e-mail capability.

SURVEY PROJECT

Overview

I named the project "survey project" because students conducted surveys through e-mail. I used this lesson plan in the Japanese II Honors class. There were two classes, and the total number of students was 39 (20 and 19 students in each class). The reasons I used these classes were that students in honors classes were more motivated and capable, and I was the only teacher teaching this class, so I had no conflict with other teachers. Most students had two years of Japanese in junior high school (equivalent of one year in high school). Most of them were ninth graders, including some sophomores, two juniors, and one senior.

As I mentioned, I hoped to overcome the shortcomings of isolated classrooms using CMC. Through their surveys on using CMC, I wanted to provide them an opportunity to use what they had learned. I wanted them to use their language learning strategies when they read authentic writings that contained vocabulary and sentence patterns they had not learned. I hoped that students would gain some confidence in their Japanese skills through communicating with real Japanese people. I also wanted them to self-discover Japanese culture and awareness of their own American culture.

Project Description

In this section I describe the survey project step by step, including actual examples from students.

As a preactivity, students were taught Japanese word processing skills in class by actually using a Japanese-capable computer.[1] There was only one computer capable of typing in Japanese in this room. I taught the whole class how to type in Japanese briefly and gave each student opportunities to type while other students were engaged in other activities. Sometimes I received help from a student assistant who knew how to type in Japanese.

Because this activity was conducted while working with a conventional curriculum for the class, I could not afford to spend much classroom time on this activity. Much work was done outside of the class as homework.

---

[1]The two types of software "Japanese Language Kit" and "Japanese Teach Text" were used on a Macintosh computer to type in Japanese.

Project History

A handout describing this project was first given to students. Because this was a group activity, three or four students formed each group. One topic was chosen by each group according to their own interests. Topics chosen for this activity were, for example, music, sports, travel, transportation, food, entrance examinations, seasons, and so forth. Students then discussed the topic and created a hypothesis. I encouraged students to use Japanese during the discussion to practice their oral skills.

Second, students wrote their hypotheses in Japanese. They then discussed the hypotheses to create questionnaires. I asked them to ask at least 10 questions. They submitted their drafts to me before they typed their surveys in Japanese using a Japanese-capable computer. Each questionnaire included a brief introduction of their project, the date by which they needed to receive the answer, and questions and names of students, all typed in Japanese.

Third, I sent students' surveys to Japan via e-mail. As mentioned earlier, I was the only person who had an e-mail account. I found Japanese contacts using the Internet.[2] Messages were sent to various Japanese people, such as college students, college professors, high school and junior high school students, and some of my personal friends.

I could have done this activity using the conventional mail system if I did not have to worry about its cost and time. My access to the Internet was free through an educational institution. This activity was done within a quarter (about two months) including the preactivity and the postactivity; therefore, the research time (time to receive responses to students' surveys) was limited to about a week. Because this class was a novice class and many Japanese contacts were studying English, we asked them to respond in either Japanese or English. Students received some responses written in Japanese. Because I was the only person with access to a Japanese e-mail-capable computer, I sent and received messages for students.[3] I printed out e-mail messages for students and gave them to each group.

---

[2]Except my personal contacts, the following listservs helped me to find Japanese contacts: (a) Japanese teachers and instructional technology (address: jiti-l@psuvm.psu.edu To subscribe, send an e-mail message "subscribe jtit-l" to listserv@psuvm.psu.edu); and (b) Intercultural E-Mail Classroom Connections (K-12) (address: iecc@stolaf.edu To subscribe, send an e-mail message "subscribe" to iecc-request@stolaf.edu).

[3]Eudora-J 1.3.8.5 was used on a Macintosh to send and receive Japanese messages. A Macintosh has to be able to handle Japanese to use this software. Eudora-J 1.3.8.5 is shareware and available at ftp://ftp.taiiku.tsukuba.ac.jp/pub/eudora/.

At the same time, students interviewed at least one Japanese person orally using the same survey for their oral practice. Students had to record one interview for their evaluation.

After gathering responses, each group discussed the results of their surveys in Japanese to prepare for their oral presentations. They compiled the responses and compared the results with their hypotheses.

During the oral presentation each group talked about their hypotheses, results of their surveys, about whether their hypotheses were supported, and their conclusions. The quality of their presentations was evaluated; therefore, many groups created various visual aids, such as posters and overhead transparencies. Some groups further investigated the topic through library research and gave the class more information including some actual demonstrations. One group imitated the Japanese TV show *Soko ga shiritai* to present their findings.

Each group submitted a written report in Japanese about the survey for their evaluation. In addition, each student turned in his or her oral interview and brief reflection written on the project.

For the last activity, students wrote and sent a thank you note to respondents electronically. Some respondents returned another e-mail to students with words of encouragement.

Outcome

I believe this activity was generally successful because most students responded to this project positively. Many liked to work in groups. They said that because this was a group activity, it was much easier and more fun than projects they had done by themselves previously. They also liked to choose their own topics. This was a surprise to me because many groups struggled to come up with a theme. I recommend that teachers suggest themes, but let students choose their own topics.

Students really enjoyed receiving responses from Japan via e-mail. Many students were amazed to receive so many responses in such short time. Language learning strategies such as guessing and cooperating with others were used to accomplish this activity. Many mentioned knowing Japanese people and culture better and accepting the inaccuracies of stereotypes that were frequently expressed in their hypotheses.

The following are some comments on this activity. (excerpts from students' reflections):

> I have enjoyed working on this quarter project above all others, I appreciate the chance to work in a group. This project seemed in a way easier to me. . . . Also, it was fun sending and receiving e-mail from Japan, especially trying to understand what some wrote in response. What is nice about working in a group is the fact that everyone pitches in, and works to complete a great product in the end.—Valerie, ninth grade

I like the method of interviewing many people and receiving answers through e-mail. This way, a broad spectrum of answers are received and it represents more of an accurate sampling of the Japanese opinion.—Kristin, ninth grade

I'm glad we had opportunity of interviewing students by e-mail because you really get to know what is going on in Japan.—Jamie

It [the activity] gave up an opportunity to communicate with and learn about Japan and its people; a chance we normally would not have if we didn't have this project. It also was a valuable time for us to apply what we had learned in the classroom to the outside world where it really counts.— Elizabeth, ninth grade

The letters we received from the Japanese students by using the e-mail also helped to improve my reading skills. Some of the words and kanji we hadn't learned so I had to learn to pick out the key words or phrases so I could have a basic understanding of the answer.

I think we all had a lot of fun working together on this project and I hope that we have another chance to work together again in a group project.—Megan, ninth grade

This project helped me to gain a better understanding of Japanese culture and traditions while learning factual information as well.—Emily, tenth grade

I kind of enjoyed doing this project because using e-mail was pretty interesting. I learned new facts and also new vocabulary that I never heard of like hatsumode.—Maria, ninth grade

I felt that this project was unique and interesting in that we got a chance to write and communicate with students our age in Japan. Due to our advanced technology, I find it fascinating that it is so quick and easy to communicate with people living so far away!—Erin, tenth grade

Successes

The following are a list of strengths of the project:

1. Highly motivating, cooperative, and student-centered learning took place.
2. This activity cultivated greater cultural awareness among students.
3. Various language learning strategies were actively used.
4. Students could apply classroom learning to real communicative situations.
5. It was possible to conduct this sort of activity in a short period of time.

Failures

As for failures, the lack of time for students and lack of equipment were major obstacles. Only minimal classroom time was used for this activity. Many students had to meet outside of class to complete this activity. Some groups had a difficult time meeting together because of their different schedules. More integration to the usual curriculum would be a way to solve this problem.

Because there was only one Japanese-capable computer available for all Japanese students in my school, students had to wait for a long time to use the computer. This will be solved when the school installs more Japanese-capable software in more computers.

DISCUSSION

General Observations

In this activity, CMC was used as a tool to gather information from Japan. The use of CMC is only a part of the whole activity, yet it played an important role. Without CMC I would not have been able to find Japanese contacts as quickly, and without it my class would not have finished this project within one quarter. I could finish everything during this quarter from the preactivity (learning to type in Japanese) to the postactivity (oral presentation and writing a report) while covering the usual curriculum.

The convenience of sending and receiving mail electronically made it possible for one person (me) to handle the huge amount of correspondence. In the future, when students have their own accounts, I will not have to do this. Students can find Japanese contacts by themselves.

This activity is applicable to any other language and level. Teachers should suggest appropriate topics depending on students' proficiency level.

Uses for Language Teaching

It is possible to use this activity to reinforce certain grammatical forms. During this quarter, students learned comparative and superlative patterns. One of my instructions was that students had to use the comparative and superlative patterns in their questionnaires. Students used comparative patterns in their questions and received authentic Japanese using those patterns. From the various responses from Japan, they experienced the use of these patterns in different contexts.

Through this activity, some students' stereotypes of Japanese were changed. Many of my students recognized that there were many different types of Japanese people. It is crucial to have a flexible attitude without negative stereotypes when we communicate with a person from a different culture. Without cultural understanding, students will not be able to achieve communicative competence (Ross, 1990).

This activity is just one example of CMC use. CMC has much more potential use in education (Cummins & Sayers, 1990). The more technology progresses, the more dreams will come true. At the same time, secondary teachers in particular are often less fortunate than college-level instructors in terms of the availability of technology. My use of CMC was limited, yet the problems of traditional classrooms were overcome even by this small use of CMC. I hope this case study encourages some of the teachers who only have limited access to CMC.

REFERENCES

Beauvois, M.H. (1992). Computer-assisted classroom discussion in the foreign language classroom: Conversation in slow motion. *Foreign Language Annals, 25*(5), 455-464.

Beazley, M.R. (1989). Reading for a real reason: Computer pals across the world. *Journal of Reading, 32*(7), 598-605.

Brown, H.D. (1987). *Principles of language learning and teaching.* Englewood Cliffs, NJ: Prentice-Hall.

Cohen, M., & Miyake, N. (1986). A worldwide intercultural network: Exploring electronic messaging for instruction. *Instructional Science, 15*, 257-273.

Cononelos, T., & Oliva, M. (1993). Using computer networks to enhance foreign language/culture education. *Foreign Language Annals, 26*(4). 527-533.

Crookall, D., & Wilkenfeld, J. (1985). ICONS: Communications technologies and international relations. *System, 13*(3), 253-58.

Cummins, J., & Sayers, D. (1990). Education 2001: Learning networks and educational reform. *Computers in the Schools, 7*(2), 1-29.

Davis, B.H., & Ye-Ling, Y. (1994). Long-distance collaboration with on-line conferencing. *TESOL Journal, 4*(2), 28-31.

Kelm, O.R. (1992). The use of synchronous computer networks in second language instruction: A preliminary report. *Foreign Language Annals, 25*(5), 411-451.

Kroonenberg, N. (1994). Developing communicative and thinking skills via electronic mail. *TESOL Journal, 4*(2), 24-27.

Ommagio, A. (1986). *Teaching language in context: Proficiency-oriented instruction.* Boston, MA: Hainle and Hainle.

Oxford, R. (1990). *Language learning strategies: What every teacher should know.* New York, NY: Newbery House Publishers.

Reynolds, F.C. (1992). Bringing Minitel to the French classroom and integrating EDUTEL *CLASSE into the existing curriculum. *The French Review, 66*(1), 20-25.

Riel, M. (1987). The intercultural learning network. *The Computing Teacher, 14*(7), 27-30.

Riel, M., & Levin J. (1990). Building electronic communities: Success and failure in computer networking. *Instructional Science, 19,* 145-169.

Ross, S. (1990). Culture in the foreign language classroom. *ERIC/CLL News Bulletin, 14*(1), 1-12.

Sanaoui, R., & Lapkin, S. (1992). A case study of and FSL senior secondary course integrating computer networking. *The Canadian Modern Language Review, 48*(3), 525-552.

Sayers, D., & Brown, K. (1987). Bilingual education and telecommunications: A perfect fit. *The Computing Teacher, 14*(7), 23-24.

Shires, N.P. (1992). Computer-mediated lists for foreign languages. *Foreign Language Annals, 25*(6), 533-539.

Soh, B., & Soon, Y. (1991). English by e-mail: Creating a global classroom via the medium of computer technology. *ELT Journal, 45*(4), 287-292.

Southworth, J.H. (1986). The Hawaii Global TELEclass project and multimedia computer-based educational telecommunication (CBET). Learning tomorrow. *Journal of the Applied Education Advisory Council, 4,* 273-298.

Widdowson, H.G. (1978). *Teaching language as communication.* London: Oxford University Press.

Wollstein, J.D. (1986). TELEclass: The bottom line in second language learning. *CALICO Journal, 3*(3), 9-10.

15

THE *DEUTSCH GOSSIP COLUMN*[*]

Justus H. Lewis and Uta Morse

BACKGROUND

The Deutsch Gossip Column (DGC) is a computer group conference that uses a local area network. It was initiated by one of the students from the five beginners and one intermediate German classes in this study and remained an optional but strongly encouraged part of the German language teaching program. At the invitation of the students, the class teacher participated as a co-contributor. Subsequently she conducted a short survey of students' views on the DGC. The learning of German in Singapore is part of a general orientation toward Western cultures that originated with the then Prime Minister, Lee Kuan Yew, in 1990.

For many of these students, studying a foreign language formally (a language representing an unfamiliar culture) is a new experience so they approach the task with few preconceptions about

[*]This chapter is based on data collected by the class teacher, Uta Morse, and is analyzed and written up jointly by both authors.

grammar, style, and the target to be achieved. Acquiring a new language (the language of a culture with which they are acquainted to some degree), however, is a familiar experience. These students live in a multilingual society in which English, Mandarin, Malay, and Tamil are all recognized and commonly spoken as well as Singlish (the distinctively Singaporean "local dialect") and a variety of other dialects such as Hokkien and Teochew. Language switching (combining two or more languages within a sentence) and code switching (from colloquial to formal, for example, Singlish to standard Singaporean English) come naturally. Unlike Westerners, they have no inhibitions or qualms in these matters; in one sense, learning a new language is simply a matter of adding some extra words and phrases to their existing multilingual vocabulary.

WHAT WAS THE *GOSSIP* ABOUT?

Students used the DGC to discuss matters of general interest, particularly concerning the university and issues relating to Germany; to ask questions about and practice the language; and to raise matters of academic concern. The DGC is:

1. A forum for "gossip." Gossip also included matters of general interest relating to Germany and things German, for example, the wrapping of the *Reichstag* in Berlin, *Steffi Graf*, the German Film Fest in Singapore, German football players, and German technology.
2. An opportunity to use the language in a *real* context and to ask for help. ("I have difficulty figuring out which object is male, female, neuter, are there any gay objects?") One student posted a request for help in translating a postcard. This was duly provided from another student.
3. A platform to raise matters of common concern such as class tests and examinations and to air fears and concerns relating to the learning of the new language.

WHO WAS GOSSIPING?

Although the teacher identified herself by name, students, at least initially, assumed fictitious names: Phantom, Devil's Advocate, Herr Umlaut, Friedrich der Grosse, and Pumpernickel.

We discovered that the students who participated were highly communicative. Their interest in expressing themselves and saying something in the DGC was greater than their fear of not being correct. They switched to English when their knowledge of German was insufficient. This is typical of the Singaporean propensity to language switching noted earlier.

All students at the university have access to e-mail, and its use has been actively encouraged by senior academics. Computer conferencing links have been established with similar groups of students in Germany and the United States. Nevertheless, it is still new technology for many, with all its attendant stresses and challenges. The survey results attested to this by indicating that some of those who did not participate lacked confidence in their ability to use the computer and the Notes Conferencing System. In a later discussion with a group of students who had been among the most active contributors, it was found that these students all knew how to access and find their way around the Web and how to download files from online sites before being introduced to the DGC.

THE EFFECT OF THE *GOSSIP*

The most noticeable effects of the DGC was on the group dynamics of the classes. It fostered a sense of pride, promoted a positive attitude to the language and culture, motivated students to spend more time on German, encouraged the adoption of metacognitive strategies consistent with earlier findings (Fowler & Wheeler, 1995), and provided an environment for cooperative learning.

The DGC improved the classroom dynamics by providing students with a sense of belonging to an exclusive group which was entirely their own creation as well as a sense of pride of achievement: "This is our very own column; Only German language students can read it."

It provided further topics for both class and online discussion of the language (for example, German word formation; the longest German word, adjectival endings, and the problematics of the dative versus the accusative case).

The classroom provided feedback to the DGC and this process also worked in reverse. For example, one student "flamed" the group by suggesting that the DGC reduced German to a bunch of greetings and superficial statements as students' grasp of German was insufficient. This led to a discussion in the classroom and a later riposte in the DGC in which one of the students took a modern poem (incidentally demonstrating the use of possessive pronouns) and rewrote it to reply to the original student.

It provided incentive and motivation for students to spend additional time studying the language, not only at the time they entered their postings but also in planning and preparing what they were going to write. Despite the apparent spontaneity of the column, we learned in subsequent informal discussions that at least a few students spent some considerable time either separately or in discussion with friends, in advance planning of their postings.

It generated a sense of discovery and excitement as bewilderment with the new language gave rise to a metacognitive examination of students' own learning strategies and an interest in the learning strategies of others. "What was it that hit me?" was one posting title, followed by the observation: "I think I better start planning b4 I write my German sentences—what do the rest of u guys do? Type them out as u think?"

It sensitized students to formal and informal registers and styles of the language. It was noticed that the language needed to "chat" in the DGC was very different from the German taught in the classroom to pass the examination: "It is a different issue that when I try to write German the outcome isn't the German that Frau Morse teaches us!" It also, because they did not usually have their dictionaries with them when using the network, forced them to make do with their existing knowledge of the language and encouraged them to adopt the predictive, guessing strategies that are typical of "good" language learners.

It led to animated postings that made comparisons among the different languages with which the students were familiar; for example, the derivation of "tea" in Hokkien, Mandarin, Hindu and Tamil; the lack of tenses and articles in Mandarin; and letters that looked similar but behaved differently. This discussion was fueled when one of the group downloaded a lengthy extract from Mark Twain from the Web, in which he makes some unflattering comments on the German language. Students found this highly amusing and responded with a number of observations of their own.

It encouraged cooperative learning by providing a forum in which problems could be articulated and appropriate advice dispensed by a peer member. As students became aware of their own learning needs, it was possible to admit to having difficulties: "Mein Deutsch ist bad." Advice ranged from how to find the special characters used in the German "Umlaute" on the keyboard to psychological support and encouragement: "Aller Anfang ist schwer . . . (A translation of a Chinese proverb, "All beginnings are hard," which is also, as it happens, an everyday idiom in German) so don't be scared." This availability of friendly advice appeared to reduce the sense of isolation and allay the feelings of anxiety and insecurity that are common among language learners.

THE APPEAL OF THE *GOSSIP*

The use that students made of the DGC and their responses to the survey suggested that the gossip appealed to them in a variety of ways and provided an outlet that was not otherwise readily available for discussion of the language and investigation and sharing of their strategies for language learning in a metacognitive context.

Anonymity

The anonymity of the contributions was nonthreatening. Particularly in Asian society, in which loss of "face" is a serious social embarrassment, the opportunity to make an unidentified contribution that would not be subject to teacher correction was welcomed. Interestingly, as students became more confident and their mastery of the language increased, anonymity was superseded by a kind of reveling in the oratorical opportunity to address a "mass" audience. This was epitomized in one later posting that began, "Friends, Germans, Singaporeans . . . " It seemed that the initial anonymity may have contributed to building students' confidence in their ability to communicate in German.

Control of the Learning Situation

Related to the issue of anonymity was the ease of undoing or deleting what they had written. Unlike a classroom situation in which the spoken word cannot be unspoken, it is easy to delete a written phrase. This put the students more in control of the learning situation to the extent of being able to delete a note completely if they felt it was too outspoken. As their mastery of German increased and they "tried on" the roles of guru or orator, bold assertions would be followed up with blanket apologies lest the writer had inadvertently offended the susceptibilities of any of the group. Sometimes the apology would be posted at a later stage. In a classroom situation, this would be much harder, if not impossible, to do verbally.

Pride in Group Achievement

Being in control was enhanced by the knowledge that it was their own group, created by themselves. This fueled a sense of pride in the group effort: a sense that all were working on it, all belonged, and all were in the same position as beginning students, sharing the same kind of problems. Most Singaporeans attach great value to such group efforts. Further evidence of this pride was seen later in an almost proprietary interest in developing the language. It was observed that Singlish (the local English dialect) could be derived from the coupling of "SINGapore + EngLISH," so why not perform a similar process on "SINGapore + GerMAN" to derive SINGMAN? This obviously captured the imagination of a number of participants who proceeded to invent fanciful and amusing combinations of German and local words to represent how a SINGMAN would express him- or herself in various situations.

Voluntary Participation

The DGC was entirely voluntary. The suggestion that any part of the formal compulsory teaching such as homework should become part of the DGC met with a strong negative response. Being voluntary and created by the students, the postings took an informal, chatty tone that was more like a conversation than a piece of writing. The distinction between written and spoken language became blurred: "The column is there for us to gossip, to chat, to create." The DGC provided a contrast to the strongly goal oriented character of their formal academic studies, and the students seemed to experience a sense of relief in being able to "talk" in this informal way. According to one group, they often feel guilty if they indulge in what seems like inconsequential chatter: "We never sit together and just talk."

Using the DGC they could talk about the language as well as talk in the language and experiment with the language. The focus of discussion was very much on how German affected them personally rather than any academic or abstract view of what German might be (see the SINGMAN example discussed earlier). There was a sense of excitement as the students experienced the creative use of language in a context that was meaningful and relevant to them. A genuine interest in German and things German was kindled, which seemed likely to endure when the examination was long over.

GOSSIP FOR THE TEACHER

Although the Gossip, being voluntary and nonexaminable, demanded a substantial commitment from students, it also involved a tremendous amount of work for the teacher, who at the start was herself relatively unfamiliar with the technology. Nevertheless, she found that the benefits outweighed the costs, not only because the DGC extended and enhanced what could be provided in limited classroom time, but also because it helped beyond the classroom in the administration of the course.

The teacher was made aware through the DGC of problems that students had with the language but were unwilling to admit to in class. This was characteristic of the initial stages of the column.

The DGC extended and broadened the necessarily somewhat restricted classroom horizons by providing a channel to impart cultural and background information for which there was insufficient class time, thus encouraging a positive attitude to the language and culture. As speaking skills were not tested in the final written examination, it compensated for the small amount of class time that could be allocated for conversational German.

The DGC also provided a replacement for the simulation normally done in language teaching. It was a true-life situation in which learners were forced to struggle with their limited knowledge of the language to manipulate it to put their meaning across and to learn from their peers. As they did this, other sides of their personalities were revealed: They became more complete human beings, with likes, dislikes, and idiosyncrasies rather than just "typical" students.

As it gathered momentum the DGC eventually seemed to transform the role of the teacher to the point of apparent redundancy. Prior to the examination students began to post tables of verb endings and detailed explanations of, for example, the use of *Ihr* and *Sie*. It seemed that they were now comfortable with providing and accepting basic grammatical assistance from each other and no longer felt the need to rely on the expertise of the teacher. This is another example of the pride of ownership discussed earlier. Students having isolated particular points of difficulty for themselves worked through these points and then, with much pride, shared their newfound knowledge with their peers.

This development presented itself to us as a watershed in the DGC. The students had taken the column completely into their own hands, no longer seeing themselves as needing to refer to the teacher for advice on grammatical problems. Now their teacher-directed queries focused more on cultural questions and issues, a gratifying development from the teacher's point of view.

5. In administrative matters, the DGC provided a valuable medium to assist in the coordination of part-time teachers. It was used to alert co-teachers to last minute additions to the syllabus, to assist in maintaining content parity among the classes, and to encourage uniformity in teaching approaches.

SPREADING THE GOSSIP

Voluntary or Compulsory?

A major question that faced the teacher on reflecting on the outcomes of the DGC was whether it should become an integral (i.e., nonvoluntary) part of the subject.

On the one hand, it would ensure that all students had an opportunity to explore a medium that gives them a chance that the classroom does not provide to use the language in a real situation. On the other hand, the students were both contributors and noncontributors and were very much against including the DGC as a formal part of the course.

Need for Training

One major deterrent to voluntary participation is students' lack of confidence in using the technology. This, coupled with a sense of lack of time and a need to cover the syllabus adequately to achieve success in the examination, apparently deterred a number of potential gossips. This could be to some extent overcome by incorporating a brief training session into one of the initial class meetings. At this session, the idea of the DGC could be introduced and discussed, backed up with a brief handout on how to access and use the system. After that, students could be kept informed of current discussions and encouraged to make their own contributions.

Self-help Counseling Function

Koul (1995) refers to the difficulties experienced by some students in developing countries in coping with problems that arise specifically from their studies. Their cultural background of an extended family leads them to expect that any problems will be resolved within the family. They may be reluctant to talk about problems outside the family or even to recognize that it is legitimate to seek help from professional counselors. The problems they experience with their studies, however, are new to both themselves and their families. So there is no source of advice within the families. Students in these circumstances may become discouraged and blame themselves for what they see as their own inadequacies.

Singaporean students exhibit some of these characteristics. It may be that the opportunity to share their experiences with other students using CMC and guaranteeing anonymity provides a valuable outlet for working toward the resolution of some of these academic-related problems. The ability to articulate an issue is often the first step to finding a solution and, as we have seen, the DGC "forced" students into some articulation of what they wanted to say and reduced the "isolation" that is frequently felt by language learners.

It is not only in Singapore, however, that students are reluctant to admit to academic problems and may find these problems compounded because their immediate families lack an understanding of the nature of them. This can be true in many situations and many cultures, and it may be that CMC can go some way to supplying part of a contemporary solution to these problems.

Metacognitive Environment

Pearson and Santa (1995) noted that when their students "investigated their own learning, they seemed to feel more ownership in their work" (p. 469). Although there was certainly no formal attempt to introduce students to the idea of metacognition as Pearson and Santa described how they did for their High School students, it seemed that the DGC provided a type of active learning environment that encouraged students to reflect on and share their own learning and studying strategies and certainly to experience the pride of ownership of their achievements.

In this respect, it seemed to us that the opportunities provided by the shared forum of the DGC provided a type of learning that from an instructional viewpoint was significantly different from the one-on-one communication generated by individual linkups with students in other locations.

World-Wide Web

It seems appropriate to make a brief mention and comparison of the function of the DGC, which might in Singaporean terms be described as a virtual coffee shop, with other language learning programs available to a wider audience on the Web. MOOs (Sanchez & Turbee, 1995) allow users to meet in real time rather than asynchronously to exchange information, ideas and viewpoints. MOOs are Multiple-user domains, Object-Oriented, software applications that allow multiple users to interact in a virtual reality environment by means of the computer keyboard. The experience of Venezuelan interns at Syracuse University (Lewis & Romiszowski, 1995) suggests that once the technology is mastered and initial inhibitions about interacting with strangers are overcome, access to a MOO can become a fascinating and valuable means of language learning and improvement. This may prove to be a future DGC development.

CONCLUSION

Fowler and Wheeler (1995) observed that CMC changed the educational context for students, impacting on the social organization of the classroom and encouraging patterns of cooperative learning. We have had a similar experience in studying the way that beginning language students used the DGC. In particular, we found that:

- it enabled students to appreciate and experience the relevance of what they were learning in class

- it encouraged students to take a more active and metacognitive approach to their study of German as they shared learning strategies and discovered what worked best for them
- it encouraged collaborative sharing of learning among students
- it transformed the role of the teacher.

We hope this will encourage other teachers to join us in the exploration of further uses of CMC for language learning. And as one of the most recent postings said, "Lang lebe die *Deutsch Gossip.*"

REFERENCES

Fowler, L. S., & Wheeler, D. D. (1995). Online from the K-12 classroom. In Z. L. Berge & M. P. Collins (Eds.), *Computer-mediated communication and the online classroom* (pp. 83-100). Cresskill, NJ: Hampton Press.

Koul, B. N. (1995). Trends, directions and needs: A view from developing countries. In F. Lockwood (Ed.), *Open and distance learning today* (pp. 23-31). London: Routledge.

Lewis, J. H., & Romiszowski, A. (1995, November). *Networking and the learning organization: Networking issues and scenarios for the 21st century.* Paper presented at the IDLN First International Symposium, "Networking into the 21st Century," Yogyakarta, Indonesia.

Pearson, J. W., & Santa, C. M. (1995). Students as researchers of their own Learning. *Journal of Reading, 38*(6), 462-469.

Sanchez (Guernsey), B., & Turbee (Colega), L. (1995). *MOOing to a new frontier in language learning.* Paper presented at the 1995 National Foreign Language Resource Centre Networking Symposium.

16

THE AP GERMAN CMC CLASSROOM

Werner Dobner

This course is designed for high school students who are planning to take the AP German Language Exam administered by the College Board usually sometime in May of each year. Because about 50% of this exam is written, students write texts via the computer on topics designated by the teacher or on the program.

PREREQUISITES

The nature of the course necessitates a few prerequisites: The students must be fluent enough in advanced German to be able to largely dispense with speaking and listening exercises. The emphasis is on improving writing skills. High school students should have access to a computer station with an e-mail program on a 50 minute daily basis. Students should be able to be monitored by a German teacher, who corrects their work. Many other aspects of the course are self-monitored and self-programmed.

OBJECTIVE

The program's goal is to eradicate what I have identified as the 10 most common errors made in German by Americans. A "Correction Table" has been designed, listing these common errors with the numbers 1-10. The students receive two grades for every written assignment, one grade for the way they handle German—that is, for their command of the language and their articulation—and a second grade for the correction. The teacher reads the compositions and marks the number of the error that corresponds to the "correction table," thus identifying the mistake. The students then make the correction, where the actual learning process takes place, and return it to the teacher for the correction grade. It is suggested to be rather lenient in grading the first draft but very strict in grading the second. This encourages the student to be particularly meticulous in making the correction and pursuing the correct answer. Taking off 5 points per mistake remaining in the correction is a viable procedure.

PROCEDURE

Because this idea of eradicating the 10 most common errors made in written German through the use of a correction table is so central to this program, it is important to dwell on it a bit. The correction table not only identifies the error, but also includes a summary of the rules for each of the 10 common errors. It would be too cumbersome to publish the entire list here, but the following excerpt should make the procedure clear:

> On your work I will indicate the # that identifies your mistake. When you make corrections, do not erase my number. For example:
>
> *Ich wissen* (4), *das* (7) *er kann* (1) *kommen* (1) *nach die* (5) *schule* (3) *nicht* (2).

You would identify your mistakes on the correction table, make your correction, but leave the numbers.

> *Ich weiss* (4), *dass* (7) *er nach der* (5) *Schule* (3) *nicht* (2) *kommen kann.*
>
> The only time it may be necessary to erase the numbers would be in the case of wrong word order.

Note: In e-mail programs that allow changing colors or other means of highlighting, the students make the corrections in a different color, allowing the teacher to "zoom in" on the correction without having to read the entire composition anew.

The 10 Most Common Errors and a Summary of Rules:

1. Word order:
   a. regular: subj/verb/complement (rest of sentence), e.g., *Ich gehe heute nachmittag.*
   b. inverted: complement/verb/subject, e.g., *Heute nachmittag gehe ich.*
   c. "verb last" word order occurs in a dependent clause, e.g., *Er weiss, dass ich heute nachmittag gehe.*
2. Position of *nicht*
   a. *nicht* goes after the subject, verb, or direct object, whichever comes last in the sentence. Or it goes in front of phrases that tell "where or when," e.g., *Ich kenne den Mann nicht. Ich bin nicht in Hamburg geboren.*
3. Capitalization
   a. In general, capitalize all nouns, do not capitalize pronouns or adjectives, e.g., *Mein Bruder* (noun) *und ich* (pronoun) *haben eine amerikanische* (adj) *Fahne* (noun).
   b. Capitalize all pronouns and possessive adjectives in the formal address (you, your when using a title), e.g., *Frau Schmidt, gehen Sie* (you) *mit Ihrem* (possessive adj) *Freund ins Kino*? etc.

The other seven most common errors are (4) subject/verb agreement; (5) wrong case; (6) wrong adjective ending; (7) *das/dass*; (8) *wenn, wann, als*; (9) *nach, zu,* in meaning "to;" and (10) catch all—spelling, wrong gender, wrong plural, wrong participle form, and so on.

WRITING ASSIGNMENTS

The writing exercises need to be varied in order to keep the interest of the student to a maximum. These are exercises to increase the student's volume of vocabulary. The following is a list of categories or formats in which the students may write ("Variety is the spice of life"):

1. Phone conversation: Put in an order by phone, make a date, complain about a service or a product
2. Responses: List statements to which the student must answer—Where were you at 3 p.m.? I thought we were supposed to meet!
3. Fairy Tales: Tell a fairy tale from the viewpoint of a certain character, e.g., the witch in Hansel & Gretel.
4. News: Write a report about a current headline.
5. TV: Tell about an unusual happening during a TV show.

6. Film: Discuss why did you/did you not like a certain film.
7. Opinion: Take a stand on suicide, death penalty, broadcasting trials (O.J. Simpson), red or green hair, and so on.
8. Proverbs: Explain (in German) *Luegen haben kurze Beine* [Lies have short legs], Too many cooks spoil the broth, and so on. Do not translate, explain.
9. Trivial pursuit: Describe in your own words in German: Mercedes Benz, *Loewenzahn* [dandelion].
10. Jokes: Tell a joke in German, build up to the punch line.
11. Situation: Describe what is going through your mind as you are walking alone in a dark forest, as you are buying a gift for a friend, or as you are thinking about what to cook (or eat) that night.
12. Literature: Read, for example, *An Diesem Dienstag*, by Wolfgang Brochert, and answer the following questions in essay style.

One of the most important components of the AP German Language Exam is the composition. Fifty out of the 180 minutes are dedicated to this exercise. It is therefore of utmost importance that the students get a lot of practice in writing good compositions. Sample directions for a composition are included here.

Composition: suggested time: 50 minutes. Percent of Section II score: 75%

(You see what weight is given to this particular exercise

Directions: Write in German a well-organized and coherent composition of about 200 to 250 words on the topic below. Spend the first few minutes organizing your thoughts and the last few minutes proofreading your work. Your composition should state and develop these thoughts. Your work will be evaluated for grammatical accuracy, variety, range, as well as appropriateness of vocabulary and idioms, spelling, and organization. You will receive no extra credit for exceeding the prescribed length, but credit will be deducted for compositions that are too short. NO credit will be given for compositions that do not address the topic.

Here is the topic (translation follows):

Eine Freundin oder ein Freund aus Amerika wird Sie auf laengere Zeit besuchen. Schreiben Sie ueber mindestens drei der folgenden Punkte:

1. *Die Lage Ihrer Stadt und die Verkersmoeglichkeiten*
2. *Klima und Kleidung*
3. *Freizeit und Unterhaltung*
4. *Besondere Feste*

Translation: A friend from the United States is coming to visit you for some time. Write about at least three of the following points:

1. The region in which your city is located and the means of public transportation
2. Climate and clothing
3. Leisure and entertainment
4. Special events

PARTNER OR GROUP EXERCISES

There are many opportunities in this program to get the students to communicate with each other. This can be done either by way of a bulletin board to which all students and the teacher have access or directly by having students communicate with each other individually via e-mail.

The bulletin board is well suited to expand the knowledge of a certain topic or to personalize a topic. For example:

1. Write a report (in German) about the German Karneval season.
2. Write about your personal experience with a Karneval event.

Direct communication among members of the class can be elicited through interviews or projects for smaller groups. An example of an interview follows:

1. Ask at least three of your classmates the same questions about their likes and dislikes—and write a report.
2. Form a research group with three or four of your classmates and report on the place of ecology in Germany, how are sports organized in Germany as compared to the United States, German public transportation, and so on.

Grammar and Fill-in Exercises

Some of the assignments that need only minimal intervention or interaction on the part of the teacher are grammar or fill-in exercises, as well as multiple-choice items.

Any good German grammar book may be used, as long as the teacher and the students use the same version, of course. A very good text is *A Practical Review of German Grammar* by Gerda Dippmann (Macmillan). The students do the grammar exercises and then correct their own work by means of an answer sheet sent out by the teacher after the exercise has been completed.

Literature

By using the same correcting method as for grammar or fill-in exercises, students are also exposed to good German literature. They read the text and answer questions, either multiple-choice or fill-in tests or, as mentioned earlier, in essay style.

Oral Work

Learning a language is accomplished not only in writing but also in reading and speaking. Although the main thrust of this course by e-mail is improving writing skills, the teacher may also elicit the students to make real phone calls in German to set up appointments, make reservations, or find out information. The students then make a written report about these phone calls. The AP German Language Exam has the candidates speak on tape while looking at conversation prompts, or the candidates must look at a series of pictures that tell a story and then recount that story on tape. It is an easy matter to send the students of this course copies of such picture stories and have them recount them orally to the teacher by phone.

In addition, preparation for the oral aspects of the exam is provided by phone calls to the teacher and by teacher-prepared tapes that contain texts to which the students respond in the form of multiple choice or true and false questions that are written on the computer screen. The teacher can direct the students to bring magazines containing advertisements to the phone and describe these ads to the teacher during the phone call or record them on an audiotape, which is then sent to the teacher.

CLOSING REMARKS

As is the case in any venture, the more the learner puts into the project, the more he or she will get out of it. This maxim holds particularly true for this course. Because many aspects of this course are self-programmed, the student must bring along a good measure of self-discipline and a firm desire to learn.

V

AUDIOGRAPHICS IN SECOND LANGUAGE LEARNING

17

ELEMENTARY SCHOOL USE OF AUDIOGRAPHICS FOR LEARNING LANGUAGES

Elizabeth Stacey

THE NEED FOR COMPUTER-MEDIATED COMMUNICATION

Students who learn in small sized groups, whether in remote country schools, in town and city schools with unevenly distributed populations, or in isolated situations that are only served by distance education, are often denied the opportunity of learning in curriculum areas that require specialist interactive teaching. The cost of providing specialist teachers for only a small number of students in learning content areas such as foreign languages has meant that often those students have only been offered a limited range of curriculum areas. School authorities in Australia, seeking to redress this inequality, investigated the capabilities of audiographic technology as a form of synchronous computer-mediated communication (CMC) that would enable a teacher to teach a larger number of students more frequently without the necessity of a face-to-face classroom presence (Gray & O'Grady; 1993, Stacey, 1994). Audiographics appeared to provide a communication link between school sites so that a teacher could effectively teach students in their own classroom and at remote sites simultaneously. This could provide a cost-effective, relatively easy-to-use technology that would attempt to simulate the interaction of a real classroom and engage the students in an extended "real-time" classroom (Oliver & Reeves, 1994).

AUDIOGRAPHIC TECHNOLOGIES

Audiographic technologies are a combination of telephone conferencing for an aural/oral link, facsimile use for immediate document transfer, and synchronous computer-mediated communication using specialized software for linking computer screens so that text and graphics can be shared on screen like an electronic "chalkboard." To teach audiographically, a telephone conference is established between the teacher and students at all sites using speaker phones or audio conferencing units with microphones and speakers. When more than two callers are linked, an audio-conferencing bridge is used. A visual focus for the lesson, for explaining pictures, diagrams, or maps, interacting with students solving mathematical problems, or analyzing text together as a class can then be provided with computers and software programs that are available for all computer types. These establish a shared interactive computer screen that is visible in several locations simultaneously when the computers are linked by modems plugged into telephone lines. Teachers can prepare screens before a lesson and download them at any time before or during the lesson or alternatively use a series of empty screens to develop material interactively with students during the lesson.

These technologies seemed to provide the required interactive communication link between school sites, and it was hoped that with audiographics, a teacher could effectively teach students in their own classroom and at remote sites simultaneously. However, to ensure that teaching and learning were effective in these technologically simulated classrooms, extensive trial studies and partnerships between classroom teachers, university researchers, and specialist consultants were established.

In an emerging globally focused and multicultural society, languages other than English (called by the acronym LOTE) are being viewed by Australian school authorities as a key learning content area to be offered in both secondary and elementary schools. Audiographics enabled remote or organizationally isolated schools to participate in learning languages when access to face-to-face teaching was difficult to organize. If one LOTE teacher is shared between a cluster of schools (e.g., two to three schools), and includes audiographically connected students in face-to-face classroom sessions, students can gain access to additional classes in their language. Preliminary work with audiographics showed that languages were particularly well suited to a medium that focused on the aural and oral components of a lesson with a graphic facility for further explanations.

PARTNERSHIP PROJECTS

This chapter describes how our university worked in partnership with three clusters of schools sharing resources for teaching three different languages—Chinese, Italian, and Indonesian—and incorporating the use of audiographics. The aim of the partnerships was to establish good pedagogical models for language learning using this form of synchronous computer-mediated communication.

The university team worked closely with the teachers in schools who were establishing LOTE programs with audiographic links. In the first partnership, the focus was on the introduction and establishment of audiographics into a classroom LOTE program. The teacher of Chinese was helped by a university teacher who was situated at the remote site to which the audiographic lessons were transmitted, observing and assisting technically when needed. Reflective discussions about each lesson helped the Chinese teacher and the university teacher establish effective models of audiographic teaching.

In the other partnerships, teachers of Indonesian in a cluster of schools in a country area, and a city school with an exemplary program in teaching Italian, worked in partnership with the university team to establish good models of audiographic teaching. Their classrooms were linked audiographically to the university campus where student teachers taught language lessons to small groups of children each week with staff supervision. The students later spent a period of practice teaching in the schools and further developed their skills with audiographics. The university team researched their experiences and particularly focused on developing models of good audiographic teaching and analyzing issues of professional development and staff support. The principles described for models of effective audiographic teaching and professional development and support of staff are a result of these partnership programs.

OUTCOMES OF PARTNERSHIPS

Introducing Audiographics

Developing a model of technology introduction, often a difficult process of change when a teacher is lacking in confidence with computer technology, was the goal of the first partnership. The teacher had participated in a three-day hands-on workshop to learn how to use the technology, and she initially established small groups of 6 children at two locations, who acted as one class of 12 children for an hour each week for five weeks. The teacher taught Chinese to the class from on site at one elementary school, whereas the group of children at the audiographically linked remote school were supervised and helped by their class teacher. The groups spent an hour of preparation each week learning computer skills, specific vocabulary for the lesson, greetings, and informal conversation skills prior to the telematic linkup. We used the initial trial groups to develop teaching strategies for maximizing the effectiveness of the use of telematics in the LOTE classroom and to develop an understanding of the developmental phases of introducing this technology—its effects on the classroom environment and the attitudes and adjustments of students and teachers involved in its use.

Technical Learning Phase

During the first lessons we developed skills with the use of the technology and overcame the frustration of faulty modems, inadequate speaker phones, and our own inexperience. Building in such a learning phase to any program is important as learning to use the technology can dominate early lessons and, if not recognized as a valid learning process, could frustrate teachers concerned that the language content of the initial lessons was being neglected.

Linking and Language

We used the audio link first to talk our way through the modem/computer linking process so that everyone knew what was happening. Once the linkup was made, Chinese was the language of use, with English only for technical emergencies.

Teaching Partner

The involvement of the supervising teacher at the remote end of an elementary audiographic class was crucial in encouraging the smooth running and correct pedagogical approach to language learning. If this partner teacher was an active participant in learning the language, there was a greater quality of student interaction in the lessons.

With an older student group, responsibility for organizational setup and support of the remote ends of audiographic linkups may be placed with the students. However, each school must ensure these roles are supervised by a delegated teacher in the school or organizational problems of time-tabling of the availability and readiness of equipment and resources can make the program less effective.

Preparatory Practice and Materials

The Chinese teacher found it important to give the children preparatory practice in computer use and, in conversation, teaching appropriate responses and vocabulary for the specific lessons that were to be taught telematically. She provided children with information sheets to help them through the spoken language of each lesson, and this gave the children security as they developed their conversational repertoire. This role would need to be taken up by the classroom teacher if there was no face-to-face contact with the LOTE audiographics teacher.

Classroom Contexts

The first part of the lesson was always spent exchanging greetings and personal information and conversation. A classroom had to be conceptually established with all participants aware of all the identities of other students in the lesson and their physical placement. Using the draw facility to create a classroom diagram of everyone's location helped each participant visualize the other unseen classroom environment. The development of the group dynamics of the classroom was as important for effective interaction as it is in a normal classroom.

Monitoring Participation

The teacher had to monitor each child at the remote location to ensure that they were all participating. She addressed students by name and asked for their involvement in turn in the lesson. Students improved their spoken delivery to a clear, slow style that could be understood better over the speaker phones.

Interactive Focus

Students were included in "hands-on" activities as soon as possible so that they were all involved in the interactive visual focus of the lesson on the computer screen. A sequence of lessons was devised that had the children taking turns speaking, drawing, writing, and always listening carefully. These involved students at one location giving directions or descriptions to the students at the other location, who then drew or wrote to the screen or faxed their responses. Topics included their own physical description and creating monsters or animals following oral directions with both strategies using vocabulary about body parts, shapes, prepositional phrases, colors, and size. Students also described and drew house plans and scenes that use similar vocabulary about buildings, furniture, places, and external and internal scenery. The children played games and sang songs and generally mirrored good interactive LOTE classroom strategies.

Class Size

Our trial sessions showed the benefits of keeping the total multisite class to a manageable number with the optimum group size dependent on the type of equipment being used. This had to ensure that all participants could see the screen (whether computer projection or multicomputer networking was possible) and be able to actively interact. Group size impacted on the noise level of the class that had to be managed to ensure that adequate speaker phone reception could be maintained and all spoken interactions were able to be heard.

Establishing Models of Audiographic Teaching

The partnerships that audiographically linked students at the university campuses to children in remote classrooms built on this knowledge of effective teaching, learning, and management strategies for teaching audiographically while practicing effective LOTE methodology. The study again focused on developing the technical expertise of teachers and students to an independent level of competence in handling audiographic technology with the ability to problem solve when problems arose during linkups or when software or hardware functioned incorrectly.

Student teachers prepared a range of language lessons across the curriculum in mathematics, story writing and reading, science and cultural learning. Strategies were needed that supported the children's understanding even though the distance mode limited the nonverbal clues to meaning. The use of English was limited providing a real purpose to use the LOTE.

Classroom Teacher's Support

The distance mode encouraged the children to take greater responsibility for their own learning but also relied on the classroom teacher's support for prelesson preparation. Developing strategies to establish and encourage the classroom teacher's role were important. The classroom teacher needed to be fully informed of the necessary preparation and the content of the lesson. This enabled them to support the audiographic teaching even though they may not be a speaker of the LOTE. Providing time to prepare the language charts and other support material that enabled the children to understand and use the LOTE during the linkup was vital. The student teachers also needed information on current classroom topics and content. A template for audiographic lesson planning was developed and used by a consultant group of experienced audiographic teachers working with the university team, and this was completed and faxed to the classroom teacher a week before an audiographic lesson to allow for preparatory activities and organization to occur prior to the audiographics lesson.

Effects on Students' Learning

The medium provided an authentic purpose for using the language, which is often difficult to establish in a school environment. The children were accountable for their learning when they had to speak the language to children at the remote site, and the teacher found that the children were prepared to learn their vocabulary when they had previously lacked motivation to do so.

The children responded enthusiastically and positively to telematics even when there were technical difficulties and the linkup took up a large part of the lesson time. They saw telematics as "fun" and from that perspective had few negative reactions to learning this way. The computer and related technology were motivating and contributed to the perception of telematics as fun.

The communication with unknown students motivated many students to improve their conversational skills so that they could interact effectively with these unseen classmates. The audiographics gave them a potential of a wider community of language learners—important for many isolated students. Learning was seen as relevant and purposeful, and the added small group teaching contributed to the success of the program.

The teacher education students concentrated on using their LOTE more, and the children responded to this by using their language more. They found that children "were compelled to use the language, either written or spoken rather than using hand gestures and bypassing the language," and that this medium demands "good articulation of language for communication."

The small group nature of such learning involved all the children in the group compared to many class lessons that provide minimal involvement for some children.

Children were willing to "have a go." They progressed from answering with one word to trying to use a whole sentence. Their listening skills and comprehension improved, and they had to become more organized to answer questions. Peer tutoring was an effective way for children learning to use the technology—children could even be the experts that helped the teachers.

The children perceived that they had more freedom to ask questions, they were not chastised. One said, "you don't get embarrassed." They admitted to feeling less likely to "get into trouble" when the teacher could not see them.

Keyboarding skills were important for confident and effective interaction, and time had to be allocated for these skills to be developed.

Staff Needs for Support and Development

The projects researched and analyzed the issues affecting staff incorporating audiographics into their language teaching programs. The issues identified included the following.

Professional development and technical backup. The need for teachers to receive sufficient hands-on training with the equipment, as well as learning effective strategies for teaching telematically, were seen as high priorities by all teachers in the program. Expert support needed to be available to help with problems as they arose. Such access to expert advice was essential to establishing technical confidence and competence.

Whole school support. Teachers developed negative attitudes to telematic use when they perceived a lack of support from the whole school staff. When space was not dedicated to telematic learning sessions and staff borrowed equipment and did not return it or leave it ready for a telematic lesson, the telematic teaching became stressful. Time-tabling had to be agreed on by classroom teachers at all locations so that both teachers and students did not see the telematic lesson as an intrusion into their program. "Plenty of time free of interruption " was seen as an ideal coupled with a willingness of the remote school to work cooperatively.

Model for technology setup. "Locations that allow effective use of equipment with minimal disruption to classes" was seen as an ideal, with "a quiet, controlled work space." If space was not sufficient teachers were frustrated with their attempts to run the program effectively. Some groups were held in principals' offices and school staff rooms, which presented problems and interruptions. The need for dedicated equipment that was not moved was an important factor for success of the program. Recurrent phone costs, additional phone lines, and help with setup were additional organizational issues that teachers needed to address. Situations in which teachers were unsupported became stressful.

CONCLUSIONS

The study developed a model of effective strategies for introducing audiographic technology and incorporating it into effective language learning programs. Issues of professional development and support of staff were also identified and discussed.

The supervising teacher at the remote location as a partner in the telematics lesson was essential. Teachers had to plan ahead, send material to the classroom teacher well before the lesson, and be organized. Audiographics is a very accountable medium, unforgiving if materials are not at hand or well thought out. Supervising teachers were informed of the lesson content and any necessary preparation prior to the lesson. They gave the students the time and opportunity for preparing materials and activities in preparation for the telematic lesson. Often this was material they needed to refer to during the linkup. It would be displayed around the computer or brought to the lesson.

The environment was important at both ends of the linkup. Charts and pictures were displayed around the students' computers to provide context clues as in face-to-face language lessons. Student teachers referred to labeled photographs of their students at the remote site while teaching the lesson to help establish a real rapport and relationship despite the distance.

Interactive lessons that replaced the usual visual focus of the classroom by an involvement with the computer screen were important. Lessons were designed to ensure that all children were speaking, drawing, writing, and actively listening.

Teachers required good professional development and technical and school support to successfully incorporate audiographics into their teaching. Time for learning to teach with the technology, to experiment and adapt exemplary models of audiographic teaching into their programs, was essential for effective audiographic implementation into language learning.

REFERENCES

Gray, A., & O'Grady, G. (1993). Telecommunications pedagogy for effective teaching and learning. In G. Davits, & B. Samways (Eds.), *Teleteaching* (pp. 307-316). North-Holland: Elsevier Science.

Oliver, R., & Reeves, T. (1994). *Telematics in rural education: An investigation of the use of telematics for the delivery of specialist programmes for students in rural schools.* Perth: Intech Innovations.

Stacey, E. (1994). Technology overcomes Australian distances. *Technological Horizons in Education Journal, 21*(6), 56-59.

18

CHALLENGES TO TEACHING HIGH SCHOOL CLASSES OVER DISTANCE LEARNING SYSTEMS

Stephen W. Zsiray, Jr.

Distance learning has the potential to expand high school curricular offerings by giving students access to programs from an unlimited number of remote locations. The EDNET program, a statewide distance learning initiative, has the goal of placing a two-way, interactive, fiber-optic-based distance learning center in each Utah High School. EDNET literally stands for "education network," which allows schools to interface, using a televised interactive system, offering classes that would not otherwise be available to students.

For the past two years the Cache School District has pioneered the development of programs offered on the system. A unique partnership has developed that has enabled high school students in Utah to learn Russian, a most important strategic language. This partnership involves the Cache County School District, Utah State University, and the Utah State Office of Education.

Two very successful programs are the Introduction to Russian 100 and 200 series. These courses are offered as concurrent enrollment classes through Utah State University. Concurrent enrollment classes give high school students the opportunity to earn university credit for classes taught on the high school campus by a university-approved teacher. The courses originate from Mountain Crest High School,

Hyrum, UT and are broadcast to five other locations in Utah. Russian classes are now available to any high school in the state of Utah with an EDNET receiving system.

A comprehensive instructional sequence has been developed that utilizes the features of the distance learning system. The instructor utilizes the Elmo multimedia delivery system to access overhead transparencies that contain graphic advanced organizers, to highlight important segments of information contained on the transparency, and to switch cameras to focus on student interactions. In addition, videotape and videodisc sequences are delivered to students through traditional delivery systems. During the school year, CD-ROMs will be used as a means to deliver multimedia materials such as slides, video, computer-generated graphics, and computer-based instruction. Students also utilize an interactive Russian software package designed to reinforce the conversational aspects of the language and basic vocabulary. This software will run on either Macintosh or PC platforms.

This chapter describes the elements of distance learning systems, the EDNET system, and some of the administrative issues involved in its day-to-day management. It concludes with a case study description of our Russian language instruction.

ELEMENTS OF DISTANCE LEARNING SYSTEMS

Generally speaking, distance education takes place when a teacher and students are separated by physical distance, and technology (i.e., voice, video, data, and print) is used to bridge the instructional gap (Willis, 1993). Three key elements of distance learning systems must be satisfied in order for successful instruction to occur: student expectations, teacher expectations, and classroom environment (Utah Education Network, 1994; Zsiray & Menlove, 1994). In addition, administrative expectations must also be considered.

Student Expectations

A high degree of student decorum is necessary in a distance learning classroom. It is difficult to manage a multisite classroom. For the instruction to be successful in this electronic medium, students need to be courteous and polite in the classroom. Students should be highly motivated and self-disciplined, especially when they are receiving instruction from a remote location. Students participate in class by interacting with the instructor and the students at the other sites. This interaction involves the ability to work with individuals from several locations simultaneously broadcast over the system. Students work more independently by watching programs and reading printed materials.

Teacher Expectations

Distance learning courses have the same academic content and student outcome requirements as regular high school or college (on-campus) classes. Quality is not compromised but delivery is a new process for teachers. Significant training efforts are needed to bring the teacher up to speed on the use of the technology used to support the instruction. Training programs have emerged as a result of efforts by the Utah Education Network (Utah State Office of Education, 1996). Teachers will also need to customize and adapt instruction to not only meet student needs but to facilitate efficient delivery of instruction over the distance learning system. Teachers expect students to be highly motivated. Students must be able to sometimes function as independent, self-directed learners, especially if the system is down. Teachers must have a solid support network established that includes the school and district administration, department heads, technical specialists, and parents. Teachers must be flexible due to changing high school schedules and expect sites to be connected at different times. This translates to students entering and leaving the class according to the schedule of the various receiving sites.

Meaningful Interactive Instruction

Meaningful interactive instruction is interpreted as the way in which the teacher at the origination site designs the instructional sequence of the lesson to give the students in the remote/receive site a feeling of teacher presence that extends beyond the video screen and the audio speaker. Creating an environment for learning simultaneously at both the origination and receive sites is a challenge. The teachers in the system recognize that the key to a successful learning experience for the student is to actively engage the students from the origination and receive sites. Meaningful learning in an electronic classroom extends beyond the information in contained in the class syllabus but extends to formal and informal discussion between students and teacher, and dialog between students from around the globe who are interested in the same topics and ideas. A motivated teacher who understands course content, methods of teaching, and appropriate use of the technology, can build meaningful interactive instruction.

Classroom Environment

Teachers must be familiar with the technology employed in the electronic classroom. Both the origination and the receiving sites should have a trained paraprofessional or technician to manage the technical aspects of the classroom. These include video cameras, microphones, and the control console. Students in the receiving sites need to know how to use the microphones properly. Classes of 30 students sharing six to eight microphones becomes a logistical nightmare if students are not properly trained to use these devices. Furthermore, students from receiving sites also communicate with the instructor during class using telephones, faxes, and e-mail.

Administrator Expectations

Administrative personnel can be categorized as both external and internal to the school district.

External to the school district. A clear communication link needs to be established between the originating and receiving sites with the data hub site. The data hub serves as the conduit from the originating to the receiving sites. It is crucial that in the case of hub site administration there is a "real-time" person to speak to about concerns relative to the operation of the signals.

Internal to the school site. Several key positions need to be identified in each school to make the distance learning system operate smoothly. These include: a district office administrator willing to serve as the system coordinator, who could be an assistant superintendent or a curriculum director, and a distance learning administrator at each school high school site, who is usually the assistant principal or department head. Training for administrators must include the design of the schedule of classes, building logistics, teacher training, and a general knowledge of the important characteristics of the distance learning system.

The distance learning technician, a person who understands electronic systems, is needed in each site for purposes of maintaining the operational quality of the system as well as making sure that microphones are connected and the system is running. This individual could be a teacher already on staff who has an affinity for electronics and is willing to learn, but we recommend that a new staff position be created and a trained paraprofessional employed. Training will also need to be provided for the technician.

IDENTIFICATION OF TEACHING STAFF

Identifying the teaching staff is critical. We have looked for the "risk-taking," "change agent"-type teachers and determined whether the subjects they taught meet the needs of students. The system needs are based on classes required by students that they would not normally have access to in the conventional high school schedule. Usually, the classes are offered in the larger urban or suburban high school or in cases in which a teacher on staff may have a special expertise to teach the class.

It is important to provide these individuals with training opportunities to learn the important characteristics and nuances of the system. Local school districts in collaboration with agencies such as State Offices of Education, local universities, and the private sector (e.g., U.S. West Communications) provide additional training options. More comprehensive programs are needed to train teachers. Teachers in the Cache School District have developed a training manual for prospective teachers (Obray, Zsiray, & Menlove, 1994). We need to continue to develop responsive teacher training needs. A mentor teacher program has been established to allow the veteran EDNET teachers to assist the new teachers in preparation of class materials, and methods of instructional delivery. Regional teacher development centers must be established to give teachers formal training and support opportunities to develop expertise in the use of distance learning technologies to support effective instruction (Zsiray & Wilde, 1995).

ESTABLISH SCHEDULE AND FUNDING STRUCTURE

Alignment of high school schedules is a complex and controversial topic. Many school staffs have spent considerable time on a schedule that uniquely fits the needs of the school. To fit the needs of several schools linked together by distance education requires a convergence of philosophies and common interests. When trying to correlate a five-period trimester schedule with a four-period A/B rollover schedule, a high degree of flexibility is in order. Furthermore, classes may also be placed outside the school schedule, either before or after regular school hours. Funds must be built into the district budget for teacher compensation. Some guidelines developed are that teachers are paid $1,500 to develop a new class and $250 each time the class is taught over a trimester (10-week period).

OPERATIONAL ISSUES

After two years of operation, we have some preliminary findings regarding the use of the system. We are presenting an ideal system and one that we hope to implement this next school year. To operate an efficient distance learning program, the following criteria must be considered.

Cost

It is extremely critical that funds be expended to adequately equip an electronic classroom to effectively teach the course content to students. The following hardware and software in Table 18.1 is representative of a minimal system.

Communication Lines

To date, US West Communications is providing the communication lines through an agreement with the Utah Education Network. High schools are equipped with either T-1 or fiber-optic lines, depending on the availability of the fiber optics.

Interactivity

We will conduct studies to determine the needs of teachers and students so they can better communicate with each other in the electronic classroom. Issues such as hardware requirements, number of microphones, monitor size, and presentation software will be investigated.

Table 18.1. Hardware and Software Used by the EDNET System.

Hardware

- fiber-optic or T-1 transmission system
- electronic visual presentation system (in our case the Elmo system)
- two 27" television monitors
- large-screen data/video projection system
- Pentium-based or Power PC system with multimedia capability
- direct telephone line for Fax and Internet connectivity
- room modification for air conditioning
- tables for the rooms
- fax/copy machine
- videotape player
- videodisc player
- printer

Software

- presentation package (PowerPoint, etc.)
- word processor
- spreadsheet
- electronic mail interface (eg., Interslip connection)

Linkage with Other Distance Learning Systems

There is a need to offer courses and programs simultaneously through both systems and through some other satellite-based services such as TI-IN.

Organization of the School Day

Schools need to coordinate schedules, mini schedules, and assembly programs to other participating receiving sites in the system. It becomes extremely difficult to maintain instructional continuity without knowledge of schedules.

RUSSIAN LANGUAGE INSTRUCTION CASE STUDY

The instructor of the program, Marina Parsegova, describes a typical day in her electronic classroom in this section.

The first minutes of instruction on the EDNET system are always spent getting all the sites coordinated and organized. So, I have to make sure all schools involved are online. We greet each other, and I start the class. Students from the other sites show me their homework, and we discuss problems and questions faced by the students in completing the assignment. This is a highly interactive process. After homework issues are resolved, I usually explain the new material using the Elmo projection system to show the new words and to explain new grammar usage. When a student asks a question, I place the camera on the person who is asking the question. The camera is controlled by a remote touch screen. Then I usually use slides, transparencies, and "realia" in structuring my response to the students. Realia is an everyday object used as an instructional object. If I am teaching about Russian artists, I would bring into the classroom some pictures, religious icons, perhaps a copy of a Fabergé egg, some Matruska (nesting) dolls, and art prints. The Elmo projection system would allow me to display these objects on the screen for students at the receiving site.

It is convenient to store information on the computer-based instructional delivery system. This would also include line drawings and other overheads, video, and other forms of media. We either scan the information into the hard drive or create a CD-ROM disc of photographs and slides. These materials are then retrieved using presentation software. All it takes is just to select the visual and send it to the monitor. It can be seen from all the sites, and I can point to anything I want on this visual and discuss it with the students.

So, the Elmo system works like an overhead projector, but easier, and each site can see the visual well. If I need to show any videotape on a particular day, I can select the "video" camera on the system and send the video to the monitor in the classroom and through the system to make it visible for students at each site. After I am done with the explanation, we do a few quick written exercises, then some oral drills, taking turns with all the sites. At the end of the class, we usually have free conversation in Russian that is centered around the new topic of the day. I let students talk to each other, creating situations in which they would use the new words or constructions. This way they can see how important it is to use what they learned that day, and also appreciate the system that allows them to interact with their friends from different parts of Utah and to learn the language better.

Furthermore, it is possible for students to use computers with Internet access in labs at both the originating and receiving sites. In discussions with Russian students on the Internet system, some of the key questions asked by U.S. students are:

- How do spend your spare time; what do you do for fun?
- What do you think about Americans?
- What do you think about the future of Russia?
- Which sports do you like?
- What do you want to do for a career in the future?

Some key questions asked by Russian students are:

- What do you think about Russia?
- Do you think Russian or American students are more alike?
- What do you do with people who cannot start their own businesses? How do you support them? What happens to the poor and unemployed?
- Do you like capitalism or not?
- What do you like about Western society?

The students are also very interested in various cultural activities such as holidays, birthdays, home life, the "social scene," life in the cities, life in the country, or food likes and dislikes. Many classroom discussions have been generated as a result of the student to student interactions over the Internet.

Evaluation of the Program: Methods of Instruction

Students were asked to describe the effectiveness of such methods as lecture, case study, audiovisual aids, class discussion, and the EDNET system itself. Some general comments about the class follow:

- Creative use of audiovisual aids (video, realia, overhead materials) was used by the teacher to teach the Russian language and culture.

- It took too much time from class instruction to have to constantly fiddle with the EDNET system. The EDNET system needs to be up and running in a reliable manner.
- The class length was not long enough to sufficiently cover all the material adequately (55 minutes).
- The teacher's ability to deliver instruction was impacted by the sloppy EDNET service as it detracted from the learning experience.

EFFECTIVE USE OF THE SYSTEM IN HIGH SCHOOLS

As we begin to better understand how to organize and afford this system, three organizational scenarios are suggested: swapping classes, split enrollments due to low class size, and split enrollment due to high class size (Zsiray & Menlove, 1995).

Swapping Classes

Currently, Mountain Crest and Sky View High Schools have each offered an equal number of classes that are exchanged between schools. Each trimester two to four classes are offered. Teacher compensation issues are minimized as teaching load is equalized.

Split Enrollments: Low Class Size

Multiple site access to a given class enables school administrators to offer classes despite low class size at a given site. In this case the cost of the system will be based on each participating school transferring a percentage of a student's weighted pupil unit (WPU) to the sending site. A WPU refers to a weighted pupil unit that is the amount of funding given to each student enrolled full time in school. In Utah a WPU equals $1,739. If a student from a receiving site in southern Utah enrolls in a class offered by the Cache School District in northern Utah, theoretically a percentage of this money will be transferred to the originating site. Students in rural schools, lacking in numbers to hire teachers of specialists subjects such as Russian, are able to access quality instruction.

Split Enrollments: High Class Size

Classes with large class sizes would not only require payment to the sending site-based student WPU but also an added adjustment factor to account for the time and preparation needed with these class sizes. For example, if 75 students were registered for a class the amount paid the teacher would increase. Of course, careful control of the type of courses offered is needed when class sizes are in this range.

THE FUTURE

We have the potential to establish an interactive network of extended learning opportunities for every high school. Governor Leavitt of Utah speaks of the electronic high school and the ability to give some students the opportunity to move through the system at a faster pace. This notion can be extended to the community college level. Rather than build more university and college facilities in this state, a more creative solution is possible. With the advent of Advanced Placement (AP) programming, Concurrent Enrollment Classes, extended day lengths and electronic delivery systems such as EDNET, traditional and nontraditional students will have greater access to higher education possibilities. In our quest to allow our students to expand intellectually, do not forget their social, emotional, and physical needs. Advanced intellectual pursuits as well as school-to-work pursuits can be encouraged, and students will still be able to participate with their peer groups in student government, band, and athletics. At the end of grade 12, with the inclusion of extended school days and 220-day school years, many students will have earned the equivalent of two years of college or receive credentialed applied technology training.

Do not forget those other adults in the community who could come back to the high school campus and pick up college-level classes. This configuration could benefit these nontraditional learners who may have family needs to juggle along with the need to acquire the training to attain a better job or a college degree. It is exciting to develop a responsive high school program that will meet the needs of students and meet challenges posed by global competition, giving them skills to successfully compete in a system of networks and interconnection.

REFERENCES

Obray, M., Zsiray, P., & Menlove, R. (1994). *EdNet: A classroom to classroom connection—the school perspective.* North Logan, UT: Cache School District.

Utah Education Network. (1994). *Distance learning: A resource guide for K-12 students.* Salt Lake City: Utah Education Network.

Utah State Office of Education. (1996). *Preparing teachers for EdNet technology.* Salt Lake City: Utah State Office of Education.

Willis, B. (1993). *Distance education: A practical guide.* Englewood Cliffs, NJ: Educational Technology Publications.

Zsiray, S., & Menlove, R. (1994, March). *A case study of the Cache School District use of distance learning systems.* Presented at the Utah Council for Educational Technology Annual Meeting.

Zsiray, S., & Wilde, G. (1995). *Teacher development centers for the support of distance education programs.* Unpublished manuscript.

VI

RESOURCES

19

COMPUTER NETWORKS AND NETWORKING: A PRIMER

Mauri P. Collins

"It would be nice," I thought, "if I could just understand what she is saying!" The earnest young person at our academic computer services help desk had, from the tone of her voice, answered my question. And I heard all the words, but it sounded almost like a foreign language. I had recently bought a modem for my home computer and had been told that it would open whole new world to me—but it was turning out to be a frustrating place with a baffling language that did not make very much sense to me. I had asked the consultant what I thought was a relatively simple question. I needed just enough information to get my computer at home connected to my account on the university's mainframe computer. I was looking for an answer in terms of "Put this disk in your drive (or copy these files onto your hard-drive) and click on this icon." The consultant seemed to be assuming that, because I was asking the question, I could understand the answer. Not so! And I wondered how many of our readers have the same problems with the Internet's technical terminology and the acronyms that it seems almost impossible to avoid.

By the end of this chapter you should know enough about the various information management tools to recognize their names (FTP, TELNET, ARCHIE, GOPHER, VERONICA, WAIS, WWW, etc.), have some understanding of what they can do for you, and sufficient vocabulary to understand your computer support person's responses to your questions. For further information, there are introductory books available almost anywhere books are sold (including, I noticed, at my local grocery store), many online guides to the Internet, and "Internet/WWW in a box" software packages.

Developers of World Wide Web Browsers (Netscape, Mosaic, etc.) are making their products the umbrella delivery systems that will include most computer-mediated communication (CMC) information management tools and do so transparently to the user. However, the browsers require a high-speed connection to the Internet for optimal performance and computers with large hard drives and lots of memory. Not all K-12 classrooms or schools are so equipped, and many teachers have to start out using some very basic tools. This chapter follows the chronological development of the Internet information retrieval tools, which have become more and more complex in operation as their interfaces have become easier and easier for the user.

THE INTERNET

The very first wide-area computer network in the United States was known as the ARPANET and linked research universities and military installations together so researchers could communicate with one another and share expensive resources (like computers and databases). Over the years this initial network was joined by an ever-increasing number of regional and local networks. The Internet is made up of over tens of thousands of these individual networks connecting tens of million users worldwide. Used generically in this chapter, the term Internet refers to any collection of networks of computers, external to a specific organization, that are connected to the worldwide "network of networks," using the Internet Protocol (IP) and other, similar protocols (sets of rules for communications). Access to the Internet from most academic institutions is mediated by some form of "mainframe" computer or network server, although the size of such machines has decreased sharply as their computing capacity has risen.

When thinking about information storage on the Internet you can liken it to a vast and rambling school district, constantly producing and acquiring information but without a central library or filing system responsible for its storage and management. In this analogy each school or central office compiles their own information collection as would libraries and Centers for the Study of (fill in your topic of choice). Teachers, classes, or even individual students might gather very specific collections of information pertaining to their own interests, as might the various student organizations. Then there is a mass of administrative information concerning the school unit itself, its resources, constituents, rules and regulations, protocols, and processes. Of course, all this information is stored in various formats, in different locations and with varying degrees of availability and access.

Imagine trying to use such an information system! How on earth would you ever find ANYTHING? Fortunately there is help available from your computer system support persons and from some Internet information management tools, but first you have to get onto the Internet.

MAKING THE CONNECTION: A MODEM

Connection to the Internet is often accomplished via a modem. A modem (modulator-demodulator) is piece of electronic equipment that turns characters into sound and back again, so that messages typed on a computer can be sent over a phone line to communicate with other computers and other computer users. My modem processes information at 36.600 bits per second. (A "bit" [binary digit] is the smallest piece of information that can be processed, and it actually represents an on or off electrical pulse. It takes a series of these bits to represent a single character.) This is fast enough for my needs at home, although the computer I use at work has a hard-wired connection (a direct line from the back of my computer to the mainframe computer) that transmits information back and forth via a fiber optic line at almost the speed of light.

COMPUTER CONNECTIONS

Of all the terms a new user of computer-mediated communication has to deal with, *network* may be one of the most confusing. One use of the word refers to computers and the fiber-optic cables, microwave links, satellite connections, gateways, telephone lines, and software that form the connections between and among the *machines*. Another more general use of the word refers to the connections between and among *persons* that can be made using that network of machines and the access people have both to each other in virtual meeting places and conversation forums and to "network resources"—the information stored in myriads of files, databases, library catalogs, and Web pages.

Computer Networks

The computer networks come in all sizes from local area networks (LANs) of two or three machines linked together in a single room to international, composite wide-area networks (WANs) that span the globe and include satellites and microwave transmissions to move the information. The physical setup of networks can be likened to a variegated patchwork of independent telephone companies, each serving their own areas and yet linked together so that they can exchange the virtual equivalent of long-distance phone calls between distant locations.

TCP/IP

With as many different kinds of computers and operating systems and software that are in use, it has taken a great deal of cooperation to come up with a common language and set of standards that could be used to exchange electronic information. One of the most commonly used standards is TCP/IP (Transmission Control Protocol/Internet Protocol). *Protocols* are specific sets of rules followed by computers for the transmission of data. The TCP/IP protocols also provide several useful services to users, including FTP and Telnet.

Networks of directly linked computers such as UUCP (Unix-to-Unix Communications Protocol), which uses another set of protocols, are connected to the Internet by "gateways," which are computers that translate alternative protocol languages into something TCP/IP can understand. They do it in a way that is transparent to the user.

Transmission Lines—T3

The backbone of the Internet in the United States is made up of high speed data transmission lines permanently connecting the major routing computers in the network. These lines can be considered as the superhighways of data transmission. They have recently been upgraded from T1s, which carried 1.544 megabits (million bits of information) a second to the T3s, carrying 44.736 megabits a second. This has significantly increased the available "bandwidth," which translates to the number and complexity of messages that can be carried simultaneously. Initially all messages transmitted were just text: characters and words. Now data sent over these lines encode everything from plain text to interactive, two-way audio/visual teleconferencing.

IP Numbers

Each computer, large or small, that is permanently connected to the Internet has its own address or IP number. Each site with a national network connection is given a specific range of numbers that it can use for its internal machine addresses. The numbers are in the format of 123.456.789.123, with the last one or two triads pointing to a specific machine. This is done so that mail and other traffic can be routed correctly and machines can be identified when their user logs onto other computers. We rarely use the IP numbers in addressing mail or anything else, usually preferring to use machine names in our addresses. I use a Sun SparcStation with the friendly name of Wilbur, who is known on the Internet as 128.118.058.011. *Nameservers* are computers that hold the lists that match the IP numbers to computer names and locations and make these translations transparent to the user. It is a good idea to know the IP numbers of some of your favorite destinations as there will inevitably come a time when you want to go somewhere and the nameserver is off line and no translation from machine name to IP number can be made.

Moving Traffic

When messages and files are passed through permanently connected networks of computers such as UUnet, the message "hops" from one computer to another that "stores and forwards" messages in a linear fashion, rather like a bus that stops at every bus stop on its route. If a machine is temporarily offline (broken in some way or being fixed or upgraded), the messages just sit patiently until the way is open again. Despite the fact that electronic communication *can* move at the speed of light, I have sometimes had messages take 16 hours to get from Virginia to Nevada, and four hours from Washington, DC to Pennsylvania. Yet at other times transmission between Pennsylvania and Australia appears to be nearly instantaneous.

Some sites have Internet connections, some have UUnet connections, some have both, and some have neither, but there are an increasing number of "gateways" from one network to another and to commercial service providers. Some sites have leased telephone lines that tie them to the nearest major switching center. The lines are always open and available for traffic, and their cost is usually shared by the connected institution and various commercial telecommunications providers.

Fidonet/Dial-up Connections

Some sites run bulletin board software (bbs) that dials the nearest switching center during the early morning hours, collects all the files and mail that are waiting, and delivers all the mail that it had collected during the day. That one phone call may be the only connection with the outside, networked world. "Fido" is one example of this kind of software. "Fidonet" is the collective name for the thousands of computers owned by amateur computer hobbyists throughout the world that use the Fido software. Each computer is again assigned its own specific address so that messages can be routed to the correct place. The existence of Fidonet is not dependent on universities or government funding. There are no permanent, fixed connections between these computers; all traffic goes over ordinary phone lines, and the cost is usually paid out of the individual system owner's pocket. It does not matter where you are in the world, there is probably a Fidonet node within easy dialing distance. Fidonet provides person-to-person electronic mail, file sharing, and hosts a large number of discussion groups called conferences.

PEOPLE CONNECTIONS

Electronic Mail

As soon as I had my modem set up, I immediately used it to send and receive electronic mail (e-mail). In my own case, I used my modem and home phone line to reach my account on one of Penn State's computers. However, I could have just as easily (but for a fee) used my modem to dial the local access number for any one of a number of commercial computer communication service providers, like CompuServe, America Online, or Prodigy, or to access Microsoft Mail from Windows. Electronic mail is referred to as "asynchronous" messaging because both parties do not have to be online at the same time in order to communicate.

The first thing you have to know when you want to send e-mail to someone is the address, and always the easiest way to determine that is to ask the person you want to send mail to—perhaps by using an interactive voice network device commonly called a telephone—or ask them to send you a note so you can simply "reply" to theirs. Electronic mail addresses look very different from ordinary post office addresses (called "snail mail" by e-mail users).

To send "snailmail" to my home address you need to know:

my name	mauri collins
my house number and street	NAU Box 5751
my city	Flagstaff
my state and zip	AZ 86011-5751

To send electronic mail to my Internet address you need to know:

a login name (or userid)	mauri	mcollins
a machine	@star	@giaec.cc
a location	nau	.monash
a domain	.edu	.edu
a country code (outside US)		.au

My addresses are:

mauri@star.nau.edu

or mcollins@gaiec.cc.monash.edu.au

Remember the periods or "dots" between the different parts of the address (it reads out loud as "mauri at star dot nau dot edu"). Computers are confused by blank spaces in e-mail addresses so you will see the underscore or hyphen sometimes used as a spacer as in mauri_collins@machine.location.domain. You just have to remember to copy addresses carefully or to use the "reply" feature on the mail program on your computer. It can generally be relied on to take the correct information from the "header" on the mail you have received, but it is always an excellent idea to check.

Different Internet address domains you may see are .com for business or industry, .mil for military address, .gov for governmental addresses, .org for nonprofit organizations, and .edu for educational organizations. Addresses outside of the United States usually require a two-letter country designation (AU = Australia, HK = Hong Kong, ZA = South Africa, etc.).

Discussion Groups

One of the more popular uses of networks, after the exchange of electronic mail between individuals, is to join and read the incredible variety of discussion lists or groups and newsgroups that are available. Discussion groups come in many forms. Some are like the bulletin boards in the local grocery stores. Messages are posted and left for people to read and comment on; some groups focus around particular topics, others are strictly for announcements; whereas others read like the transcript of a cocktail party.

Discussion groups have been likened to newspapers or talk radio. Many people read or listen or, to use the networker's term, "lurk," and a relatively small number of people contribute. However, readership in a discussion group can bring people together from all over the world, who might never have a chance to meet and talk; it fosters the exchange of ideas and information and engenders a sense of cooperation and friendship (Berge, 1994).

LISTSERV

Many of these discussion groups are handled by a program called LISTSERV, written by Eric Thomas. The groups are often called discussion lists because essentially what the listserver software deals with is a subscription list of electronic mail addresses. When a message is received the listserver, depending on the instructions it has been given, will forward it to the moderator/listowner, or, if the list is unmoderated, copy the incoming message to each of the addresses on its subscription list (Berge & Collins, 1995).

If the list is moderated, the moderator will check the message against whatever formal or informal criteria exist that govern what goes to the list's readership and either send the message on, edit or delete it, or return it to the sender. Most moderator's see their primary role as "controlling the signal-to-noise ratio." This involves making sure that the discussion is kept with the limits set forth in the group's charter, and that discussion is conducted in a civil manner (Berge, 1995).

One unfortunate and often unpleasant aspect of unmoderated discussion and NetNews groups is the occurrence of "flaming." With no available indication of body language, tone, or mood (except for the ubiquitous emoticons :-) (tip your head to your left shoulder to see the grin) it is very easy for misunderstandings to arise and to escalate very quickly. Free from the sanction of others' immediate presence (and the fear of a pop on the nose for running off at the mouth), there are those who tend to run off at the finger tips and whose language often becomes hostile, vulgar, and profane. Then there are those who choose to communicate in that tone all the time. If a calm and reasoned attempt to clear up the misunderstanding is unsuccessful, a gracious exit from the communication situation is often the best remedy, as censure or argument often seems to exacerbate the problem.

Usenet/NetNews

Usenet/NetNews can be defined as "a virtual network of computers that exchange messages with Usenet headers." Usenet newsgroups number in the thousands and are divided into a number of major streams, for example alt (alternative), comp (computer), soc (social), rec (recreation) and so on. No matter what your interest you can probably find a Usenet group that discusses it; if not, you can gather some like-minded correspondents and start one. Some newsgroups are of local interest, such as psu.jobs that advertises employment available on Penn States' campus to soc.women, which is carried worldwide. Many of the commercial online access providers not only carry NetNews but also have their own forums, using the same kind of format.

Differences Between Listserv and NetNews

There are some significant differences between Usenet/NetNews and listserver managed discussion groups. A user subscribes as an individual to a listserver and similar discussion groups and the messages that the listserver forwards are delivered to his or her personal mailbox. In order to read the NetNews newsgroups one's site or Internet access provider has to receive some part of the "feed," the stream of NetNews messages that can be measured in tens of megabytes each day. The messages are stored at a central location, in a bulletin board format on the site's mainframe; the reader must log in and use some kind of "reader" software to read and respond to the messages. Messages are held for whatever period of time the site administrators decide is appropriate, and this is often dictated by the amount of storage space available. A site may receive some, all or none of the newsgroups.

The first word in the name of the newsgroup is a kind of "family" name to indicate which of the main topic divisions the group belongs to: comp.misc is a computer-related group, soc.women is from the social science grouping, rec.fishing deals with recreational topics, talk. indicates discussion groups, bit.listserv indicates groups that are mirrors of Internet listserv groups.

THE CLIENT-SERVER MODEL

Many of the Internet information management tools work on a "client-server" model. A computer somewhere is set up as a "file-server." Information in machine-readable form (text files, sound, graphics, computer programs etc.) is stored and made available for general (or restricted) retrieval. In order to access these files, there has to be a "client" program running somewhere between your keyboard and that storage archive. Krol (1992) describes a "client" program as one that "knows how to work on your behalf to extract some service from a server somewhere on the network" (p. 356). He further suggests the analogy of your own telephone as a "client" and the telephone company as the "server" as an illustration of the client-server model. Examples of such client-server programs are FTP, Telnet, Gopher, Netscape, Mosaic, Lynx, and so on.

Some guides I read in preparation for this chapter suggested that if you do not have a particular "client" program available on your site's system, you find one in an archive somewhere, make a copy of it in your own account, and use it. Please do not. First, talk to your computer support people. They can be very particular about the integrity of their systems and often have rules concerning the kinds of programs users are allowed to run from their accounts. They may also have installed the particular client program on a systemwide basis or will do so at your request and can give you directions for its use.

File Transfer Protocol and Anonymous FTP

TCP/IP protocols provide users with FTP (File Transfer Protocol). This service is most often encountered in the phrase "anonymous FTP." Many sites worldwide have set aside computer space as FTP servers to archive (store) files and computer software, and by using "anonymous FTP" these files can be retrieved almost as easily as if they were on a local machine. You do not have to have an account at an archive server site nor do you to pay for access, but you must have an FTP client program and access from your site (check with your local computer gurus to find out if you have). The "anonymous" part of the name indicates that you may be asked to log into the computer before you can download files. Your login would be "anonymous" (you must spell it out and spell it correctly), and your password is your login in full (I type mauri@star.nau.edu usually with some difficulty as it doesn't show on the screen as I type!)

Netscape and other Web browsers use FTP to retrieve and download files, but do it transparently, usually in response to "Click here to download." You may notice your web browser downloading from an address like ftp://machine.com rather than http://machine.com. Computer usage at most sites is heaviest during the local daytime hours, so please be polite. To get faster service, FTP your files in the evening, night, or early morning hours at the FTP site, if at all possible.

Telnet

Telnet is another basic TCP/IP service that gives you an interactive connection with another machine. Telnet is both a protocol (TCP/IP remote login protocol) and a program. Telnet is used for two major purposes: to remotely log into a machine that you have access to (i.e., a userid and a password) so you can use it as if you were actually at that site, and to remotely log into public access catalogues and databases.

I use Telnet to log into my accounts in Australia and Baltimore from my computer account here in Arizona. When I am traveling (with laptop computer in hand), I dial up the local number of an international Internet access provider and Telnet back to my home machine to keep up with my mail.

Some of the remote sites you can Telnet to, such as library catalogs and computers holding public access databases, need a login name, but it is usually published with information about the service. These login names are case-sensitive, so type them exactly as they are listed.

Watch carefully as you log into a site for something that says "Escape sequence: ^]" This means that if you get into difficulties you can type control-] (or whatever else it said) to return you to the Telnet> prompt or your own system prompt. From the Telnet> prompt you can close the connection with "close" or "quit" or "exit."

Archie

There are anonymous FTP sites all over the world, each with its own collection of stored files. But how do you find what you are looking for? One of the first global answers to this question was the Archie program, developed by students and volunteer staff from McGill University's School of Computer Science.

Archie is an automated indexing program that contacts each registered FTP site (over 1,500 FTP servers, archiving over 2 million files) about once a month and collects a complete directory listing from each FTP server. This is held in a master index of file/program names.

To find a file you have to know, or guess, a word or phrase that is part of the file's name. It soon became clear than many files had obscure, nonintuitive names, so FTP site operators were asked to send information on the major packages they had archived. The "whatis" service is comprised of this list of alternative indexing keywords and can be used to locate files and programs even if their name has no connection at all with their content.

There are two ways to access Archie's master index or the "whatis" service. First, check with your computer support personnel to see if you have an Archie client installed at your site. If so, they will give you site specific instructions, but usually it is sufficient to type Archie <keyword(s)> at your system prompt. The next alternative is to Telnet to a public Archie server, preferably one close to you. Krol (1992) suggests the following:

Name	Suggested Usage Area
archie.rutgers.edu	Northeastern U.S.
archie.sura.net	Southeastern U.S.
archie.unl.edu	Western U.S.
archie.mcgill.ca	Canada
archie.au	Australia and the Pacific Basin
archie.funet.fi	Europe
archie.doc.ic.ac.uk	United Kingdom

Telnet to your chosen host name and then log in with the name "Archie" (without the quotes). When you see the Archie> prompt, type in your keyword. Archie servers can get very busy, so do not be surprised if you are told that you have tried to access the server when it was at its limit for concurrent sessions. Just try again later. Several of the Web search engines not only search their own index of Web pages, but also check the Archie database.

Gopher

Gopher was developed at the University of Minnesota (U of M), whose mascot is the "Golden Gopher." (Gophers are small, burrowing rodents, and "go-fers" are staff members who fetch and carry on demand.) The system was designed so that campus offices and departments, widely distributed over the U of M campus, could each maintain and control their own files stored in their own chosen text or binary formats. A system was designed with a series of "point and click" menus so that users, with no prior training, could find information, regardless of the actual location of the actual files. These menus were arranged by topic so it would appear as if access was to one, large database instead of a myriad small ones. It did not take long for the potential inherent in Gopher as a information organizer to become obvious. It did not matter if the FTP servers that Gopher was referencing were distributed on a single campus or over the whole Internet.

Only the Gopher program knows the exact location of the particular piece of information it displays, and it has the capability of searching for that information in FTP archives, library catalogs, listserv and Usenet discussion group archives, campus phone books and directories, course catalogs, and online syllabi. When queried, Gopher reaches out, searches its sources, compiles a list of files (and their locations) that match the requested item, disconnects from its sources, and presents that new menu of choices to the user. The user can then choose to search further or have displayed on the screen the contents of the individual files Gopher has found. When appropriate files are identified, the user can then save the file to their account, have it mailed to them or to any e-mail address they chose, or continue their search, all with the touch of a single key (following the single line of instructions on the screen).

Many campuses have chosen to make Gopher their CWIS (Campus-Wide Information System) of choice. Penn State made all the information from course catalogs, the library, NetNews, and PSU weather, available via a Gopher interface, connecting the many different FTP sites and Gopher servers on campus with each other and the rest of the Internet world. The Penn State Web pages (http://www.psu.edu) now serve as a "front-end" access point to the Penn State Gopher system.

Gopher is a client-server program and to use it, you must be logged into a computer connected to the Internet that is running a Gopher client program. Again, consult your computer support personnel for information on the particular implementation for your site, if there is one. If your own site does not have a Gopher client program, unless you are a systems operator, please do not try installing one on your own. To try out Gopher you can Telnet to the main Gopher server at boombox.micro.umn.edu, log in as "gopher" (without the ""), and follow the menu instructions.

The amount and kinds of information now stored in gopherspace is truly incredible. You can spend many hours just browsing different sources, and new ones seem to come online daily. While preparing this article I asked Gopher to find what was available on "networks and networking" and it turned up a number of copies of a promising file—which turned out to be an article that I had written for the *Interpersonal Computing and Technology* online journal several year ago (Collins, 1993). Many institutions have now linked their gophered files to their homepages and a Web browser can be used to access them.

You may notice your browser downloading from an address like gopher://machine.com.

VERONICA

To provide even more help in finding Gopher resources, VERONICA (Very Easy Rodent Oriented Network Information Computerized Archives) was developed at the University of Nevada, Reno, and is a "Main Menu" selection on many Gopher servers. Every week or two, VERONICA, fashioned on the archie model, contacts all the registered gophers in the world and requests a copy of all their menus. These menus are maintained in a single database, and a user can request that VERONICA search it for keywords. The results are presented in the style of the familiar Gopher menu. Veronica documentation is available via Gopher. Many of the Web search engines also check the VERONICA database and can retrieve files directly.

WWW or WORLD-WIDE WEB or Just THE WEB

This ambitiously named service was developed in Switzerland at the CERN (European Laboratory for Particle Physics) research center as a way for physicists to share their work and to access community information, using single, consistent interface. It has become the fastest growing information service in the world.

The Web is another client-server system with Webservers and Web client programs known as *browsers*. (Again, check with your systems operators to see if one has been installed at your site, and, if so, what the site specific access instructions are.) The most common browsers are Netscape, Mosaic for Windows, and Lynx, which operates in text-only mode. The online commercial access providers have their own browsers built in. Browsers know how to access just about any resource on the Internet. They can set up a file search, read Usenet articles, send e-mail, access Gopher and anonymous FTP servers, initiate Telnet sessions, deal with registration and other kinds of forms, and so on.

Web "pages" are hypertext documents. Embedded in the text are "hotlinks" indicated either by color (often blue or purple) and/or by underlining. Pointing to or clicking on a link will cause the browser to activate that link and present you with the Internet resource at the other end of the link. This may be another text document, but could be a graphic, a video clip, an animation, a sound file, or binary versions of computer programs, spreadsheets, or word processing files.

Sophisticated indexes ("spiders"), some with several million entries, and search engines (Web crawlers) have been developed, and access to them is built into most Web browsers. You can keyword search for anything you want. The results of the search are generally presented to you in the form of an index that sometimes includes the first 20 words or so of a resource. Clicking or pointing to an index entry will retrieve the document or resource.

HTML (Hypertext Mark-up Language) is used to "tag" documents for the Web and presents a "strong suggestion" to Web browsers about how an author wants a document to be displayed. Each browser is a little different so it is wise when preparing Web pages to use several different ones to look at a document to be sure it looks approximately the way you want it to. HTML editors are proliferating, downloadable from the Web, and are incorporated into the latest versions of the most popular word processing packages to make conversion a matter of simply saying "Save As. . . HTML."

The Web is an emerging and fast growing technology and is constantly being added to and refined, with the browsers setting the de facto standards for information posting and retrieval. Maintaining the links in a document is an ongoing effort as sites appear and disappear. On the Web anyone can be a publisher, even without benefit of editorial review.

Web pages number in the millions and are rapidly proliferating. Browsers are becoming more powerful and the latest versions have very large footprints, requiring up to 12 megabytes of RAM to function efficiently. With increasingly large numbers of users, sometimes popular sites refuse connections or files download very slowly. Heaviest use occurs between 11 a.m. and 3 p.m., so those are good hours to avoid, if you can.

GUIDES TO MORE INFORMATION

Always the very first source of information on anything that pertains to access to the computers at your site, how they are set up, what programs are installed, and how to run them is your own site's computer support personnel. They are most knowledgeable about the idiosyncrasies of the equipment and programs they support and can provide you with instructions, written guides, access to training classes, and so on. Often your own site may have a Web page or Gopher or FTP server set up from which information, files, and programs can be downloaded (copied from a server to your personal computer).

There are a host of extraordinarily good guides to the use of computer-mediated communication and lists of such guides. One comprehensive beginner's guide is the work of John December at Renssalear Polytechnic Institute and is available from http://www.december.com. Another is Scott Yanoff's "Internet Sources Guide." This is updated biweekly and is posted to the NetNews group alt.internet.services or is available by anonymous FTP from FTP: csd44.csd.uwm.edu in File: pub/internet. services.txt. Both guides can be found by searching for the author's name with any Web search engine (AltaVista, Yahoo, etc.).

SUMMARY

I have introduced, very briefly, some of the more common Internet information management tools. Each has their benefits and limitations, and it is more than worth your time to spend a few hours exploring each one. There is a wealth of information residing just on the other side of your computer screen, waiting for you to call it forth and use it. What else is information for?

REFERENCES

Berge, Z. L. (1994). Electronic discussion groups. *Communication Education, 43*(4), 102-111.

Berge. Z. L. (1995). Facilitating computer conferencing: Notes from the field. *Educational Technology, 43*(1), 22-30.

Berge, Z. L., & Collins, M.P. (1995). Computer mediated scholarly discussion groups. *Computers In Education, 24*(1), 1-7.

Collins, M. P. (1993). Networks and networking: A primer. *Interpersonal Computing and Technology: An Electronic Journal for the 21st Century, 1*(1). (Archived as COLLINS IPCTV1N1 at listserv@listserv.georgetown.edu or http://star.ucc.nau.edu/~mauri/moderators.html).

Krol, E. (1992). *The whole Internet user's guide and catalog.* Sebastopol, CA: O'Reilley & Associates.

GLOSSARY

Zane Berge, Mauri Collins, and Michael Day

Acceptable Use Policy. A written document setting out the terms and conditions for using internal and external computer networks.

Address. There are two forms of machine addresses that commonly identify any computer connected to the Internet. They appear as either words or as IP numbers in the form of dotted quads (1234.1234.1234.1234). For instance, GUVAX, a VAX computer at Georgetown University, is known as either 141.161.1.2 or guvax.acc.georgetown.edu.

Anonymous FTP. A form of FTP (*see* **FTP**) which allows unregistered users (those without passwords to the account) access to files. When using anonymous FTP, one logs in as "anonymous" and uses one's email address (e.g., BERGE@UMBC2.UMBC.EDU) as the password.

ARPANet. A packet switched network developed in the early 1970s. The "grandfather" of today's Internet. ARPANet was decommissioned in June 1990.

ARCHIE. An internet service which allows users to search the indexes of many FTP sites. Archie tracks the contents of over 800 anonymous FTP archive sites containing over 1 million files stored across the Internet. Two archie sites are archie.ans.net (147.225.1.31) and archie.unl.edu (129.93.1.14). Logon as "archie."

ASCII. American Standard Code for Information Interchange, pronounced "ASKEE." A standard data transmission code which the computer uses to encode alphanumeric and other characters into a binary file.

Asynchronous. Transmission by individual bytes, or packets of bytes, not related to specific timing on the transmitting end. When used to describe computer-mediated communication, it indicates that communication can take place without both parties being logged on at the same time, as messages can be left for subsequent reading (e.g., email).

Backbone. The primary or trunk connection on a distributed hierarchical network system such as the Internet. All systems connected to the backbone are assured of being connected to each other. This does not prevent systems from setting up private arrangements with each other to bypass the backbone for reasons of cost, performance, or security.

Bandwidth. Used generally to refer to the capacity or throughput of a communications link. High bandwidth implies high data throughput, which can provide a very high speed to a few users at a time, or lower data rates to many users.

Bitnet. Acronym for "Because It's Time Network." Begun in 1981, BITnet is a world-wide academic and research network that connects many universities, colleges, and collaborating research centers and is restricted to the noncommercial exchange of information. It is operated by EDUCOM. Bitnet differs from the Internet in the types of services (e.g., FTP and telnet) its users can access. Bitnet uses the RSCS protocol set and provides electronic mail, file transfer, and "Tell/Send" messaging. GATEWAYS are computers that link Internet and BITnet sites.

Bookmark. A navigational shortcut that takes one directly to a resource, often used by WEB browsers to keep track of a user's frequently visited Web sites.

Boolean searching. A method of searching in some electronic databases which allows the searcher to combine terms and/or phrases by using the Boolean operators "and," "or," and "not."

Browser. A software client program that lets you access the Web (e.g., Mosaic, Netscape) and display and/or retrieve information (text, images, and sounds).

Bulletin-Board Systems (BBS). A network-based file sharing system into which users may enter information, usually in the form of messages, for others to read or download. Many bulletin boards are set up according to general topics and are accessible throughout a network.

Campus-Wide Information System (CWIS). A tool that allows users to navigate through and retrieve data from a variety of campus sources (e.g., library, news bureau, events center, admissions and registrar, computing center), commonly implemented using WWW or Gopher.

Client/Server software. In network terminology, "client" can have two meanings. Sometimes it is synonymous with "user." Other times it is used to denote a relationship between two computers in which one computer is a "host" and serves a "client" machine. In this situation, the client computer requests data or other resources from the host, or server, machine. The program on the client machine that provides the user-interface for those resources is typically called the "client" software.

Client-server interface. A type of computer connection, typically over a network, in which the host computer, or server, provides files or services to remote computers, called clients. An example of this interface is the WWW and it can be found on LANs, WANs, or the Internet.

Client/server network. A Local Area Network (LAN) situation in which one computer acts as a server, or host, for all other client computers on the network. This type of network commonly provides clients with access to services such as common databases, network printers, and so on.

Compression. Files can be compressed to reduce the amount of storage space they occupy on a computer or the amount of BANDWIDTH they occupy when being transmitted across a network. Compatible software is required at compression and decompression locations.

Computer-Based Instruction (CBI) or Computer-mediated Instruction. Refers to using computers to instruct human users. CBI includes Computer Assisted Instruction (CAI; tutorial, review and practice, simulation, etc.); computer-managed instruction (diagnostic and prescriptive testing functions); and electronic messaging, which is generally associated with networked computer classrooms.

CMC. Computer-mediated communication. An acronym that refers to the entire range of electronic networking activities and includes electronic mail, computer conferencing, informatics, and computer-based instruction.

Courseware. Software, including documentation and workbooks, that is marketed for educational purposes.

Cross-Posting. Posting a BBS message to multiple subject groups or conferences.

CU-SeeMe. A desktop video-conferencing software program, available from Cornell University and many NASA sites, that allows users with the appropriate cameras and video equipment to transmit video over the Internet in real time.

Cyberspace. A term for immersive virtual reality, sometimes used to denote the Internet or the area behind one's computer screen in which one interacts with other users, computers, databases, and so on.

Daemons. Small "mainframe" programs that follow what is happening in a system. Mail daemons are often activated when mail is bounced; idle daemons track user's logon time and disconnect sessions with no activity after a predetermined length of time.

DEC VAX Notes. *see* **Vax Notes.**

Domain. Usually the last term in an address (q.v.). Domains are usually functional or national. Functional domains in the United States include EDU for education, GOV for government, COM for commercial, MIL for military, NET for network related, and ORG for nonprofit organizations. National domains are country codes such as CA for Canada, MY for Malaysia, SG for Singapore, and TH for Thailand.

Download. The electronic transfer of information from a remote computer to a local one, or from a personal computer's hard drive to a floppy disk. *see* **UPLOAD.**

EFF. Electronic Frontier Foundation. An organization established as a clearinghouse for open discussion and analysis of the many legal and social implications of the increasing role of computer communications in the world. EFF maintains a Gopher and a WWW server and is based in Washington, DC.

Electronic Bulletin Board. *see* **Bulletin Board Systems (BBS).**

Electronic Emissary Project (EEP). The Electronic Emissary Project is an Internet-based interpersonal resource that has been online since February 1993. The Emissary is a "matching service," based in the College of Education at the University of Texas at Austin. that helps teachers with access to the Internet locate other Internet account holders who are experts in different disciplines, for purposes of setting up curriculum-based, electronic exchanges among the teachers, their students, and the Subject Matter Experts

Electronic Journal (ejournal). An electronically distributed publication which, like a print journal, includes a table of contents, numerically defined issues, and an ISSN number. Recipients can reformat text as they wish and print only those articles or issues they want to read or save in hard-copy.

Electronic Mail (email). Transmitting textual and nontextual messages in machine readable form using an electronic mail program (like Pine, Elm, or Eudora) from one computer terminal or computer system to another. A message sent from one computer user to another is stored in the recipient's mailbox, a file on the host machine where that person receives mail.

Emoticon (smiley). The typical communication style on the internet is "written conversational" and this type of communication does a poor job of expressing emotion, hence "emoticons" were invented.

They are electronic text likenesses of human faces used in mail and news to indicate a variety of emotions and reactions. :-). Tip your head to your left shoulder to read the smile. The most common emoticon is :-) connoting a smile or happiness. One also often sees :- (or :-| meaning sadness or disappointment and ;-) ("winky") meaning irony or sarcasm.

Encryption. The act of making a readable file secure. Used on the World Wide Web for the transmission of credit card numbers or other sensitive information.

FAQ. *see* **Frequently Asked Question.**

Fiber optics. The technology of connecting or networking communication devices such as computers by means of optical fiber (glass) cable instead of copper wire.

File Transfer protocol (FTP). A TCP/IP protocol and program that one can use to transfer files over the network. *see* **Anonymous FTP.**

Finger. A program that identifies a user by name and last login time.

Firewall. A software security measure that helps to limit pirate attacks by preventing access to some locations from other locations on a network or a computer.

Flame. A confrontational, emotionally charged email message usually couched in language that is vulgar, sarcastic, or profane.

FrEdMail Network. Free Educational Electronic Mail. One of the pioneering networks of microcomputer-based BBS systems serving K-12 educators, FrEdMail was begun in 1986 by Al Rogers in San Diego, CA, and has spread to include more than 150 electronic bulletin boards systems across the United States and as far away as Australia and Ireland. FrEdMail offers collaborative activities designed to help students become better writers and learners and promotes the sharing of resources and experiences among teachers. FrEdMail can now be accessed through the internet. For more information, contact Al Rogers, FrEdMail Foundation, P.O. Box 243, Bonita, CA 91908-0243.

Frequently Asked Questions (FAQs). A document containing answers to frequently asked questions about some service, application, or function. These documents are generally updated as users gain experience with the service, application, or function. (Pronounced"fak".)

Freenet. Community-based bulletin board or Gopher information system, some with email and conferencing capabilities. Based on the public television/public radio model of community access and support.

FTP. *see* **File Transfer Protocol and Anonymous FTP.**

Full Text Delivery. The ability of an information server, like Gopher, to deliver the full electronic text of a document to a patron.

Gateway. A computer or device that acts as a connector between two logically separate networks. It has interfaces to more than one network and can translate data so that it can pass from one network to another, possibly dissimilar, network in a way that is transparent to the user.

.gif (Graphics Interchange Format). A platform-independent file format developed by CompuServe, the GIF format is commonly used to distribute graphics on the Internet and especially on the World Wide Web. (Often pronounced "jiff.")

Gopher. An information management tool that allows users to search for specific kinds of information over a wide-area network by using a series of menus. Gopher was developed by the University of Minnesota and is freely available in client and server form for MAC and DOS platforms. Many Gophers serve as useful front-ends to Internet databases, FTP archives, and CWISs.

Groupware (Group Conferencing Systems). A program (often marketed for business) that permits simultaneous work on a common file by more than one networked user. All the users can see the changes made by any other person as they occur.

Home page. The first page of any site on the World Wide Web. This page typically contains links to other pages at the site and may contain links to off-site locations. Each user or account at a Web site may also have their individual home pages.

Host computer. In the context of networks, a computer that provides service to a user who is typically running "client" software which turns their computer into a "terminal" of the host. On the Internet these host computers are known as NODES>.

HTML. Hypertext Markup Language; a document-formatting language used to write World Wide Web "pages." HTML consists of "tags." These are formatting commands read by Web browsers that control the appearance of documents on the reader's screen and the links to other resources they contain. HTML documents are basic ASCII files so they can be read by most word processors and text editors.

HTTP. Hypertext Transport Protocol; the protocol of the Web that allows text, images, audio, and video to be combined into a single document. HTTP also allows the linking of documents and document components.

Hypertext. A method of embedding links into documents that provide connections with related data (text, images, or sound) at either local or remote locations. The World Wide Web is based on hypermedia applications.

Hytelnet. A menu-driven version of Telnet that serves as a guide to online library catalogs and other information sources, updated 2-3 times per year. It can be downloaded by Anonymous FTP and placed on a local machine. Information on Hytelnet is available from: hytelnet.src.

Informatics. A general term describing network-accessible information servers. These include data archives such as anonymous ftp sites, interactive databases such as library OPACs, and client/server systems such as GOPHER and WAIS.

Intelligent Agent. A program that searches the network looking for items that match criteria one specifies; also called KNOWbots.

Internet Relay Chat (IRC). A world-wide synchronous multiuser chat protocol that allows one to converse with others in real time. IRC is structured as a network of servers, each of which accepts connections from client programs, one per user. Jarkko Oikarinen, a Finnish programmer, created Internet Relay Chat. IRC is a free program, which means that anyone with access to the internet can get a client program and use it to talk with others.

internet. A collection of computer networks interconnected by a set of routers that allow them to function as a single, large virtual network.

Internet (note the capital "I"). The largest network in the world consisting of large national backbone nets (such as MILNET, NSFNET, and CREN) and a myriad of regional and local campus networks all over the world. The Internet uses the Internet protocol suite, including the TCP/IP protocol set that includes electronic mail, TELNET, and FTP. To be on the Internet you must have IP connectivity, that is, be able to Telnet to—or ping— other systems. Networks with only e-mail connectivity are not actually classified as being on the Internet.

Interoperability. What allows different computer models from different manufacturers to communicate meaningfully with each other.

IP (Internet Protocol). *see* **TCP/IP.**

IP Address. The numeric address (a dotted quad) of a computer connected to the Internet; also called Internet address. It has the form 255.255.255.255. Guvax.georgetown.edu, to other computers and the network routers, is 141.161.1.2.

IP (Internet Protocol) name. A structured, numeric-based unique name for a computer on a network. The number includes four sections separated by periods. Often there is an alphabetical equivalent to the numeric name. Example: 128.04.12.62 or abc.lib.uma.edu. *See also* domain.

IRC. *see* **Internet Relay Chat.**

.jpeg (Joint Photographic Experts Group). A filename extension used to mark JPEG compressed images.

KIDSNET. Has been renamed KIDSPHERE. *see* **KIDSPHERE.**

KIDSPHERE. The major mailing list for the discussion of K-12 computer networking. It was established in 1989 with the name KIDSNET by Bob Carlitz. In Spring 1993 is was renamed KIDSPHERE with this statement of purpose: "to stimulate the development of an international computer network for the use of children and their teachers. The first pieces of this network have already begun to take shape, and the mailing list now helps to guide its continuing evolution. Subscribers to the list include teachers, administrators, scientists, developers of software and hardware, and officials of relevant funding agencies." To join the list, send your request to Bob Carlitz <joinkids@vms.cis.pitt.edu> and ask to be added to the KIDSPHERE mailing list.

LAN. *see* **Local Area Network**

Listserv. Listserv and its clones are the software that manages electronic discussion groups or computer conference distribution lists. These discussion groups are often called "lists" because, using what is called a "mail exploder" and a subscription list of electronic mail addresses, Listserv sends messages directly to the electronic mailboxes of many subscribers. Participants subscribe by sending a message to the Listserv hosting the list of interest. Eric Thomas originally wrote the Listserv software for IBM mainframes, but he has since migrated it to most available platforms.

Local Area Network (LAN). A network connecting machines at one site, often through a single server.

Logon or Login. A set of commands to gain access to another computer, network, or online service that often includes some kind of identification in the form of a user name and password.

Lurking. Reading or "listening" to a mailing list discussion or USENET newsgroup without actively participating (i.e., without contributing to the discussion). Lurking is encouraged for beginners who wish to learn the history and habits of the group. In course-related discussion lists, lurking is discouraged because to be silent is to be invisible.

Mail Exploder. Part of an electronic mail delivery system that allows a single message to be delivered to a list of addresses. Mail exploders are used to implement mailing lists. Users send messages to a single address (e.g., mygroup-L~somehost.edu) and the mail exploder takes care of delivery to each of the individual subscribers to the list.

Modem (MOdulator/DEModulator). A device that converts the digital signals in your computer to analog signals, and vice-versa, to enable computer communication through analog telephone lines.

Moderator. The person who is "in charge" of a Listserv or Usenet newsgroup. On a moderated list, the moderator reads the messages prior to posting to the list, may edit them, and forwards them to the list for general distribution. On an unmoderated list, the moderator just steps in when discussion get out of control. On private lists the moderator may also subscribe and unsubscribe people.

MOO (MUD, Object Oriented). Offers a more complex, object-oriented virtual interaction among participants than a MUD. Usually participants take on a role and interact in character. The "objects" they create remain after a particular user has logged off.

Mosaic. The name of a popular Web browser from National Center for Supercomputing Applications (NCSA) for accessing the Web; the first BROWSER invented for the Web.

MUD. Multi-User Dungeons/Domains are text-based, virtual environments evolved from "Dungeons and Dragons" type games that allow multiple users to gather and interact together in real time. *see also* **MOO.**

MUSE (Multi-User Simulation Environment). A virtual reality interaction via the Internet that combines the elements of Internet Relay Chat (IRC) and a MOO. Participants may choose and create their own reality or participate in ongoing games.

National Education and Research Network (NREN). The National Research and Education Network is a proposed national computer network to be built on the foundation of the NSF backbone network, NSFnet, the current internet backbone. NREN would provide high-speed interconnection between various national and regional networks.

Netiquette. A contraction of "network" and "etiquette" referring to socially acceptable communication behaviors on a computer network, often in the form of a written document.

Netnews. *see* **Usenet.**

Netscape. A graphical Web browser that currently offers many cutting-edge HTML features.

Netweaving (netweaver). Netweaving occurs when connections between these networks are not automatic and messages must be individually moved by a human volunteer—who then becomes a netweaver.

Network. A group of computers connected together so they can transmit information to one another.

NIC (Network Information Center). An internet host computer designated to provide useful information services to network users.

Node. A computer that is attached to a network; also called a HOST.

NREN. *see* the **National Research and Education Network.**

NSFnet (National Science Foundation Network). TCP/IP-based network that is the backbone for data transmission in the United States.

OPAC. (Online Public Access Catalog). Most large academic and many public libraries have converted their card catalogs to electronic or "machine-readable" format. These online catalogs may be searched from remote locations via modem or remote login, and so truly have become public reference sources.

Peer-to-peer network. A LAN situation in which every computer on the network has equal status with every other computer. Users can share files or resources (e.g., printers) between any combination of computers, and typically no single computer acts as a host, or server. This type of network is often referred to as a workgroup.

Pirate. A software pirate; someone who steals computer programs. Usually pirates will sell or give away the programs they steal.

Postmaster. The person responsible for answering questions about users and electronic mail addresses at a site. Can sometimes be reached by sending mail to "postmaster@host.subdomain.domain" if you are having trouble reaching someone at that host machine or subdomain.

Protocol. A formalized set of rules governing the format, timing, and error control of transmissions on a network. The protocol that networks use to communicate with each other. TCP/IP is an example of a network protocol.

Remote Access. The ability to access one computer from another—from across the room or across the world. Remote access requires communications hardware, software, and actual physical links, although this can be as simple as common carrier (telephone) lines or as complex as a TELNET login to another computer across the Internet.

RFC (Request for Comments). The document series, begun in 1969, in which the Internet's standards, proposed standards, and generally agreed-upon ideas are documented and published.

Robot. An automated program that will go out and search or retrieve information for the user.

SEND. The interactive real-time messaging protocol for BITnet-connected VAXJVMS systems. (*see* **TELL** for the equivalent protocol for IMB mainframes)

Server. A dedicated computer that shares its resources, such as files and applications programs, with other computers on a network. *see* **CLIENT**.

Shareware. Microcomputer software, distributed through public domain channels such as ftp, for which the author expects to receive some compensation. Users are typically allowed a free 30-day evaluation, after which they can discard the software or are expected to pay for it. This free evaluation period and the ease of distribution by "everyday people" makes shareware a powerful means of distributing software and rewarding authors.

Signature (often .sig). The three or four lines at the bottom of an email message or a Usenet article that identify the sender. A .sig is a short file created in a mail program that often contains addresses, telephone numbers, e-mail addresses, and, sometimes, ingenious graphics built from keyboard characters. Large signatures (over five lines) are generally frowned on.

SLIP. Serial Line Internet Protocol. A communications protocol for internet connections over a serial line like phone lines with a modem.

SMTP. Simple Mail Transfer Protocol. The Internet standard protocol for transferring electronic mail messages from one computer to another.

Snail Mail. A pejorative term referring to the postal service.

Synchronous. Data communications in which transmissions are sent at a fixed rate, with the sending and receiving devices synchronized. Synchronous communication occurs in real time (e.g., with two or more users communicating online at the same time to one another.

Sysop, sysops. System operator, person in charge of maintaining a host, server, or network.

Talk. A protocol that allows two people on remote Unix computer systems to communicate in real time. When one issues the "talk user@machine.place.domain" command, and if the individual is logged and accepts the request, the screen display divides horizontally and one can type at each other in real time.

TELL. The interactive real-time messaging protocol for IBM mainframes running VM/CMS and with BITnet connections. (SEND is the equivalent protocol for BITnet-connected VAXNMS systems). At the system prompt one types

tell (or "send") user@machine a single line message

and the message will appear on user~machine's screen if they are logged in. It is unwise to send TELL or SEND messages to persons one does not know because, depending on the rank and mood of the recipient, it could result in revocation of one's access privileges.

TCP/IP (Transmission Control Protocol/Internet Protocol). The set of transmission standards on the Internet that provide the reliable communication service on which many applications depend for accurate data transfer. It allows the transfer of data between computers that use TCP/IP, and it supports other services (protocols) such as Telnet, FTP, and SMTP. TCP/IP is also often used for other networks, particularly local area networks that tie together numerous different kinds of computers or engineering workstations.

Telecommuting. The practice of employees working partially or primarily from home, using microcomputers and modems to access information systems and perform their daily duties without regard to their actual physical location.

Telnet. A basic function provided by the TCP/IP protocol on the Internet is Telnet, or remote login, or remote terminal connection service. This allows a user to interact with another computer as if she or he were directly connected to the remote computer.

Terminal Emulation Software. Communications software that permits one's personal computer or workstation to communicate with another computer or network as if one's machine were a specific type of terminal directly connected to that computer or network (e.g., VT100 or TN3270).

Terminal Server. A computer that connects terminals to a network by providing host TELNET service.

Thread. A series of postings to an electronic bulletin board, or other discussion group (e.g., Listserv), that have a common subject heading. A thread normally consists of responses to an original posting to a discussion topic, or an offshoot of another thread.

TN3270. A version of Telnet required by some IBM mainframes for remote logins.

UNIX. An operating system developed by Bell Laboratories that supports several users logged into a computer or workstation at the same time, and which supports multi-user and multitasking operations. That is, this operating system allows many people to share the processing capabilities of the computer on which it is running and to use several programs at once. Unix is case-sensitive so most commands to UNIX hosts must be typed in lower case.

Upload. Transfer electronic data from a local to a remote computer, or from a floppy disk to a hard drive on a personal computer. *see* **DOWNLOAD.**

URL (Uniform Resource Locator). A technical description of a resource's Internet address. A URL specifies what type of resource (a document at an FTP site, on a gopher, a WWW site, etc.) is being described and its location on a machine connected to the Internet using a standardized format. Most web browsers allow the user to enter a URL and gain access to the specified site. (Pronounced "earl."). *see* **HTTP**

Usenet (NETNEWS). A computer bulletin board system, originally distributed over computers running the Unix operation system to which many computer systems on and off the Internet now subscribe. Whereas Listserv software delivers discussion group messages as mail to individual mailboxes, messages from some or all of the over 2,000 Usenet newsgroups are typically stored on a site's mainframe computer. Readers can then log in to read the accumulation of messages which may amount to 15 to 20 megabytes of text a day. With the number of groups growing daily, there is truly something of interest to everyone on Usenet.

UUCP (Unix to Unix Copy). A protocol used for communication between Unix systems, on which mail and Usenet news services were built. Internet has largely taken over the transmission of such date exchange.

VAX (pl. VAXen). Mainframe and personal computers manufactured by the Digital Equipment Corporation and in wide use on the Internet. One of the prevalent terminal emulations used on the Internet is named for the VT100, an early DEC video terminal.

VAX Notes. VAX Notes is essentially a computer bulletin board set up with a series of topics numbered 1, 2, 3, and so on. Replies to each topic are attached to each topic note. Replies to topic 3 would be numbered 3.1, 3.2, and so on. This permits users to read, conduct, and respond to several different discussion topics simultaneously. It also saves and stores all topic notes and replies, permitting readers to connect at any time, even after a several day hiatus and catch up on the entire series of transactions.

Veronica (Very Easy Rodent-Oriented Net-wide Index to Computerized Archives). A search tool/utility used in gopher; performs a keyword search of the menus or documents of many gophers. Search results (these vary widely; sometimes many retrievals, sometimes none) are then displayed via newly created menus.

Virus. A program that infects other programs and computers, resulting in some sort of malfunction.

Virtual Reality. Systems that transform the computing environment by immersing the user in a simulated world, which also can include movement and tactile control. Virtual reality systems permit users to interact with computer systems in a manner that more closely mimics how humans naturally operate in the real world.

VMS. A Digital Equipment Corporation operating system for VAX machines.

VT100. A standard protocol for terminal emulation. This is the most common and often required protocol used when telnetting to a remote host. It is a bare-bones, lowest common denominator terminal emulation that does not usually allow for commands and features which are available with a workstation-based client

WAIS. (Wide-Area Information System). An information retrieval tool developed by Thinking Machines, Inc. WAIS provides a simple-to-use interface that allows a patron to search multiple sources for information with a single natural language question.

Web Crawler. A program that moves along the Web looking for URLs or other information; a type of intelligent agent. Used to build the search indexes available through Web browsers.

Web. *see* **World Wide Web.**

Web Server. Server software that allows an information provider to make documents (image, text, sound) available using a variety of platforms (DOS, Unix, Macintosh, etc.).

Wide-Area Network (WAN). A distributed network spanning hundreds or thousands of miles, connecting a number of Local Area Networks.

World-Wide Web (Web or WWW or W3). A global, hypermedia-based, distributed information system created by researchers at CERN in Switzerland. It allows users to create, edit, or browse hypertext documents containing text, images, and sound. The clients and servers are now easily accessible and available.

SOURCES USED IN THIS COMPILATION

Ask ERIC InfoGuide. (1993). *K-12 educators and the internet*. Available via anonymous FTP at ericir.syr.edu.

Cook, D., & Sellers, D. (1995). *Launching a business on the web*. Indianapolis, IN: Que Corporation.

Day, M. J. (1993). Private correspondence.

Jacobsen, O., & Lynch, D.. (1991). *A glossary of networking terms*. RFC 1208.

Kehoe, B. P. (1992). *Zen and the art of the internet*. Available for anonymous FTP on host FTP.CS.WIDENER.EDU, directory PUB/ZEN, filename ZEN-1.0.PS (Postscript file) and other formats.

Krol, E. (1991). *The whole internet user's guide & catalog*. Sebastapol, CA: O'Reilly and Associates, Inc.

Lamb, A., & Johnson, L. (1995). *Cruisin' the information highway: Internet in the K-12 classroom*. Evansville, IN: Vision To Action.

Longley, D. (1986). *Dictionary of information technology* (2nd ed.). NY: Oxford University Press.

Malkin, G., & Parker, T.L. (1993). *Internet users' glossary*. RFC 1392.

Mitchell, M., & Saunders, L. (1992). *Glossary*. Sent via private correspondence .

Mulliner, K. (1993). *Internet glossary*. Prepared for a workshop in Columbus, OH. Sent via private correspondence.

University of Wisconsin-Madison Libraries. (1995). *Basic internet glossary of terms and acronyms*. Madison, WI: Author.

Other miscellaneous glossaries and individual entries from unidentified sources that were sent to us as private correspondence.

AUTHOR INDEX

SUBJECT INDEX